The Grimace

of Macho Ratón

Artisans, Identity, and Nation

in Late-Twentieth-Century

Western Nicaragua

Les W. Field

Duke University Press   Durham & London

1999

© 1999 Duke University Press

Printed in the United States of America on acid-free paper ∞

Designed by C. H. Westmoreland

Typeset in Sabon with Gill Sans display

by Tseng Information Systems, Inc.

Library of Congress Cataloging-in-Publication Data

appear on the last printed page of this book.

Frontispiece: A mask of Macho Ratón, given to the author by Flavio Gamboa in 1993. Flavio estimated the age of the mask as at least one hundred years. (Photo by Gia Scarpetta)

For the Nicaraguan people and their futures
In memory of George Field y todos los antepasados

Many complain that the words of the wise are always merely parables and of no use in daily life, which is the only life we have. When the sage says: "Go over," he does not mean that we should cross to some actual place, which we could do anyhow if the labor were worth it; he means some fabulous yonder, something unknown to us, something that he cannot designate more precisely either, and therefore cannot help us here in the very least. All these parables really set out to say merely that the incomprehensible is incomprehensible, and we know that already. But the cares we have to struggle with every day: that is a different manner.

Concerning this a man once said: Why such reluctance? If you only followed the parables you yourselves would become parables and with that rid of all your daily cares.

Another said: I bet that is also a parable.

The first said: You have won.

The second said: But unfortunately only in parable.

The first said: No, in reality: in parable you have lost.

—Kafka, "On Parables"

Contents

Acknowledgments

It is unfortunately true that even now the most important people with whom an anthropologist works "in the field" are personally credited, often warmly so, in the acknowledgments to a book, but somehow do not appear as individuals elsewhere in that book. The text of this book is the product of a number of long-term collaborative projects and friendships with Nicaraguan individuals. Some of their own texts, in the form of essays, letters, family journals, and informational pamphlets, appear, in translation, in the chapters that follow. Other individuals contributed their words through conversations and interviews that I transcribed and translated as well. All of these individuals are named and credited throughout what follows, so much so that it seems to me that to acknowledge them here is to mislead the reader about the nature of this text. Nevertheless, I will formally thank them here, hoping the reader will agree to suspend her or his disbelief and trust that these individuals will play a larger role in what is to follow than is conventional.

In Monimbó: Flavio Gamboa

In San Juan de Oriente: Orlando Gallegos, Catalina Bracamonte, Agustín Amador, Digna Gallegos, Roberto Potosme, Juanita Bracamonte, Bladimir Nororís, Ester Bracamonte, Patricia Gallegos, Gregorio Bracamonte, Ena Bracamonte, Silvio Gallegos, Joséfa Nicoya, and María Isabel Nicoya

In Matagalpa: María Esthela Rodríguez Pineda, Carmen Rodríguez Pineda, Benita Pineda

In Jinotega: Silvia Pineda de Castro, María Dolores Castro Pineda, Ramona Castro Pineda

In addition, the following individuals working in the contemporary indigenous movement helped me enormously to understand that movement; they also appear in the text: María Josefina Jarquín Moreno of Estelí, Enrique de la Concepción of Sutiava, Christina Hernández and Hipolito Lopez of El Chile, and Jorge Hernández of Sebaco. I also must thank the following individuals from the Ministry of Culture under Sandinismo who do not appear in the text but whose interest in my projects enabled me to become a resident of Nicaragua: Olga Marta Montiél, Marta Zamora, and Lidia Forbes. The most supportive people of all in so many ways have been Felipa Cerda Padilla of Masaya and her children, Lester, Cinthia, Lisania, and Jorge. They are truly the most faithful of friends.

I am very happy to take this opportunity to finally and formally thank the many people in the United States who have supported this project over the course of almost fifteen years. It is a pleasure to name the intellectual mentors who have guided and inspired me and who I hope are not disappointed with what they will read in this book: Carol Smith, Richard Fox, Virginia Domínguez, Katherine Verdery, and Brackette Williams. I have been fortunate indeed to find additional guidance and support among the colleagues at the universities where I have worked (University of New Hampshire) and where I currently work (University of New Mexico): Nina Glick Schiller, Stephen Reyna, Louise Lamphere, and Carole Nagengast. Michael Kearney has been an attentive sounding board at various stages of this project and always provided insightful suggestions. Finally, I am immensely grateful to two Nicaraguanist scholars whose work has been a continuing source of inspiration and who have provided an endless stream of constructive comments on the many drafts of this book and the chapters therein that have appeared elsewhere as articles: Charles Hale and Jeffrey Gould. Without them, this book surely could never have been completed.

There are many friends and family members in North Carolina, Seattle, the Bay Area, New Mexico, New Hampshire, and elsewhere who financially, emotionally, and creatively supported this project in its myriad stages. I would like to thank Adam Stern, Frank Henderson, Charlie Zechel and Mari Snow, Mark Fleisher, Theonia and Wes Boyd, Rebecca Stith, Andy Fox, Dan Kozarsky, Dave Hirschman, Grace Nordhoff, Ruth Ziegler, Marcie Pachino, Alison Seevak, Wendy Jacobs and Michael Meredith, Paul Holmbeck and Helle Ørsted Nielsen, Alisa Johnston and L. D. Burris, Molly Mullin, Tom O'Connor, John Bratton, Phillip Williams, Thereza Przekota, Jo Montgomery and Ruth Conn, Jamo Wright and Denise Hammer, Wendy Cadden and Barbara Nylund, Joe Kinsella, David Craven, Karl Benedict, Maria Firmino-Castillo, Marta Henriksen, Philip Laverty, Angelle Khachadoorian, Jenny Sanborn, Sonia Stern, Sam and

Vee Dysart, Reinaldo Scarpetta, Maruja Scarpetta, Andrea Scarpetta, Jenny Dysart, my mother Frances Field, and my grandmother Sylvia Gitelman. I also want to thank Margaret Randall for her support before I ever knew her, and more so since we have become friends. Ken Wissoker and Duke University Press have been very encouraging, friendly, and above all timely in their treatment of this work, which has made an experience I expected to be intimidating actually pleasant.

The most essential person to the research and writing of this book has been my life partner, Gia Nina Scarpetta. During the 1980s, Gia and I worked as a research team. In the past few years, I have returned to Nicaragua alone, but she has continued to be the key person with whom I discuss all of the ideas and analyses contained in this text. This is an astonishing feat, for our lives have been utterly transformed by the presence of our children, Lukas, Simon, and Maia. No better partners in adventure can be found, and I thank them all profoundly for the constancy of love that I never knew could exist.

A substantially different and briefer form of chapter 2 appeared in *American Ethnologist* 24, no. 3 (1995): 786–806, under the title "Constructing Local Identities in a Revolutionary State: The Cultural Politics of the Artisan Class in Nicaragua, 1979–1990." Some aspects of that article also appear in chapter 3, and some of the ideas introduced in the article appear in chapter 4 in greatly elaborated form.

A much briefer and different form of chapter 4 appeared in *American Anthropologist* 100, no. 2 (1998): 431–443, under the title "Knowledge and Truth about Post-Sandinista Ethnic Identities in Western Nicaragua."

Prologue

Historical

A certain familiarity with the past century of Nicaraguan history will prove useful for readers of this book who are scholars neither of Central America nor of twentieth-century revolutionary movements. Therefore, I summarize here the period of Nicaraguan history that constitutes most of the setting for the ethnographic, literary, and analytic explorations that follow.[1]

As in much of Latin America, the late nineteenth and early twentieth centuries in Nicaragua were dominated by military, political, and economic contests among elite families who labeled themselves Liberal and Conservative parties. The substance of these battles revolved around competing versions of national identity, internal economic development and international economic relationships, and the form of the state. Briefly, the Liberals sponsored capitalist development, integration into the world economy, and secular political and cultural policies, whereas the Conservatives favored a nationalist politics and culture flavored by paternalistic social relations, an alliance with the Church, and an economy dominated by already existing agricultural development. In the case of Nicaragua, the Liberal-Conservative struggle effectively prevented the formation of a unified state and delayed the coalescing of a national identity. At the end of the nineteenth century, a Liberal dictator, José Santos Zelaya, finally welded together a functioning state using an expansionist nationalism[2] and an aggressive agro-export developmentalism. He was deposed in 1909 by a conspiracy supported, perhaps even devised, by the United States, thus setting the stage for the rest of the twentieth century.

The United States sent its first military forces to Nicaragua in 1912, after full-scale Liberal-Conservative warfare had resumed. General Augusto César Sandino, the illegitimate son of an Indian mother and a Liberal landowner, underwent a profound transformation as a result of U.S. intervention. Sandino admired the nationalism of the Mexican Revolution, having spent time in Mexico as a worker in the petroleum industry, and he emulated the revolutionaries' romantic glorification of the Indian past. At the same time, he became convinced that North American imperialism was largely responsible for Nicaragua's prostrate economy and political abasement. Whereas both the Liberal and Conservative parties had always forcibly conscripted troops from local rural areas, Sandino's army was made up of volunteers, most from agro-export coffee plantations of northern Nicaragua. If Sandino did not specifically represent the interests of Nicaragua's poor majority, he was, on the other hand, the first national leader who did not represent only the interests of the elites.

Conflict continued between various Liberal forces, including the Sandinistas (followers of Sandino), and the Conservative army until 1927, when the United States formed the Guardia Nacional (National Guard). Intended to act as the foundation for a new unified Nicaraguan state, the U.S.-trained force immediately set out to destroy the Sandinistas. Under Anastasio Somoza García, the Guardia became a means to pursue political power and personal enrichment. Somoza used U.S. backing to adroitly play Conservatives against Liberals, and became president of the republic in 1937. In the meantime, his forces had abducted and murdered Sandino and his inner circle after inviting them to negotiate a permanent truce.

The Somoza family—first Anastasio, then his son Luis, then his other son Anastasio Debayle—ruled Nicaragua through co-optation and repression until 1979. Somoza García parceled out bureaucratic positions in the new network of state ministries to both Liberals and Conservatives, and never threatened the economic base of the elites. Instead, he embarked on a program of agro-export economic development that fulfilled Zelaya's dreams. Top officials of the Guardia and compliant sectors of the old elites participated in a modernization of the coffee industry, an expansion of the cattle industry, and, especially under Luis and Anastasio Debayle, the creation of an immense cotton industry. The associated financial and construction booms drew in other fractions of the old elite and enriched a new upper class whose loyalties to Somocismo lasted almost until the 1970s.[3] The Somozas never hesitated to use armed repression against laborers, unions, or wayward individuals of the upper classes.

By the 1970s, the majority of the Nicaraguan workforce was employed in agro-industries and associated service sectors, none of which provided year-round employment or any semblance of security. Immiseration of the working classes gave Nicaragua the lowest standard of living in Central America. This desperate situation shaped the reemergence of a radical anti-imperialist, anti-Somoza movement in the 1960s, which called itself the Frente Sandinista de Liberación Nacional (Sandinista National Liberation Front), known as the F S L N or Frente. Led by both disaffected sons and daughters of the elite classes and individuals from the vast impoverished sectors, the F S L N called for a violent overthrow of Somocismo. The first ten years of struggle against the much more numerous and better-armed Guardia were singularly unsuccessful. The turning point in the fortunes of both the F S L N and the Somozas arrived with the devastating earthquake of 1972, which destroyed Managua, the capital city.

The disaster afforded Somoza and the Guardia a unique opportunity to enrich themselves from international aid and to extend their control over agro-industries, construction, and banking. Huge residential and commercial districts of Managua became wastelands, and large numbers of people either deserted Managua or were moved wholesale to the desolate outskirts of the city where they were left to fend for themselves. The avarice of Somoza's inner circle destroyed the Somocista social contract with the upper classes, encouraging business leaders and public intellectuals to break with the Somozas and engage in an increasingly cordial dialogue with the F S L N. At the same time, the Frente's recruitment among Managua's refugee population, service sector workers, students, and women, as well as among rural agricultural workers and artisans, expanded tremendously. A broad class alliance emerged in the middle and late 1970s, leading to the victory of the Sandinista forces over the Guardia in 1979.

Tensions within this class alliance emerged very quickly. The upperclass alliance with the Frente was only tenable as long as economic policies pursued by the revolutionary government continued to support the expansion of agro-export industries. Yet the Sandinistas were also obligated to their much closer allies: landless rural agricultural workers, subsistence peasants, artisans, the huge informal service sector in Managua, and the large pool of unemployed and underemployed persons also in Managua—sectors that expected massive redistribution of land and other social wealth, social benefits, human rights for all disadvantaged social sectors, and a national culture that reflected the needs and aspirations of the poor majority. The leadership of the revolutionary government had also been shaped by the legacies of Liberal and Conservative politics and their competing visions of national identity and development. Contradictions within the revolutionary bloc caused oscillations in Sandinista economic policy from the beginning, which were exacerbated by the hostility of the United States that emerged openly after the election of Ronald Reagan in 1980. Armed, trained, and ideologically abetted by the United States, counterrevolutionary armies (or contras) initiated warfare against the Sandinistas in 1982. The United States declared an economic boycott of Nicaraguan exports and blockaded U.S. imports to Nicaragua in 1985. A series of draconian economic policies, repression of anti-Sandinista political parties and social movements, and the military draft all contributed to the decline in support for the revolutionary government and its increasingly confused social transformation.

Nevertheless, the FSLN won an election in 1984 in which it competed with five vocal opposition parties. In 1990, however, the effects of economic hemorrhage, the war, and distrust of the Frente's leadership culminated in electoral loss. The opposition coalition, Unión Nacional Opositora (UNO), had received millions of dollars in aid from the United States and elite Nicaraguans exiled primarily in Miami. The UNO government attempted to roll back many of the Frente's reforms and accommodate the United States; at the same it is no longer possible to silence the poor majority in the post-Sandinista era. New contestations over national identity and economic development are ongoing, and although an even more elitist government emerged in 1996, social and cultural movements and changes at the end of this century suggest that radical reconfigurations of the Nicaraguan nation and state are not by any means over.

Dramatic

About *El Güegüence:* For an uncertain length of time exceeding two hundred years, a drama called *El Güegüence* has been performed by elaborately masked dancers in the streets of small towns in the provinces of Masaya and Carazo, located in the center of Pacific coastal Nicaragua. The script of *El Güegüence* exists in several forms, but all of the original manuscripts were written in a mixture of Nahuatl and Spanish; these manuscripts were then translated into Spanish several times, each time with different emphases.

Nicaraguan intellectuals from the Liberal and Conservative elites, and later from ranks of the radical, Sandinista intelligentsia, have understood *El Güegüence* as a parable for Nicaraguan national identity and its formation. A parable differs from an allegory in important ways: in an allegory, each fictional character and event stands for or symbolizes another character or event that exists in historical time. The allegory's story tells its audience about real events and characters through a symbolic narrative. In parables, no such exact correspondences are used. The parable is a narrative with a point or several points. Events and characters in a parable endure transformations that are instructive to an audience, often with respect to historical time, no doubt, but not exclusively so. The purpose of a parable is to inform audiences, but the lessons thereby taught are always open to divergent interpretations.

In brief, both Conservative and Liberal intellectuals have understood *El Güegüence* as a parable about the defeat of Indian identity in Nicaragua and the domination of a new, Hispanic Nicaraguan identity. Such an interpretation has fueled the nation-building projects of late-nineteenth- and early- to mid-twentieth-century state elites. By contrast, Sandinista and other radical intellectuals made of *El Güegüence* a parable of class and anti-imperialist struggle that, at least in part, rescues the Indians of Nicaragua from total defeat.

I too will use the parable of *El Güegüence* to explore and explain Nicaraguan national identity and its transformations since the victory of the Sandinistas, focusing on one very salient sociocultural group, Nicaraguan artisans. First, I need to summarize the action of this drama which, as I have noted, exists in multiple versions and interpretations as it has passed through the metamorphoses of linguistic translation.[4] Telling the story of *El Güegüence,* describing the main characters and the action that occurs, will enable me to show in later chapters how various intellectuals have focused on key phrases and characters to illuminate their versions of Nicaragua's national culture, versions that provide the backdrop for the cultural transformations about which I will have much to say in this volume. One such character, Macho Ratón, bears immediate attention, as his name is part of the title of the play (*El Güegüence, or Macho Ratón*), and of this book as well. Macho Ratón may or may not be the alter ego of Güegüence, given the play's title. In most of the interpretive literature it seems that Macho Ratón names the dance of the machos, or mules, that occurs toward the end of the play, rather than a particular masked dancer. But among the actors and other persons presently involved in the promotion and performance of the play, whose lead I will follow, Macho Ratón names any and all of the individual dancing mules. Their words, and my attendance at several partial performances of the play in the streets of Masaya and Monimbó, have led me to interpret the entire play in ways that both coincide with and diverge from what Nicaraguan intellectuals have written and said. I have seen the frozen grimace or rictus on the masks of the machos as an expression of forbearance with the constancy of oppressive conditions, frustration at the absurd limitations posed by authority, sarcasm and cynicism about change and what passes for change, and a lascivious enjoyment of carnality and sensual pleasure. The grimace tells about living with disjuncture and multiple kinds of uncertainty, particularly about personal history and identity. If this seems too much of a late-twentieth-century sentiment, then that too is part of the pleasure of reinterpreting parables.

A Summary As the play begins, the Spanish governor, Tastuanes, formally greets his constable. They bemoan the impoverished state of the Royal Council, and ultimately blame a traveling merchant (an Indian, it seems, although some have called him a mestizo) named Güegüence. Ruling that no one may enter the province anymore without a permit issued by him, Tastuanes orders that Güegüence be brought before him immediately to answer a variety of charges.

Güegüence and his two sons, Don Forsico (who is his biological child) and Don Ambrosio (who, we are led to understand, is the illegitimate child of Güegüence's former consort and another man), are actually nearby and within earshot. Güegüence repeatedly pretends to mishear whatever the constable says to him, constantly twisting his words so as to insult him. When Tastuanes reenters, he demands to know how Güegüence is traveling about without a permit. The Indian contrives a lewd reference from this question, then proposes to share his immense wealth with the governor. Tastuanes is doubtful, but Don Forsico carries on convincingly about his father's riches, detailing an interesting and heterogeneous hoard of gold, imported and silk cloth, silver, beaver hats, and feathered capes.

Then the governor queries Don Ambrosio about his family's alleged riches, but this son denounces his father as an impostor and a layabout. Güegüence answers these allegations indignantly, and Don Forsico excoriates his brother for not having the same blood as he and his father, which indeed he is not.

Tastuanes tries to settle the question of Güegüence's wealth by looking in his traveling shop. Güegüence diverts the governor's attention by offering him ridiculous things (the morning star, a syringe of gold), and then starts loudly praising his son Don Forsico. Tastuanes inquires about Don Forsico's talents, including his ability to dance. So, Don Forsico dances with his father and brother, and again with them and with the governor and the constable. Once again the main characters dance, this time accompanied by perhaps a dozen masquerading machos, dancers who wear the masks of grimacing mules. The machos, who never speak, include Macho Viejo (old Macho), Macho Guajaqueño (Oaxacan Macho), Macho Mohino (melancholy Macho, offspring of the female donkey), and Macho Moto (who lost his mother while still nursing). Throughout, Güegüence makes thinly veiled obscene references to sexual activities of various kinds.

Suddenly, Güegüence insinuates that he is asking for the hand of the governor's daughter, Lady Suche-Malinche, in marriage. Tastuanes is offended, but at this point appears to believe in Güegüence's self-professed wealth. Güegüence then changes his tune and proposes that Don Forsico marry Suche-Malinche. Suche-Malinche enters with an entourage of women, and Don Forsico grumbles that his brother Don Ambrosio has already impregnated a few of them. Don Forsico indicates his approval of Suche-Malinche, who never utters a word throughout. For no apparent reason, the governor agrees to their marriage, and Güegüence becomes morose over the loss of his son.

The governor and the constable let it be known that it is up to Güegüence to provide fine wine for the wedding. Güegüence is on the offensive again and deliberately misunderstands, for it is apparent he cannot possibly procure such treats. Don Forsico assures his father that he can provide the wine, which leads his father to accuse him of selling favors to a male benefactor. Another series of rather crude phallic jokes ensue, as the machos reappear dancing and the wine is loaded onto them.

The action draws to a close. Again, Güegüence's mood shifts. As the constable endeavors to hurry him, Güegüence speaks nostalgically of days gone by, using several obscure and allusive references. Something is changing, has already changed, and Güegüence knows this. Nevertheless, his last words are that once again he and his sons have pulled off a successful ruse, having gotten something for nothing.

The Grimace of Macho Ratón

Introduction

Regarding Macho Ratón

A Cultural History

This book is a cultural history of a sort. It focuses more or less on one region of western Nicaragua, but not exclusively so. It concerns itself with artisans, potters to be more precise, but imbricates other groups of peoples whose histories intertwine with those of the potters about whom I have much to say. And although it focuses on factors of class, ethnicity, and gender in the transformation of artisans' identities within the past fifteen or twenty years, it makes reference to a much longer period of history, stretching back to the arrival of the Spaniards in the area that became Nicaragua.

How these histories, which include events far back in time and those of the past two decades, have been woven together is hardly straightforward. In many instances, neither I nor anyone else is sure exactly who is responsible for events that occurred during certain historical periods, nor can anyone assert that certain kinds of responsibility will ever be irrevocably established; but this, I would argue, is not the point.[1] The *effects* produced by what has been and continues to be said, written, dramatized, and interpreted by individuals and groups, in books and in various art forms, concerning the entity "Nicaraguan culture" and its histories are much more important for my purposes. These effects have produced incongruent, unexpected, and contradictory outcomes, from both my perspective and the perspectives of many of the people with whom I have worked since 1980, some of whose thoughts, written as texts that I have translated from their Spanish into English, form a key part of this volume.

I am focusing on the changing *identities* of the artisans, by which I mean the constantly transforming and always incomplete production of, knowledge about and ways of expressing self and social being, under stratified systems of power. Alberto Melucci, a theorist of contemporary social and cultural movements, writes:

Collective identity is an interactive and shared definition produced by several individuals and concerned with the orientations of action and the fields of opportunities and constraints in which the action takes place: by "interactive and shared" I mean a definition that must be conceived as a process, because it is constructed and negotiated through a repeated activation of the relationships that link individuals. The process of identity construction, adaptation and maintenance always has two aspects: the internal complexity of an actor (the plurality of orientations which characterizes him), and the actor's relationship with the environment (other actors, opportunities and constraints). (In Escobar 1992: 72)

The identities of the artisans with whom I worked have been writ upon the canvas of Nicaraguan culture as that entity has been shaped by elite groups and their constructions of the Nicaraguan nation-state and Nicaraguan national identity. I will underscore the fairly stable notions about Nicaraguan culture, particularly its ethnic and racial character, extant among Nicaragua's intellectual elites during the previous century, notwithstanding notable ideological differences among influential elite individuals and political groupings. Let us define the *state* as the institutionalized, organizational apparatus that governs a group of individuals defined as citizens within a variously conceptualized spatial territory, and the *nation* as a collective political and social entity bounded by particular and inclusive constructions of history, territory, language, and daily practice. In effect, although the nature and form of the Nicaraguan state has changed considerably in this century, ideas about the Nicaraguan nation propagated by intellectual elites have remained in many ways consistent for about a hundred years. This historical matrix is no doubt related to the fact that Nicaragua's intellectual elites, of varied ideological shadings, have been and largely remain the scions of old, wealthy, and powerful families from the preeminent colonial cities of western Nicaragua, León and Granada, among whom both violent rivalry for control of the national polity and near monopolistic control over successive agro-export economies have been determinant forces in Nicaraguan history.

This book describes the historical demarcation of Nicaragua's cultural canvas by these elites, which is part of the national project of the class that has controlled the state, and how this project transmuted under the cultural policies of the Sandinista years. I will also focus on how artisans' identities have formed and transformed within and against those demarcations, in a country and in a time in which ethnic identities, like palimpsests, materialize out of highly obscured histories, where gender identities are either silenced or voiced but not as gender discourses, and class identities formed during Sandinismo's triumph have since dissolved in its eclipse. Part of Sandinismo's legacy, however, was to unleash the production of discourses of identity by local intellectuals who never before had challenged elite intellectuals. Unexpectedly for the Sandinistas, the perspectives voiced by local intellectuals challenged many of the assumptions of the revolutionary state. In this complex milieu, the making of artisans' identities in the past two decades has alternately burst apart the borders defining Nicaraguan culture, remained within those borders, and proceeded as if those delineations had little or no relevance.

A central strategy I use to contextualize artisans' identity within the demarcation of national culture by intellectuals from the classes that have controlled Nicaraguan nation-building is the exegesis of *El Güegüence o Macho Ratón*[2] and the numerous textualizations of it by Nicaraguan and foreign intellectuals. During the past century, many Nicaraguan intellectuals have argued over the meaning(s) of *El Güegüence* while agreeing that the tale it tells is a parable of the historical appearance of the Nicaraguan nation and a paradigm of Nicaraguan identity. If the play also operates as a parable for my ethnographic descriptions and a paradigm for the arguments I will make, it does so in complex ways. While divergent interpretations of the play set the stage for contested elaborations of Nicaraguan culture and the positioning of ceramics artisans in the Masaya-Carazo region during Sandinismo, the grimace of Macho Ratón and several declamations from the play also serve as inspirational tropes for my own understanding of Nicaraguan history. My interpretation of the play metaphorizes the arguments about Nicaragua's cultural past, present, and future made in several chapters.

All of this makes for a very messy analysis of recent Nicaraguan cultural history. I am trying to show that cultural identities in western Nicaragua have formed on a fabric woven by elite Nicaraguans and authoritative outsiders, but that since 1979, artisans caught up in cultural processes have made rips in that fabric and have rewoven its pattern in unpredictable ways. Each chapter describes processes in which particular individuals (including, in a minor way, myself) and key texts have played out multiply interpreted roles in reproducing and changing key components of the entity called "Nicaraguan culture." Obviously, I am placing a premium on remaining faithful to complexity, but that is a decision I have felt quite obliged, under the circumstances, to make.

Theoretical Tools and Concerns

My focus on the historical contexts underlying and events occurring during and after the Sandinista Front's negotiation of cultural policy obliges me also to engage in a more general treatment of "culture," the mascot of anthropology. Many anthropologists write and speak as if, on the one hand, it is crucial that our discipline decisively define culture, perhaps to arrive at some sort of consensus, and as if, on the other hand, arriving at a consensus defining culture would make a difference to people in the world beyond ourselves. (For example, the exchanges in 1995–96 over science and the study of culture in the *Anthropology Newsletter* appear to reflect such assumptions.) Perhaps there is some truth to these assumptions, although the theories, methods, and best intentions shaping anthropological texts seldom if ever change the difficult circumstances confronting the people with whom and the places where we work. In Nicaragua and other (formerly) revolutionary, socialist, and (currently) Third World countries, however, anthropologists' ability to control the meanings given to the term "culture" and the uses to which those meanings have been put has become minimal, apart from those (very few) circles in which anthropologists predominate. Whatever role — and that role was inarguably important — our discipline played in unleashing upon the world the idea of culture and its many possible interpretations, substantive control of its conceptualization as it is operationalized across the face of the planet is mostly not in anthropologists' hands at this point in time. Culture is now, I would argue, less a broadly descriptive term, like the word "society," and more a situationally charged and contentious term, like the word "democracy." For better or worse, our work may have less to do with studying culture per se than with how the concept of culture is sociopolitically operationalized and thereby played out in the relationships shaping the lives of very different peoples, all of whom live in a world of nation-states. Such a conclusion may reconcile what seem to be disagreements among contemporary theorists, such as Appadurai (1996), who argues against any sort of discussion of the "primordial" essences of ethnic and national identities, and Verdery (1996), who shows how nations and ethnic groups utilize essences, particularly in the idiom of kinship, to "primordialize" cultural identities.

Of course, the term "culture" still always describes certain phenomena to which anthropologists have historically paid attention: weblike structures of signification; norms of behavior and the values upon which norms are based; rituals and rites of passage that socialize individuals from generation to generation; symbols, collective understandings, and worldviews; aesthetics, art, and drama; and much more. But this laundry list and debates over whether to stress behavioral or ideational components in defining the term do not objectively define culture and its components, regardless of what we (and I include myself most assuredly) tell undergraduates year after year. Culture cannot be defined definitively, because it is a term that is and has been defined by "the social organization of meaning" (Friedman 1994: 211). As Friedman confesses, culture must be redesignated "as a phenomenon to be accounted for rather than one that accounts for" (27). And insofar as anthropologists still play the game of defining culture, Friedman warns:

The most dangerously misleading quality of the notion of culture is that it literally flattens out the extremely varied ways in which the production of meaning occurs in the contested field of social existence. Most atrociously, it conflates the identification of specificity by the anthropologist with the creation and institutionalization of semantic schemes by those under study. It confuses our identification scheme with theirs and trivializes other people's experience by reducing it to our cognitive categories . . . [Culture's] usefulness resides entirely in its classificatory properties and these are highly suspicious . . . In global terms the culturalization of the world is about how a certain group of professionals located at central positions identify the larger world and order it according to a central scheme of things. (207–8)

In the histories and ethnographic narratives composing this book, culture exists as an inextricable part of systems of power embodied by constructions of nation and national identity by elite groups. I do not merely assert that we cannot talk about culture and cultures apart from what people in nations say/write/believe, but that culture *is* exactly what people say/write/believe, and almost always with reference to a laundry list of ideas and behaviors that anthropologists indeed had a great deal to do with establishing. It goes without saying that "people" means not just any people, but powerful people. Part of the power exercised by elites who set up and rule nation-states and own the greater share of their economies is the business of constructing national identities, that is, defining what is and is not national (majority) and (ethnic) minority culture, as well as high and low culture, good and bad culture, and so on. Recent work by anthropologists has focused on how, on the one hand, nation-state elites employ and control intellectuals to do such work (see Verdery 1991), and on the other hand, how local intellectuals from subaltern groups define subnational oppositional positions through both political organizing and writing (see Rappaport 1990). Influenced by these moves in contemporary ethnology, my work has had less to do with how our discipline defines culture and much more to do with what the Ministry of Culture defined as culture during the Sandinista period, and the deep roots of those definitions. In uncovering the relationships between the Ministry's definitions of culture and past elite definitions, and the ways that artisans worked with, rejected, and reformulated the realm of culture in their lives, I also situate pottery within the historically textualized demarcations of Nicaraguan culture, especially in the Masaya-Carazo region. Thus, I show how pottery's relationship to elite discourse concerning Nicaraguan culture has danced a strange and complex dance with the transformations of identity among the artisans with whom I have worked since 1980.

For the purposes of understanding cultural processes in Nicaragua, I make use of analytic frameworks concerned with national and ethnic identity formation, and the relationship between power and knowledge outlined by recent theorists. The Comaroffs' (1992) five "propositions" concerning ethnicity describe it as an effect of two dialectically intertwined factors of the postcolonial world. On the one hand, ethnicity is a social classification organized around axes of cultural differences, even if these differences and their cultural content may be to a greater or lesser extent consciously constructed to emphasize and exaggerate social boundaries. On the other hand, ethnicity also names the unequal division of labor among social groups that have been assigned positions within the stratified political economies of nation-states. The dual cultural and politico-economic nature of ethnicity elucidated by the Comaroffs well describes the post-Conquest appearance of "Indians" in the Americas: a subaltern "ethno-class" position (Rasnake 1988; Sider 1994) created in the wake of colonialism's destructive incorporation of indigenous civilizations from Alaska to Patagonia. Brackette Williams (1989) summarizes this process: "the ideologies we call nationalism and the subordinated subnational identities we call ethnicity result from the various plans and programs for the construction of myths of homogeneity out of the realities of heterogeneity that characterize all nation building . . . ethnicity labels the visibility of that aspect of the identity formation process that is produced by and subordinated to nationalist programs and plans—plans intent on creating putative homogeneity out of heterogeneity" (428, 439). In the Americas, the processes by which previously autonomous local and large-scale societies and social groups were dominated by European colonialism and later by elite-dominated, stratified political economies of nation-states recreates the disempowered social groups as ethnicities. Alonso (1994) intimates that processes of national and ethnic identity formation are intrinsically linked to knowledge-producing projects: "Nationalism is partly an effect of the totalizing and homogenizing projects of state formation. These projects produce an imagined sense of political community that conflates peoplehood, territory, and state . . . In contrast to nationalism, ethnicity is partly an effect of the particularizing projects of state formation, projects that produce hierarchized forms of imagining peoplehood that are assigned varying degrees of social esteem and differential privileges and prerogatives within political community" (391).

Foucault (1980) elucidated the evocative term "regime of truth" precisely to describe elite power over knowledge:

Truth is to be understood as a system of ordered procedures for the production, regulation, distribution, circulation and operation of statements.

Truth is linked in a circular relation with systems of power which produce and sustain it, and to the effects of power which it induces and which extend it. A "regime" of truth.

This regime is not merely ideological or superstructural; it was a condition of the formation and development of capitalism. And it's this same regime which, subject to certain modifications, operates in the socialist countries. (133)

However, the lack of historical dynamic, the absence of conceptual, spatial, and temporal room for *change* in Foucauldian concepts of power such as regimes of truth, power/knowledge, epistemes, and so on poses problems for those who try to deploy these concepts analytically. Edward Said (1983) has observed that "[t]here is always something beyond the reach of dominating systems, no matter how deeply they saturate society, and this is obviously what makes change possible, limits power in Foucault's sense, and hobbles the theory of that power" (246–47). As an alternative to the apparent unassailability of power as congealed in regimes of truth, Said offers Gramsci's concept of hegemony, which also describes the reach of power into the most minute aspects of everyday life under capitalism. Gramsci linked his analysis of hegemony to a political program of resistance to its domination, resistance that would reach its highest form in a revolutionary counterhegemony paving the way to a socialist transformation. Yet, hegemony theory has also been criticized by some authors along lines similar to Said's complaint about Foucault: "The possibility of an alternative hegemony seems to presuppose a social order in which the existing hegemonic apparatus is not so powerful and pervasive as to disrupt all organized, collective challenges and yet which is sufficiently dependent upon that hegemonic apparatus for its stability so that an alternative hegemony would pose a serious threat. That would seem to be an unlikely combination, and one, in any case, at odds with Gramsci's own suggestions about the nature of the advanced capitalist state" (Adamson 1980: 179).

These discussions lead me to ask specific questions relevant to the Nicaraguan case as well as to many other Latin American milieus. If regimes of truth, or hegemonic systems of knowledge, about local and national identity do indeed constitute "a sense of reality" (R. Williams 1977: 110) "taken for granted as the natural, universal, and true shape of social being" (Comaroff and Comaroff 1992: 28), how do human beings ever come to understand their lives differently? How can resistance by subaltern groups lead to thinking new truths about individual and sociocultural identities, thereby constructing alternative knowledges about those identities?

Florencia Mallon (1995) has described the very different formation of national and of ethnic identities in Peru and Mexico, respectively, during the late nineteenth–early twentieth century, a period of intensive local rebellions and elite nation-building in both countries. The value of her historical reconstruction for the Nicaraguan case is its illumination of the complex relationships between elite and local intellectuals in the processes by which national (dominant) sociocultural identities co-opt or marginalize local (subordinate) sociocultural identities. She defines "local intellectuals": "In the villages, local intellectuals were those who labored to reproduce and rearticulate local history and memory, to connect community discourses about local identity to constantly shifting patterns of power, solidarity, and consensus . . . village intellectuals spoke for the villages, then, not because they represented them or took advantage of them in some pure way but because a local political coalition had been built through processes of inclusion and exclusion" (12). Mallon has drawn attention to the necessity of understanding how certain individuals come to be, *can* come to be, intellectuals in local environments, in order to understand the larger relationships between elite and local intellectuals in the articulation of national and local identities. My investigation of the transformation of regimes of truth and hegemonic knowledge in Nicaragua probes the possibilities and conditions under which local intellectuals have defended, defined, avoided, and transformed local social and cultural identities. Lomnitz-Adler's (1992) discussion of the term "internal articulatory intellectuals," that is, those individuals who both elaborate identities internally to their communities and articulate their communities' political demands to the elite-dominated state, helps to explicate those possibilities and conditions in Nicaraguan history.

In the following chapters, I argue that the complex effects of revolutionary social processes conditioned the emergence of internal intellectuals in artisan communities who became articulatory. The formation of these intellectuals led to challenges to the national regime of truth that had been elaborated by elite intellectuals, whose views I see congealed in the discourse about *El Güegüence* and Nicaraguan national identity. In describing the limits of the cultural field generated by Nicaraguan intellectual discourse and the class project of nation-building within which it is inscribed, this framework does *not* propose a set of keys that will "truly explain" Nicaraguan culture better than what other authors (anthropologists, literary critics, and other academic or Nicaraguan elite intellectuals) have proposed. This book does not offer a last word concerning Nicaraguan culture from a self-styled new authority on the subject and its history. Moreover, I realize that my framework and its questions do not always have much to do directly with how the people with whom I worked have made sense of these situations. If that was not already clear to me, it became crystalline when I returned to Nicaragua in 1993, realized my previous obsessions had been concerned with brief historical moments, and decided to investigate the post-Sandinista development of class, ethnic, and gender identities among artisans. At that point, I reconceived the nature of relationships with my many friends and informants in San Juan and in the north, and initiated a process of including in the writing of this book essays written by key individuals that present *their* perspectives on the same cultural processes I have also attempted to analyze. This decision and its outcome raises another set of dilemmas; about coauthoring, "giving voice," and the empowerment of subaltern, native intellectuals.

Working in Nicaragua, Constructing the Text:
Insider/Outsider Dilemmas and Empowering "the Other"

After more than fifteen years of going back and forth between Nicaragua and the United States, sometimes staying and living in Nicaragua for extended periods (February 1984–June 1985) and sometimes for shorter intervals, I have tried to take stock of the ways I approached my research in that country, arrived at research objectives and methods, and faced the numerous paradoxes and dilemmas this work entailed. In probing these processes, I have been helped and prodded by a literature I began using in order to teach ethnographic methods to graduate students, a literature that in the main stems from feminist scholarship in anthropology (see Haraway 1991; Visweswaran 1994; Spivak 1988; D. Wolf 1995; Brettell 1996; Behar and Gordon 1995; Patai 1991; Kondo 1990). But although I find a rich panoply of ideas in this literature that have clarified and greatly problematized all that I have done and intended to do, this is explicitly an ex post facto process of finding other scholars whose insights helped me to unearth my own conclusions, rather than a revisiting of texts and ideas that motivated my work in the first place.

Additionally, it has taken me some time to find a position of real comfort in reflexivity, notwithstanding the reflexive qualities my work has taken from early on. Greg Sarris (1993) invokes the attractions of the reflexive move in social science:

what I explore is . . . a specific kind of dialogue, or conversation, that can open the intermingling of the multiple voices within and between people and the texts they encounter, enabling people to see and hear the ways various voices intersect and overlap, the ways they have been repressed or held down because of certain social and political circumstances, and the ways they can be talked about and explored . . . reflexivity ask[s] ethnographers to account for their conclusions, for their notions of truth and knowledge, and for the political and historical consequences of their work. They argue that for cross-cultural communication to be open and effective, interlocutors must be aware of the limits on and possibilities for understanding one another in the exchange. That is, in understanding another person and culture you must simultaneously understand yourself. The process is ongoing, an endeavor aimed not at a final transparent understanding of the other or of the self, but at continued communication, at an ever-widening understanding of both. (5–6)

Recent feminist scholarship drives to the heart of the limits of reflexivity, as when Daphne Patai warns that social scientists' reflexivity "does not redistribute income, gain political rights for the powerless, create housing for the homeless, or improve health" (1991: 35) and Diane Wolf adds that "[t]he challenge remains to write a text that does not position the researcher on center stage while marginalizing those being researched" (1995: 35). These are cautions that guide this discussion of methods, theories, and above all my positioning, which (again in retrospect) constitutes a series of conscious, half-conscious, and unconscious strategies, or what Haraway (1991) names "partial perspectives," based on the "multiple personalities" (Sheehan 1993) that straddled the insiderness and outsiderness into which I grew during my research. But if the multiplicity of personas the ethnographer lives and uses in her or his work means that ethnography is by necessity "a rescripting and reperforming of self" (Henriksen n.d.: 10; see also Probyn 1993), then I have struggled to make sure that this elaboration of self is only one aspect of research for and writing of this book, and that the reflexivities of others, both authors and speakers, carry weight as well.

In viewing my work in the context of these ideas, I have become aware that my friendships in the field facilitated reciprocities that might also be considered synonymous with forms of mutual exploitation. I am left with the upper hand because of the very nature of ethnographic research (see Patai 1991; di Leonardo 1991), and thus that the notion of empowering informants in the course of either research or write-up may be another way for an ethnographer to expand the range and legitimacy of her or his texts (see Spivak 1988). Nevertheless, I have decided to imagine that the effects of my partial perspectives, experimental textualizations, and different field persona have created an autonomous interstice described by Brackette Williams. Notwithstanding my pale-colored skin, a stature and physique radically different from the people with whom I worked, my maleness compared to the femaleness of female informants and conceptualized very differently by me than by male informants, my U.S. citizenship during the period the United States waged war on Nicaragua, and my relative material wealth with respect to everyone I knew in Nicaragua, Williams (1995) seems to describe what occurred:

> If the anthropologist is successful in getting informants to ignore the requisite aspects of his or her identity features, then he or she can sometimes ignore those aspects of the social order of power relations that too severely constrain his or her construction or participant-observation to permit it an autonomous role identity. To select the requisite features to be ignored in fieldwork requires the anthropologist to continually situate himself or herself in the local order of status distinctions and to be aware of their symbolic, historical, and ongoing economic connections to his or her "own society" and its place in the social order of power relations. (93)

The fact that thousands of foreigners, especially North Americans and Western Europeans, flocked to Nicaragua following the triumph of the Sandinista Front on July 19, 1979, and that these foreigners were officially accorded a semi-insider status as *internacionalistas* (foreigners in solidarity with the revolutionary process), masked numerous internal contradictions and variations in that status. By so recognizing sympathetic foreign leftists, the Sandinista Front created, to abuse Lila Abu-Lughod's (1992) term, a political "halfie" status: you are like us because of your politics, but because you are from foreign rich countries perhaps you can help us out, even if (perhaps especially if) the government of the *internacionalistas estadounidenses* is the main culprit for our problems, past and present. Yet, how many *internacionalistas* did not even speak Spanish? How many were escaping unemployment, marginalization, and in some instances criminal charges in their home countries? How many came with political agendas further to the left than, more to the right than, or simply irrelevant to the revolutionary processes of an impoverished country recovering from year after year of war and economic contraction? Probably everyone who went to Nicaragua has her or his own impressionistic accounts with which to answer such questions and their many corollaries; but in my case the position *internacionalista* afforded me a semi-insider's entry into Nicaragua, an acceptable persona in a place where in 1980 I knew no one, spoke no Spanish, and considered myself in the main a student of Marxism.

After a month there, communicating with people in a way I still do not entirely understand in retrospect, I decided to go to graduate school in anthropology to carry out a period of extended fieldwork in Nicaragua. In my mind, this was mainly a *political* decision; the Nicaraguan Revolution was from my perspective the most interesting event in the world and the most aligned to the politics I had derived from my undergraduate studies. Moreover, when in the years to come I spoke with various officials in the new government's Ministry of Culture, I perceived that any study I would be permitted to undertake would be approved only insofar as my research yielded useful information to Ministry personnel. Sandinista officials with whom I spoke told me in no uncertain terms that the condition for doing anthropological fieldwork in Nicaragua was gearing research toward activist and action-oriented ends in the overall service of the revolutionary transformation. By accepting, indeed embracing that condition, I again conceived myself as an insider, a "militant anthropologist," in Scheper-Hughes's (1992) terms. I also believed that as a graduate student in anthropology I would gain a sufficiently sophisticated theoretical armature to understand what was occurring in Nicaragua, and that anthropology alone of the social sciences required the kind of firsthand research I wanted to do. During the next three years I returned to Nicaragua twice for a month at a time and composed a research project that put together several strands of personal, political, and academic interests and imperatives, each strand with its own set of contradictions and dilemmas that developed during the period of dissertation fieldwork (February 1984–June 1985).

By 1983, I had decided to work with a pottery production cooperative and to focus on changes in men's and women's work roles and routines stimulated by the revolutionary process. The cooperative is located in the village of San Juan de Oriente, about six kilometers south of the city of Masaya, the capital of the province (*departamento*) of the same name. Masaya is the artisanal capital of the country, and along with the neighboring province of Carazo (and part of

Granada province as well), forms a region composed of numerous small villages, or *los pueblos,* as Nicaraguans call them. The choice to work with potters derived from the time I had spent studying pottery in Mexico and North Carolina, a study that derived from a life-long infatuation with the craft. Here, I was obviously setting up another insider strategy: "they" did pottery, and so did I. We would obviously have much to talk about and immediately so. My decision seemed legitimated by the extensive anthropology literature on artisanal production, made readily accessible to me by my academic advisor, Carol Smith, and by the small number of Marxist ethnographies of work exemplified by Harry Braverman (1974) and Richard Pfeffer (1979), which motivated me to base my own research around a workplace and the daily experience of work. Deciding to focus on gender issues and changes brought up more complex issues. I considered myself a feminist and had tried to shape my personal relationships on that basis; unsurprisingly, I felt extremely uncomfortable with Latin American machismo. Initial conversations in San Juan and elsewhere in Nicaragua in 1982 and 1983 showed that, at least on the official level, the government and mass organizations were calling for changes in gender roles and an attack on the most grotesque aspects of machismo. This provided some comfort to me; I now realize that at the time I believed that I would get along better with women than with men in my research. That belief proved partially right and mostly wrong in several circumstances.

In working out the details of my project, I had discussed Gramscian theory with individuals at the Ministry of Culture, particularly Marta Zamora and Olga Marta Montiél, women educated in the United States and Europe and from the revolutionary fraction of Nicaragua's elite. The Marxist discourses we shared in common facilitated the Ministry's approval of my work, or so it seemed to me. Our relationship was likely also facilitated because I did not challenge or even mention certain limiting factors in my research design. For one thing, I never petitioned the resource-starved Ministry for technical or any other kind of help. I also did not propose to use individual or household surveys or questionnaires, recognizing the extremely politicized nature of such methods, given two factors. First, any kind of household survey meant asking about draft-age men during the period in which the Servicio Militar Patriotico (Patriotic Military Draft) was reaching for younger and younger men and becoming one of the sorest points of contention between the populace and the Sandinista state. Second, such formal questionnaires were viewed as politically sensitive in an increasingly polarized climate, especially if deployed by a North American. I chose to stick with purely qualitative methods—ethnographies of work based on participation and mostly informal interviewing—which seemed to ease everyone's worries.

At the Ceramics Cooperative in San Juan de Oriente, Orlando Gallegos, the Co-op's coordinator, very quickly approved my plan to apprentice to the potters when I introduced the idea to him in 1983. My daily presence in the Co-op starting in 1984 was also accepted fairly immediately by several of the men who worked there, especially Agustín Amador and Bladimir Nororís, the painters of the so-called Mayan vases, as well as several other men, particularly Roberto Potosme. They called me *"un estudiante de la cultura"* (a student of culture), no doubt influenced by my descriptions of anthropology and what anthropologists did. I think my work made sense to them because the Ministry of Culture had already created a framework called "culture," already sent Ministry people to San Juan as cultural attachés, and because of the San Juaneros' perception of the Masaya region and its history as integral to the entity "Nicaraguan culture," phenomena I will detail at length in this book. So, for the first six months of my fieldwork, I sat with the men, helping them with their easier, repetitive tasks, asking about the history of the Co-op and about their lives as artisans, while they asked me about the United States and myriad questions about my life and the world. We became friends, for me a natural process, but one jarred frequently by the disparities between our lives, many of them material. Although the Co-op *socios* (members) dressed in bluejeans, T-shirts, and sneakers, much as I did, my first visits to their homes constituted an abrupt wake-up call to our differences. Agustín, Roberto, and the women with whom I later became friends lived in houses with walls of pine or even plywood planks and dirt floors. Better-built houses featured walls of cinderblock; sometimes the floor of the front sitting room was tiled. Kitchens were semi-outdoor affairs, with wood-burning cooking areas and a sink. The *socios'* houses did have running water and electricity, both of which had become universal in Masaya-Carazo during the 1960s and '70s. I did not consider my friends poor, and they, in turn, did not understand what poverty meant in the context of the United States, as Agustín made clear. "Look, Les," he declared, "we have heard that poor people in the United States have cars and televisions. Right? They have tape players. So we want to know, how can they be considered poor?" When San Juaneros visited the house we rented in Masaya, the tiny refrigerator we had impressed them less than the sheer amount of space at our disposal. Their amazement was not a positive reaction, however, as they considered so much space for two people likely to make us feel lonely and sad.

But much more than these material differences, the masculine roles and behaviors in which the male *socios* engaged and which I found repulsive separated us. When each of my friends impregnated women other than their wives during the months of my fieldwork, I never knew exactly how to react and what to say to the friend, his wife, or the other woman. The interstitial persona I occupied, however, at least relieved me of any expectation of similar behavior: I was a friend, but different. The reciprocity between us smoothed that difference and worked like this: they gave me their time and attention endlessly, and I bought them paintbrushes, oxides for glazes, and a variety of catalogues and books about pre-Columbian art of Mesoamerica, which the men used to design and paint pots. We most certainly exploited each other mutually; none of us, at least in the fieldwork situation, held all the cards, so to speak (see Patai 1991), and as my project changed that became clearer. The textualization of my fieldwork is, of course, another story, but an issue I have also tried to address.

The women whom I most wanted to talk to—Ester Bracamonte, Catalina Bracamonte, and Patricia Bracamonte, cousins who turned out literally hundreds of mugs and other wheel-spun pots daily—politely and smilingly declined to pass more than a few pleasantries with me. My relationship with women in the Co-op and with the wives of the men who had become my friends changed only after the arrival in August 1984 of Gia Scarpetta, the woman with whom I had been in a relationship for two years. The Bracamonte cousins and other women who made pottery in San Juan (in and out of the Co-op) welcomed Gia warmly; her Spanish was far superior to mine, and perhaps too, Gia's agenda was more purely friendship, uncluttered, as she put it, by my theoretical concerns. Gia's position was not unlike that of Margery Wolf when she first went to Taiwan (see M. Wolf 1992, 1995; also Tedlock 1995), in that Gia's presence, ideas, and insights enormously facilitated the process of fieldwork, particularly with the women in the San Juan Co-op. Unlike Wolf, whose visit to Nicaragua and my field sites in May 1984 spurred me to think about these issues early on, Gia has not become a professional anthropologist. She declined to write anything formal for this book, but her presence is not mute, as I refer to her ideas and presence repeatedly, as do many of the individuals with whom we worked.

After Gia's arrival, we began to visit and work with another group of potters, a large extended family living in the northern mountain towns of Matagalpa and Jinotega, among whom only women make a hand-formed, open-fired, burnished black pottery known as *cerámica negra*. My relationship with these women, Gia's relationship with them, and our relationship with them as a couple differed markedly from the parallel relationships with the San Juaneras. Both Gia and I sat at the tables with Doña Silvia Pineda de Castro and her daughters in Jinotega, and with Doña Carmen Rodríguez Pineda and her daughter María Esthela in Matagalpa and helped to prepare the clay, form the pots, and polish them at various stages of their production. Gia's presence was less remarkable than mine; the women appreciated that I took an interest in their craft, and that I was willing to do any and all of the tasks involved without commenting on what was appropriate only for men or only for women, as the men in their family had always done. I felt accepted by the *cerámica negra* women in ways that took much longer in San Juan. Nevertheless, they told Gia information about relationships with men, particularly stories of abusive husbands and lovers, which I never heard except through Gia, whereas my conversations with them centered around pottery and their relationship with the Ministry of Culture. Along these lines, Diane Wolf, using Tixier y Vigil and Elsasser's study (1976), has elaborated the complex differences between two researchers whose distinctive positionings vis-à-vis their informants enabled them to access very different kinds of information in the same fieldwork situation.

Our relationship with artisans in San Juan and up north, efforts by artisans to organize an autonomous artisans union (its acronym was UNADI) with aims explicitly in opposition to the Ministry's projects and ideas, and monthly meetings with Ministry officials about my work occasioned a new phase in our research. Both artisans and officials in the Ministry saw my work as "for the artisans," and because the latter believed that I had access to artisans' opinions and especially those of the artisans' union, I was treated and eventually functioned as a kind of go-between for the Ministry of Culture and the potters. This role gave me access to many people and more information. With this information, Orlando Gallegos was better able to plan the Co-op's production needs, while Roberto Potosme and María Esthela Rodríguez, both of whom became delegates from their respective regions to the artisans' union, used my information as a window into the Ministry's strategies. In this phase of the project, the stakes for friendship, reciprocity, and activist research climbed so high that I came to consider myself fully an insider because I perceived that I was treated that way. That perception, right or wrong, does not negate the contradictions inherent in all the aspects of my positioning. Rather than dwell on these contradictions self-importantly, it is perhaps more relevant to admit their ultimate irrelevance. I became obsessed with trying to explain why the Sandinista Front had moved to favor the artisans' union over its own Ministry of Culture during 1985 because that decision seemed to embody the possibilities for a revolutionary democracy that was moving toward a system of power sharing with and responsiveness to subaltern groups, I also believed that if I could critically describe and analyze this process, it would prove helpful to the revolutionary transformation in general and to artisans specifically. The issue became the central question both of my dissertation and of chapter 2 in this volume. After I returned from Nicaragua and since the defeat of the Frente in 1990, I have had to face the fact that what had consumed me, and all the implications I had drawn from it, had constituted a rather brief blip in the overall scheme of things.

Many changes in the economic, political, and social organization of the country surprised and disturbed me when I returned to Nicaragua in 1993, after eight years' absence, notwithstanding the many letters sent to us intermittently from San Juan and the *cerámica negra* women during that time. After having carried out several research projects with indigenous peoples in Colombia, Ecuador, and California during the interim, the existence of an indigenous movement in western Nicaragua made perhaps the greatest impression. Of course, I had been aware that San Juaneros considered themselves *indígenas* during my research of the mid-1980s, and that the Monimbó neighborhood of the town of Masaya where we lived was called an Indian barrio. But I had minimized the importance of such phenomena in my dissertation by accepting the Sandinista analysis of it: in brief, that the struggles of Nicaragua's indigenous people (not including those on the Atlantic Coast, with their totally distinct history and social mosaic) had metamorphosed into class struggles, and that the ethnic character of that struggle had faded as indigenous languages, social organization, and other cultural markers had disappeared during the late nineteenth century. In an attempt to understand the appearance of an indigenous movement in western Nicaragua, I asked Orlando Gallegos to introduce me to friends he knew in Monimbó who he believed were involved in the movement. We ended up meeting Flavio Gamboa, then the secretary-general of the Movimiento Indígena, Negro y Popular–Quinientos Años (Indigenous, Black, Popular Movement of the Five Hundred Years), one of the indigenous groups organized in the region at that time.

Meeting Flavio changed the scope of my research in Nicaragua and the way this book has been written, bringing to a new level the collaboration with artisans that had been a part of my work up to that time. The artisans in San Juan, Jinotega, and Matagalpa with whom I worked are articulate, literate individuals who actively participated in the political and intellectual processes of shaping cultural identities, and I had described them as organic intellectuals in the Gramscian vein, even as "internal articulatory intellectuals" (Lomnitz-Adler 1992). As local, organic, or native intellectuals, they have had few if any opportunities to write about, much less publish accounts of their experiences in order to analyze their participation in recent Nicaraguan cultural history. By contrast, Flavio has appointed himself the historian-ethnographer of Masaya-Carazo, and as a political theorist of the indigenous movement in western Nicaragua he has published numerous articles in national newspapers. With a ninth-grade education, Flavio is an autodidact, a man of more than sixty years whose travels in Eastern Europe, the USSR, Cuba, and North Korea were underwritten by the Nicaraguan Socialist Party in the 1960s, '70s, and '80s, and who also worked briefly as an undertaker in New York City in the '60s. The child of a family with an unusually well-documented history (described in detail later), he inherited a number of unique manuscripts: the memoirs of his father and grandfather, recording events that stretch back into the early nineteenth century. After meeting Flavio, my older project of analyzing the negotiation of cultural policy under the Sandinistas and my new project of detailing the indigenous movement in western Nicaragua in the post-

Sandinista era hitched onto Flavio's projects. He decided that both of my projects could not be attempted without an exhaustive review of the history of *El Güegüence* and the murky local history of indigenous peoples in the Masaya region.

I accepted his view. He received free travel and accommodations as we pursued our research all over western Nicaragua in 1993 and again in '95. I received access to his manuscripts, his memories, his insights. Although Flavio has appreciated the material benefits of my presence, the exchange seems to me uneven, particularly in light of other relationships between Flavio and outside researchers, in which Flavio had been given very little acknowledgment or intellectual colleagueship (see García Bresó 1992). In reaction to past exploitation of him, I asked Flavio whether he wanted to contribute his own essay to the book I was writing, which I would translate as faithfully as I could. This pleased him immensely. His essay elaborates indigenous history and identity in the Masaya-Carazo region; he was obsessing over indigenous identity and *El Güegüence* long before I showed up at his door, and we began goading each other to track down as many textual versions of this work as can be found in western Nicaragua. Thus, his essay makes explicit reference to *El Güegüence* from the vantage of his own agenda.

Flavio's influence on the organization of my thinking led me to ask several of the artisans also to contribute essays to the book, and their essays began arriving in my mailbox. Roberto Potosme, a close friend and potter from San Juan, focuses on class issues from his vantage as a founding member and delegate to the artisans' union in 1984–85. Orlando Gallegos, the former coordinator of the San Juan Co-op, also analyzes issues relating to class and revolutionary politics from a distinct perspective. María Esthela Pineda Rodríguez of Matagalpa writes about the history of her family's craft, with subtle yet pervasive thoughtfulness about issues of gender and her family's struggle against gender-based oppression. San Juanera women whom I would have liked to include, particularly Catalina Bracamonte, declined, although as a consolation to me, Catalina agreed to let me interview her repeatedly to update her extensive life history taken in 1985.

This experiment in coauthorship is nothing if not fraught with contradictions and dangers. I have not individually listed these Nicaraguans as coauthors of the book, because that would misrepresent how the book was written. I organized, edited, conceptualized, and

wrote the vast majority of this book, and I claim its overall authorship. On the other hand, I have tried to navigate a blurry middle
ground between treating the essays written by my friends as rich
ethnographic material, with which I can support my own points,
and handling them as I would a text written by another academic.
Let me elaborate. I do not claim these stories or essays as mine, in
the way Ruth Behar (1993) has done with Esperanza's story, or as
Judith Stacey's informants (in D. Wolf 1995) seem to feel she did with
their stories. It is not simply that I have limited myself to relating
only certain biographical data about each essay's author in order
to make them seem less "my" incredibly knowledgeable informants.
In the case of Flavio, he himself has limited my knowledge about
him, because he has considered our collaboration to be specifically
focused on mutual explorations of the relationship between *El Güegüence* and Nicaraguan cultural history. Many times, we agreed to
disagree—about North Korea, for example—or decided to talk more
about Nicaraguan history than about ourselves. Readers may thus
want to know more about Flavio than I know or think it appropriate
to tell. Yet our collaboration and my collaborations with the other
essay authors cannot be said to resemble what Jaffe (1993) and Sheehan (1993) described in their interactions with formally constituted,
academic intellectuals in Corsica and Ireland respectively. The power
differential between the local Nicaraguan intellectuals and me is far
more lopsided than in the case of these other authors' work. Consequently, much more so than either Jaffe and Sheehan, I have "the last
word" about Nicaraguan cultural history through this book, which
limits the collaborative glow with which I want to endow it.

As I read the essays sent from Nicaragua, I was struck by certain
similarities between their written tellings and my tellings of these
histories (see Field 1987, 1995) prior to writing this book. My accounts derived from extensive conversations and interviews, and my
reading of what they have written indicates that those same conversations have played an important role in how they wrote them
down, at least in part. In truth, I wanted our respective tellings to
differ more than they have, and so these recountings and analyses
of events no longer seem to me separated, but woven together by
the relationships formed and still forming between us. By the same
token, Flavio and María Esthela make use of essentialist notions and
what Appadurai (1996) would call primordial ideas, which I have

argued against in my work (see Field 1994a, 1996). This divergence underscores why this book should not be classified as a polyphonic ethnography, if such a creature in fact exists, along the lines Clifford (1986b) appears to favor. I agree with Spivak's (1988) warning that it is impossible for academic authors to pretend that "the subaltern can speak" through our work, whatever the experimental nature of our textual weavings. The goals adopted in Fox's (1992) recent post-postmodern anthology, particularly in the essays written by Trouillot, Abu-Lughod, and Fox himself, appear more in line with my experiment in collaborative writing. These authors argue for new cultural histories that focus on innovative individual lives (Fox), that challenge preconceived categories both within academia and in fieldwork situations (Trouillot and Fox), and that revalorize ethnography to work against the grain of Western power and its knowledges, including anthropology's obsession, culture (Abu-Lughod and Trouillot).

Thus, this book could not work without the words of these other individuals, acknowledging that as participants in this process, we do not receive equal rewards. I get a book that contributes to my anthropological career. The Nicaraguans have experienced the textualization of their thoughts and their dissemination, which I intend to translate and republish in Nicaragua, although I am aware that it may go unread or be dismissed as irrelevant, and that its interpretation by individuals involved in the making of the book as well as other Nicaraguans are beyond my control (see Rappaport 1994 for an actual case along such lines). Underlying the book is a tactical alliance between local intellectuals using essentialist ideas to defend their selfhoods and peoplehoods, and a metropolitan intellectual who is basically a social constructionist but is also committed to challenging the power relations of ethnography and interpretation. That alliance means that these essays are included with the understanding that our collaboration is limited; I do use their essays to ethnographically document my points, but I also analyze and criticize them to underscore the complex interweaving of strategy and essence in the construction of identities. The areas of agreement between us are largely based on our shared ethnographic experiences.

My larger goal in writing this book is to add to the critique of Sandinista cultural policies, as part of an overall project of eroding the manner in which various elite fractions (including, paradoxically, anthropologists) have defined and characterized what they consider

Nicaraguan culture. The fact is that Nicaragua is a destitute country, blocked from improving the lot of the majority by international capital, U.S. foreign policy, and the continued political and economic domination of its old elite. Does empowering local intellectuals to redefine identity and culture make sense in such a circumstance? Obviously I think it does, and this volume constitutes a contribution to that project directed toward reading audiences outside of Nicaragua who have had intermittent glimpses of the cultural processes going on in Nicaragua over the past two decades. Moreover, this collaboration also forms part of the larger project of bridging the work of different kinds of intellectuals. I do not agree with Friedman's recent assessment that "[c]ulture is supremely negotiable for professional culture experts, but for those whose identity depends upon a particular configuration this is not the case. Identity is not negotiable. Otherwise it has no existence" (1994: 140). Ultimately, my collaboration with local Nicaraguan intellectuals also shows that the negotiation of culture and identities has been one of the thematic characteristics of our relationships over the years.

The Importance of Nicaraguan Texts and Nicaraguan Discourse About Them: Parables, Allegories, Actors

Clifford (1986) has described as allegories the methodological choices, theoretical foci, and creative themes embedded in ethnographic texts, such as those I have described in the preceding sections. In using an expanded definition of this term, which he traces to literary deconstructionists such as Paul de Man, he argues that a "recognition of allegory emphasizes the fact that realistic portraits, to the extent that they are 'convincing' or 'rich,' are extended metaphors, patterns of association that point to coherent (theoretical, esthetic, moral) additional meanings . . . Allegory draws special attention to the *narrative* character of cultural representations, to the stories built into the representational process itself" (1986: 100). Following this usage, the allegorical subtexts in my research and writing could include cross-cultural friendship; certain romantic notions about artisanal craftsmanship; the idealism that resides in the possibility of socialist transformation; the desire to confound the macho construction of malehood and be instead a feminist man; and the hopes raised by the idea of ethnographic coauthorship raised by scholars such as Clifford himself. But although the intertwining of these allegorical themes in the narratives of this volume is no doubt informative, it is less interesting to me than the way in which parable is built into the structure and analyses I present here.

As noted in the prologue, by parable I mean a narrative that illustrates a lesson by means of analogy or comparison; the parable that I work into my treatment of Nicaraguan cultural history and the role of artisans in that history is *El Güegüence*. In organizing several aspects of my argument around *El Güegüence* and repeatedly referring to the play as a way of drawing many threads of analysis together, I believe that it is apparent how far ethnographers have come since Clifford (1986) noted, in the same essay cited above, that "it is no longer possible to act as if the outside researcher is the sole, or primary, bringer of the culture [in question] into writing . . . there has been a consistent tendency among fieldworkers to hide, discredit, or marginalize prior written accounts (by missionaries, travelers, administrators, local authorities, even other ethnographers). The fieldworker, typically, starts from scratch, from a research *experience,* rather than from reading or transcribing" (117).

During the 1980s and 1990s, Nicaraguan intellectuals have made use of allegory in the construction and reconstruction of Nicaraguan national identity, organizing their allegories around two heroic tropes: Sandino and the modernist author Rubén Darío. In the case of Sandino the allegory narrates the struggle to establish the political sovereignty of the Nicaraguan state, and in the case of Darío the story tells how Nicaragua made a major contribution to global literature, thus legitimizing Nicaraguan culture. These allegorical heroes are far more familiar to readers and thinkers outside of Nicaragua than is *El Güegüence*. Yet neither allegorical hero narrates the disjunctures of class, gender, and ethnicity in the formation and reformation of Nicaraguan national identity.

Granted, during the mid-1980s I too was almost unaware of *El Güegüence*. Little by little, and after 1993 in overpowering waves, I became engrossed with this ancient comedy-dance-drama, which was composed by an unknown author sometime, depending on which interpretation one believes, during the sixteenth, or seventeenth, or eighteenth century. As I learned, *El Güegüence* was rendered in at least four distinct nineteenth-century manuscripts written in the original Nahuatl-Spanish dialect, although its performance clearly dates back hundreds of years earlier. The play has appeared in five Spanish translations, as well as very influential, older English and Italian translations, and has been republished by three important critical essayists. It has been commented upon and interpreted by many times that number of famous and not-so-famous writers from among several fractions of elite Nicaraguans as well as by foreign authorities. Among these writers, the textualized translations and commentaries of several Nicaraguan intellectuals—Pablo Antonio Cuadra, Francisco Pérez Estrada, Alejandro Dávila Bolaños, Carlos Mántica Abaunza, Jorge Eduardo Arellano, among others—will figure most importantly for my purposes.

El Güegüence takes place in Masaya-Carazo, and has been performed there in the streets of several towns for a variously defined "very long time." It is, as we shall see, in each of its versions and interpretations a complex, simultaneous demarcation and mystification of identity, of culture, and of history in this region, and is one of the three symbols of Nicaraguan national identity in elite intellectual discourse—the other two being the poet Rubén Darío and the soldier-statesman Augusto César Sandino. Much of what Nicaraguan and foreign authors have written about Nicaraguan national identity focuses on these two historical figures, but during this century influential elite authors, especially Pablo Antonio Cuadra, also heralded *El Güegüence* as the first manifestation of Nicaraguan literature and as the dramatic nexus in which Nicaraguan national identity came into existence. In other words, Cuadra and many later writers used *El Güegüence* as a parable for the disappearance of indigenous groups from western Nicaragua and the cultural domination of the *mestizos*—in short, the people of mixed Spanish and Indian descent, the speakers of the Spanish language, and the bearers of a distinctively *Latin* American culture.[3]

Taking as valid the elite's notion that *El Güegüence* has in the past acted as a parable for Nicaraguan identity, the ethnographic information I have gathered in my work with artisans in western Nicaragua over the past decade and a half provides ammunition for two different historical hypotheses. One could surmise, given the descriptive materials I will elaborate in the following chapters, that *El Güegüence* no longer operates as a narrative for Nicaraguan national identity as it once did when much of the elite intellectual discourse about the play was written. Or, one might conclude that the elite intellectual interpretation of the play was faulty to begin with, and that *El Güegüence* does indeed possess significance to Nicaraguan national identity but in ways dominant elite interpretations have always elided. The latter conclusion is in any event already suggested by the interpretive analyses of *El Güegüence* authored by Mántica and Dávila Bolaños, both of which have had politically important consequences. It is also suggested by a new Latin American literature about social movements focused on redefining mestizo identity, which is relevant to post-Sandinista social movements in Nicaragua that I will discuss at length.

My own treatment of *El Güegüence* is twofold (at least). First, detailing the interpretative literature about *El Güegüence*, far more than analyzing Darío's poetry or Sandino's aphorisms as many others have done, enables us to understand the positioning of artisans within elite demarcations of Nicaraguan culture and national identity and therefore within Sandinista cultural policy, which itself derived from elite discourses about Nicaraguan culture. *El Güegüence*'s interpretive literature has situated San Juan and the Masaya region as culturally significant because of its artisans, including the potters, because of the linguistic complexity in regional place-names and everyday speech, and ultimately because of multiple and contradictory acknowledgments that the history of indigenous identity here remains an unfinished, or at least untidy, affair. However, this literature considers the northern highlands region, where the towns of Matagalpa and Jinotega are located, as less culturally significant, in the main because the business of indigenous identity was supposedly concluded decisively at the end of the last century.[4] Infusing the textualizations of *El Güegüence* within ethnographic analyses establishes a series of resonances between the events occurring during ethnographic research, the way that Nicaraguans themselves understand the play as illustrating their cultural identities, and the ways I have used the play's many interpretations to illuminate cultural history.

A second important weaving of the *El Güegüence* literature into this text underscores the emergence following the electoral defeat of the Sandinistas of cultural and identity discourses among artisans in Masaya-Carazo and elsewhere in western Nicaragua. I will argue that these post-1990 identity politics, under yet another regime that is attempting to reconfigure the nature of the state in Nicaragua, appear to undermine the elite construction of Nicaraguan culture and national identity. The slow collapse of an older, elite-demarcated Nicaraguan identity suggests to me the renewed significance of *El Güegüence* as a point of departure for new social and cultural movements, and perhaps especially so if and when a new Sandinismo were to assume control over the government again. Old habits of elite intellectuals of diverse ideological stripes die hard, however, as Sergio Ramírez, the former vice president under the Sandinistas and later the presidential candidate for the Sandinista Renovation Party, has underscored. Ramírez, a major contemporary novelist as well, expressed his views on Macho Ratón to William Frank Gentile in 1988:

The Macho Ratón helps to explain an aspect of the Nicaraguan character, the Nicaraguan sense of humor. The Nicaraguan puts on an armor of humor when facing difficult situations. Life here is incomprehensible without humor, without irony. The humor allows you to laugh at yourself. If you can't laugh at yourself, you really have no sense of humor at all. I think we have the ability to make light of the most difficult, the most uncomfortable situations . . . I think the Macho Ratón illustrates three things: the pride of the subjugated before the oppressor; humor as a means of defense, a kind of shrewdness; and a tremendous ability to improvise when confronted with difficult situations. These three things have emerged in the historical situations of being unequal to the superior forces we were up against, powerful forces that were capable of wiping us out completely. Intelligence and shrewdness have developed in this battle of the strong against the weak. Without that sense of national pride, we would not be able to defend ourselves. The synthesis of these three elements constitutes for me our national dignity. (Gentile 1989: 128–29)

In the same interview, however, Ramírez also named Darío and Sandino "the two poles of our national identity" (129).

During a visit to Albuquerque in 1995, Ramírez spoke to a crowd of progressive academics and graduate students, community activists and other local leftists about the way writing and politics became bedfellows in twentieth-century Nicaraguan history, thus producing parallelisms between fiction and the political imaginary particularly during Sandinismo. The central figures of the literary politics and politics of literature that have constructed Nicaraguan national identity, Ramírez emphasized, were Sandino and Darío. Apart from eliding women and women authors from his history of Nicaraguan literature and politics, he also left out *El Güegüence*. I asked him about the latter silence after he concluded his presentation, and he responded with nothing more than a politician's smile.

El Güegüence and its interpretive literature are not the only texts woven into this volume as actors in their own right.[5] Very soon after taking up residence in Masaya and beginning to work at the Ceramics Cooperative in San Juan, I realized that some books were not simply sources of information for certain individuals and groups about particular subjects of importance. Some books have played and continue to play much more profound roles, becoming powerful and authoritative in the realms of identity formation and political activity. For example, the Costa Rican Spanish-language edition of Samuel K. Lothrop's *Pottery of Nicaragua and Costa Rica* (1926), which I found at the San Juan Co-op a week after I started working there, had exercised an extraordinary influence over the development of aesthetic techniques in the production of pottery in the Co-op and in all of San Juan. Lothrop's book, based on overviews of western Nicaraguan cultural history delineated in the writings of both nineteenth-century Nicaraguan elites and foreign scholars, had fueled a reinterpretation of local cultural history and contemporary identity among the San Juanero artisans. Jaime Wheelock's *Las raíces indígenas de la lucha anti-colonialista* (1981) has also exercised a profound influence, but over the revolutionary bureaucracy's understanding of the Masaya-Carazo region. Wheelock's book, notwithstanding its denunciation of elite historiography, reproduced many aspects of the elite's views of Nicaraguan culture. In elaborating Sandinista views of national and local identities in Nicaragua, Wheelock's book helps to explain ambiguities in the negotiation of cultural policy when juxtaposed with the writings of Ernesto Cardenal, the minister of culture from 1979 to 1988. Cardenal's books have enunciated a very different Sandinista politics of culture. Written texts by Wheelock, Cardenal, and several other Sandinista authors will be cited not simply as references but as material instantiations of political discourse, allegorical subtexts, in Clifford's words, that underlie the events marking cultural policy and identity transformations since 1979.

A large volume of work of various kinds—poetry, fiction, social science analyses, testimonials, activist pamphlets—mostly written since 1990 compose a feminist literature that also behaves as active texts in Nicaraguan discourses and in the description and analysis of this book. The Nicaraguan feminist literature is perhaps the best example of how the negotiation of cultural policy under Sandinismo gave birth to a new set of possibilities for identity politics after the Sandinista defeat. At the same time, the feminist discourse, as I will show, does not necessarily elaborate the positionings of women in the artisan communities where Gia and I worked. Thus my exploration of this literature brings into relief the complexities of identity negotiation in the post-Sandinista era.

Analyses of Nicaraguan Culture Written by North Americans

In each chapter, the ethnographic material I present and my analysis of it frequently refer to the literature about Nicaraguan culture and its transformations written by non-Nicaraguans in English since 1979. This literature has been overwhelmingly dominated by authors writing in the vein of cultural critique, particularly literary criticism. I am not referring to a number of very accessible slim volumes that convey exuberantly positive impressions of Sandinismo offered by literary celebrities such as Salman Rushdie, Julio Cortazar, and others. Rather, the books in my purview critique the creative oeuvre and spoken words of Nicaraguan poets, novelists, playwrights, performers, and artists within the context of an overall analysis of Sandinista cultural policy and the transformation of Nicaraguan culture. As have I, all of these authors have carried out at least partially reflexive analyses that reflect the complex exigencies of working in and collaborating with the revolutionary process in Nicaragua. Some of these reflexivities have coincided more resonantly with this project than others.

As far as U.S. anthropologists have been concerned, however, Richard Adams's (1957) pronouncement that Nicaragua was no longer inhabited by groups who could "legitimately" be called "Indians" has exercised something of a hex over anthropological research in western Nicaragua, as well as corroborating the views of Nicaraguan elites. Adams's areal survey, mandated by the World Health Organization, was intended not merely to inform but to identify social conflicts within the Central American states and to suggest options for socioeconomic development explicitly linked to nation-building. Given that anthropologists during those decades focused almost exclusively on peoples in Latin America who could "legitimately" be called "Indians," Adams's book shaped the work, or lack thereof, that anthropologists from the United States carried out in western Nicaragua for many years. There is nothing terribly surprising about Adams's assumptions about Indian cultural identities: like other North American anthropologists in the mid-twentieth century, Adams viewed indigenous identity as trait-defined. Language, dress and other presentations of the body, and religious practices made up the most important traits against which the degree of Indianness could be mapped by an anthropologist. Anthropologists have conventionally characterized indigenous cultures as static in nature, and therefore highly vulnerable to social, economic, and technological changes. The latter inevitably erode and eliminate the former. The nearly complete absence of Indian traits in western Nicaragua, including in the Masaya-Carazo region, indicated to Adams that Indian identity had succumbed to the twin forces of acculturation and assimilation, processes anthropologists have narrated extensively during this century. Thus, Adams called the people of zones where the term Indian was still used (i.e., in Monimbó, Sutiava, and rural Matagalpa) "Spanish-speaking Indians." He argued that the term Indian marked a particular lower-class stratum among whom the process of *mestizaje* lagged compared to the majority of the poorer social sectors. Because the label had no cultural significance, Adams predicted that in time no one in western Nicaragua would be called an Indian.

Although Adams noted the performance of masquerade street theater in Monimbó, he did not mention *El Güegüence* specifically. He wrote authoritatively about rural Matagalpa, but he admitted to never having gone there himself. This accounts for his assertions that the rural folk called Indians by others and themselves in Matagalpa no longer wove cloth (they did and do), and that they made black pottery (such pottery was and is made by mestizos in the city of Matagalpa). Even in Monimbó, where he did spend time, he misidentified the source of local pottery, which of course originated in San Juan de Oriente. But more important than these quibbles, Adams's chapter described western Nicaragua as almost bereft of Indians and inhabited by mestizos whom he saw not as bearers of Nicaraguan national culture—the interpretation of a Pablo Antonio Cuadra and several generations of elite Nicaraguan intellectuals—but as somewhat pathetic specimens: "The contemporary lower class in the rural areas have dropped off most of the aboriginal and colonial Indian traits which distinguished them as Indians 80 years ago; they have not had the opportunity to take over the traits of the Ladino and upper class which required money and they have not had the social organization to develop a new series of traits. While they combine traits of Spanish and Indian origin, they have actually lost more of both. They are, like the campesinos of Panama, deculturated and the process of deculturation has left them as a part of the Nicaraguan social system, but the lowest part of it" (1957: 250). I cannot imagine a less attractive epitaph for a whole region, especially from one anthropologist directing remarks (at least in part) to other anthropologists. It is therefore small wonder that after Adams anthropologists did not set off for western Nicaragua, a land without Indians and with only deculturated mestizos.[6]

The Adams hex has been broken by only a few individuals, of whom two, besides myself, have published book-length studies. These two, Michael Higgins (1992) and Roger Lancaster (1988, 1992), have focused, respectively, on Sandinista popular organizations in a Managua barrio and the complexities of gender relations in a Managua barrio. Both have steered clear of the intertwinings between Sandinista cultural policy and the construction of local and national identities. Notwithstanding the considerable merits of Higgins's and Lancaster's work, my own work probably finds more company, if not entirely congenially, in the following three works by scholars in the field of cultural critique.

Among cultural critics, John Beverley and Marc Zimmerman's *Literature and Politics in the Central American Revolutions* (1990) offers useful insights about Sandinista cultural policy. Beverley and Zimmerman have been translating and writing introductory commentaries for Nicaraguan poets for some years now and have maintained a long and extensive physical presence in Nicaragua as well. Their insights are based on a profound understanding of Nicaraguan history and the cultural milieu shaping poetry and its production in that country before and since Sandinismo. For these authors, issues of class, class consciousness, and the shaping role of class in aesthetics and cultural production are seminal. Using such a framework, Beverley and Zimmerman reach three conclusions that I have found illuminating. First, literature as a part of culture functions as a part of the overall ideological ambience within nation-states, reflecting multiple class interests. Second, in the case of Central America and in

Nicaragua particularly, these authors agree with the elite Nicaraguan intellectual, Pablo Antonio Cuadra, who, as chapter 1 of this book relates, asserted that poetry plays a key role in the construction of national identity. Each Nicaraguan poet, according to these authors, reflects and represents heterogeneous strands of class interest and struggle, implicitly underscoring poetry's overall role as an essential glue of Nicaraguan culture. Finally, Beverley and Zimmerman recognize that the policies of the Sandinista state reflected its role as a site where such multidimensional struggles occurred. Therefore, they conclude, the battles over cultural policy (which I describe in chapter 2) cannot be depicted in stark class terms but must be understood as heavily mediated by the relative autonomy of cultural production by many individuals, the political ideologies competing within the Sandinista state, and the complex class positioning of the individuals involved in the revolutionary state during Sandinismo. Beverley and Zimmerman's theoretical framework leads them to discerning conclusions about the eventual closure of the Ministry of Culture.[7]

Margaret Randall is perhaps the best-known and most widely published author who has explored the rich vein of cultural critique from the vantage of solidarity with the revolutionary process. In Randall's case, this exploration spans several volumes. With the passing of the years, her work has moved from supportive documentation of the heroism of Sandinista women (1978, 1981) to extensive interviews with both male and female Nicaraguan writers (1984) to a sophisticated feminist critique of Sandinista politics (1994), including cultural policy, using even more extensive interviews with Nicaraguan women, many of whom are the same poets, novelists, and essayists discussed in chapter 4 of this book. Her latest Nicaragua book, *Sandino's Daughters Revisited: Feminism in Nicaragua* (1994), provides an unprecedented look into the social and cultural explosion of critical feminist analysis and identity construction among women since the defeat of the Frente in 1990. The book includes one interview with a working-class woman who is a union leader rather than a literary-intellectual-turned-Sandinista-leader; Randall has clearly spent far more time with the latter sort of person, many of whom were in fact interviewed for the original *Sandino's Daughters* (1981). Thus her interviews with powerful women like Michele Najlis, Daisy Zamora, and Gioconda Belli, who have all been integrally involved in the political life of the country, convey a depth of long-term commitment and analysis. The testimonies of these women underline their privileged position as radical yet powerful intellectuals because of their connection to the old elite social stratum. This in no way detracts either from their contributions to the revolutionary process or from Randall's focus on them. The book does, however, reinforce the impression that elite intellectuals have historically dominated Nicaraguan demarcations of national culture through mastery over written texts. If Randall highlights the unexpected ways a critical feminist consciousness emerged from Sandinista politics, which has given rise to new activism among Nicaraguan women (in the women's health movement, the A I D S education movement, the gay/lesbian organizations, etc.), her book also makes it even more imperative that new voices from among Nicaraguan women, such as the *artesanas* in chapter 4, make themselves heard.[8]

Randy Martin's *Socialist Ensembles: Theater and State in Cuba and Nicaragua* (1994) is the only work in the cultural critique literature that emphasizes the vital importance of *El Güegüence* to any discussion of Nicaraguan culture. Martin acknowledges the profound ambiguities of the play's content and the incongruity of understanding Güegüence, in the words of Cuadra, as "the quintessential national character." But although Martin's emphasis on performance and popular culture in Masaya-Carazo resonates with my own, he has not contextualized his discussion of *El Güegüence*'s role in Nicaraguan culture in terms of the wide body of interpretive literature by Nicaraguan intellectuals that I will discuss in the next chapter, or in terms of substantive ethnographic research in this or other regions of western Nicaragua.[9]

Another Reality Check: Nicaragua at the End of This Century

Some literary critics writing about Nicaraguan cultural processes (see Dawes 1993) under Sandinismo have been concerned primarily with various Marxist interpretations of class and class consciousness. Many if not most Marxist analyses during this century have considered revolutionary transformations within nation-states in light of their place in a trajectory leading toward worldwide socialist transformation. In much Marxist writing, nation-states are in effect the project of capitalist elites, and therefore socialism is naturally an international or at least nonnational project of the working and other subaltern classes under capitalism. Thus, revolutions in nations are at their best stepping stones on the way to revolutionary struggles explicitly aimed at disarticulating the capitalist world economy. I do not necessarily disagree with that conclusion, but given the position of Nicaragua in the capitalist world economy, this macro view would leave Nicaraguans and their stymied revolution waiting for the action to occur elsewhere. This view elides much of the richness of motivation, consciousness, and possibility present among the individuals I came to know during the Sandinista period.

In the current post-Sandinista milieu, the relationships between complex local identities and the cultural politics of national identity take place in the fin de siècle period of rabid capital accumulation and perpetually roving investment, a phase of capitalist development that has integrated Nicaragua into the world-system at the most abject level of powerlessness and servitude. As Manuel Castells (1986) has written, there are and will be areas of the Third World thrust into a kind of "obsolescence" by the global economy from which escape may not be possible for a very long time. Nicaragua's unenviable position is contextualized by recent historical-structural overviews of changes in global capitalist economics (see Harvey 1989; Friedman 1994) that identify the decentralization of capital investment and accumulation under a highly flexible and rapidly diversifying regime as the characterizing feature of the late twentieth century. The pre–World War II domination of the capitalist world economy by the imperialist metropolitan countries of Western Europe and North America has been replaced by a far more complex global network of capital-rich metropolises that conduct financial transactions in computer space/time as much if not more than anywhere else, but whose production home bases are as often as not scattered around the Pacific Rim. It does not take the likes of Friedman and Harvey to be aware of the juxtaposition of, on the one hand, the expanding power of global capital and the globalization of consumer products and sophisticated, "user-friendly" communication technologies, and, on the other hand, the accelerated and exacerbated development of armed, mutually hostile, localized cultural identities carving out territories for parochial, primordial, essentialist national projects. These late-twentieth-century combinations are well ensconced in much of the readily accessible popular literature.

Which is not to say that reading about these contradictions lessens the shock when entering one of three supermarkets now located on the main square of Masaya, my "hometown," where nothing of the kind had existed before 1990. Wandering the aisles, I saw rice imported from the United States, coffee from Honduras, and sugar from the Philippines—all products grown in Nicaragua but no longer available except in imported form. I also saw German beer and clothing imported from Hong Kong. Over several visits, I never saw more than four people walking around the supermarket closest to my old house, none of whom bought anything. My Masaya friends told me the supermarkets were artifacts of the UNO government's "golden handshake": the 30,000 cordobas doled out to each of the thousands of government employees fired when Violeta Chamorro became president, as part of the economic stabilization plan for the country signed, sealed, and delivered to her by the U.S. government. Many of the former employees of the state had pooled their resources to open new restaurants, ice cream parlors, and grocery stores. Too bad no one had any money to take advantage of them, as my friends pointed out. Meanwhile, back in the open-air *mercado* (market), where everyone still does their shopping, I was told that no one could sell me a cotton *cotona,* the comfortable campesino shirt; everything was made of dacron polyester now, because Nicaragua had to sell all of its cotton to other countries. Nicaraguan clothing manufacturers bought synthetic fibers from El Salvador, a measure more or less forced on the country by the Central American Common Market, whose bylaws, I was told, were written in Washington, D.C. Traveling from Masaya to visit the *cerámica negra* women in Matagalpa and Jinotega, I saw hundreds of people lining the Pan-American highway, selling wild birds and animals, archaeological artifacts, and just about anything for a few cordobas. The whole northern region was being sacked for anything that could be sold, while the former contras, still well-armed with U.S.-supplied weapons, had turned to sheer banditry, making the road from Matagalpa to Jinotega extremely risky to travel after about 4 o'clock in the afternoon.

Only a gross misunderstanding of this situation could lead one to conclude that U.S. economic and political power is in decline, even if the nature of that power has become far more complex. After all, it was during the Reagan administration, when the U.S. economy was deeply penetrated by Japanese capital and U.S. business both emulated and vilified their Japanese competitors, that U.S. foreign policymakers found it necessary to pulverize the economically puny nationalism presented by Sandinista Nicaragua in the name of continued U.S. domination of Central America. By the end of the Sandinista period, but much more since the UNO victory, it has not been U.S.-based capital that has taken the opportunity to invest in a Nicaragua made safe for business by Ronald Reagan & Co. Instead, Japanese, South Korean, and especially Taiwanese corporations have spread out across Nicaragua, looking over and buying up national assets such as gold mines, forests (see Avilés 1992), and energy resources, and even reviving the possibility of a new interoceanic canal. In the new world order, Nicaragua occupies a familiar matrix as a weak nation-state that provides raw materials at bargain-basement prices, and in which capital is always sailing away in larger quantities than it arrives. If the representatives of global capital now often have Asian instead of Euro-American faces, it is still the United States that acts as military guarantor for investment, locking Nicaragua into the same economic slot it has always occupied.

I do not know who dares to hope that this situation can be changed, at least not without much larger struggles against the ways the global economy works that must be waged on grander stages than the Nicaraguan. Of course, no one can rule out the possibility that Nicaragua's economy will improve a great deal, lifting the population out of poverty and the country out of the ranks of the world's lowest GNPs. Frankly, it is difficult to imagine how this could happen. In those African and Latin American countries where large or even modest deposits of petroleum, gold, diamonds, and other highly valued natural resources have been discovered, citizenries beyond certain elite sectors have not experienced enduring or substantial positive effects. By the same token, significant capital investment by foreign corporations and governments beyond the necessary machinery for resource extraction does not look like a good bet in Nicaragua's short-term or medium-term future. These factors frame the possibility that the Sandinistas (or some variation of Sandinismo) could return to power in Nicaragua, and more specifically pursue policies by which "culture" might both be transformed and play new transformative roles in Nicaraguan society. But if cultural policy is a means by which a new Sandinista government committed to the "logic of the majority"[10] could improve conditions of life for many Nicaraguans, cultural policy alone does not feed, clothe, or provide housing for people.

In any event, the prospect of waiting for "real" socialist revolutions to erupt in the metropolitan centers of capitalism was consistently rejected in the so-called Third World, indeed beginning with the establishment of the Soviet Union itself. Thus, many post–World War II revolutions occurred in Asia, Africa, and Latin America with the hope that significant social change could be accomplished, flying in the face of persistent capitalist power in the metropolitan countries of Europe and North America (see Ahmad 1992). Now the era of those revolutions is over, the Soviet Bloc is gone, global capital is more powerful, and the poverty of the "Third World" has been exacerbated. To countries like Nicaragua, which are more structurally subaltern than ever, the late twentieth century poses the question of whether national projects can ever become the projects of non-elite groups, even with the harsh realities of structural disadvantage. Recent anthropological literature exemplified by B. Williams (1989, 1991) and the Comaroffs (1992), which also comprehends the historical construction of national identities as the class projects of elite groups, perhaps leaves room (if not optimism) for more politically and anthropologically interesting questions than the approaches taken by the literary critics who have mostly monopolized the analysis of cultural transformation in Nicaragua. Let me be clearer: In this post–cold war era, can we imagine that the United States would simply leave Nicaragua alone militarily and do no more than ignore Nicaragua economically if a new Sandinismo came to power? Could such a new Sandinismo, making clear to the Nicaraguan people the constraints of its minimal capital, embark on a new development program that promised not much more than the goals of feeding, clothing, and housing everyone adequately, in part by deploying cultural policies to reconstruct Nicaraguan national identity? Would the majority of the people enlist in such a national project? What kind of cultural policies would avoid the problems—for example, the persistence of elite demarcations of culture that guided the revolutionary reconstruction of national identity—encountered by the Sandinista Ministry of Culture from 1979 to 1987?

Such questions have accompanied me during ethnographic fieldwork of the past three years, in reconsiderations of past fieldwork, in analysis of the existing literature about Nicaraguan culture that I will cite, as well as in pondering the nature of nation and national identity. But, although these questions underlie my accounts of ethnographic research in Nicaragua, I would not pretend that they find adequate responses therein.

The Structure of the Argument

In the first chapter, I discuss the interpretive discourse in Nicaragua concerning *El Güegüence,* after having first positioned myself with respect to the expansive academic theoretical apparatus focused on the construction of national identities and the role of literature (in the sense of fiction, epics and novels, plays, and the like) in that construction. This discussion will uncover the way *El Güegüence* has been used as a parable for Nicaragua's mestizo identity by the mainstream or dominant group of elite intellectuals, while at the same time at least two alternative interpretations of the play have also contributed to the overall demarcation of Nicaraguan culture and national identity. Within this demarcation, artisans and the Masaya-Carazo region have been situated in particular ways. In concluding this chapter, I elaborate my own interpretation of the play as a way of framing the ethnographic material in subsequent chapters.

In the second chapter, I use the materials described in chapter 1 to help explain the complexities and frequent contradictions of Sandinista cultural policy, and the dynamic that unfolded after 1979 as the Ministry of Culture, several other government bureaucracies, and the independent artisans' union UNADI contended for control over revolutionary culture. The chapter focuses on Sandinista ideas about and the politics of class and how the artisans struggled to become a revolutionary class within and against the cultural politics that were unfolding. Ethnographic work in San Juan de Oriente predominates in this chapter, and short essays by Orlando Gallegos and Roberto Potosme add to and depart from the ethnographic descriptions and analysis I elaborate. Information from work with the *cerámica negra* women of Matagalpa and Jinotega is also included.

The third and fourth chapters are concerned with identity politics that have taken shape since the 1990 elections that threw the Sandinistas out of power, although chapter 3 includes a great deal of ethnographic material from the 1980s. I argue that new discourses of identity and associated social movements derive from Sandinista political organizing and cultural policies that in effect created new kinds of intellectuals in subaltern social groups that had never had access to the means of intellectual production; here too, I will use bits and pieces of the *El Güegüence* interpretive literature to shed light on ethnographic material. Chapter 3 focuses on the development of feminist discourses in western Nicaragua since 1990, emphasizing the work of specific women authors and intellectuals, showing how feminist discourses do and do not give voice to the artisan women of San Juan and the women who make *cerámica negra*. A short essay by María Estela Rodríguez is included in this chapter, as well as sections of the life histories of Patricia Bracamonte and Catalina Bracamonte. Chapter 4 describes the post-1990 indigenous movement in western Nicaragua; the movement's constituency in Masaya-Carazo, the northern mountain region, and elsewhere; and why the artisans of San Juan do not form a part of that constituency. The written and spoken words of Flavio Gamboa play a key role in this chapter, relating to his analysis of indigenous identity and history, with themes from *El Güegüence* a constant. This chapter also includes an extensive discussion of mestizo identity, and how contemporary reexaminations of *mestizaje* illuminate the indigenous movement in Nicaragua.

In the final chapter, I speculate: Do the past two decades of changes in Nicaraguan national cultural identity shed light on an overall critique of cultural policy and the construction of national identity construction as pursued by states? To address this question, I consider contemporary analyses of state and nation-building in revolutionary and socialist states during this century. I also address the relevance of the literature about Latin American social movements, within which alternative possibilities for reshaping and reconfiguring national and local identities have been explored. This chapter highlights the continued relevance of parable and allegory for reimagining and "thinking beyond" the nation and the state in considering Nicaragua's future.

Chapter 1

A Class Project

El Güegüence, Masaya-Carazo, and

Nicaraguan National Identity

National Identity, National Literatures, and the Foreign Eye:
Theoretical Tools and the Nicaraguan Case

This chapter's roving description of the interpretations of *El Güegüence* is shaped by three analytic positionings: the exegesis of national identity as a social construction; the link between national
identities, national literatures, and literary discourses, as shaped by
state systems of power; and the legitimization of intellectual discourses in subaltern countries, such as Nicaragua, by metropolitan
authorities. Below, I discuss these positionings as they apply to the
Nicaraguan case at hand.

Benedict Anderson's (1983) characterization of nation-states as social constructions, imagined into existence through nationalist ideologies, now pervades the anthropological literature concerned with
national and local identities. Since the mid-1980s many anthropologists have grafted Anderson's insights to the analysis of class and
ethnicity in nation-states, leaning heavily on:

the Gramscian concept of hegemony, which describes systems of class
domination as reproduced and confirmed through incomplete, contested
processes of socialization and enculturation that all individuals within a
given society experience; and

Foucauldian linkage between systems of power and bodies of knowledge
that further elaborates the naturalization and internalization of domination and subordination in individual and social bodies.

Brackette Williams (1989) describes nation-building projects as
explicitly class projects, in which national identities, embedded in
nationalist ideologies, are deployed by dominant classes. Utilizing the

language of ethnicity to mark subordinate groups leaves elite domination ethnically unmarked and valorized by nationalist ideology: "ethnicity labels the visibility of that aspect of the identity formation process that is produced by and subordinated to nationalist programs and plans—plans intent on creating putative homogeneity out of heterogeneity through the appropriative process of a transformist hegemony" (439).

In recent years, the role of literature—plays, novels, poetry, and criticism—in the construction and representation of national culture and identities has been greatly emphasized, in some disciplines perhaps even more than in anthropology; my discussion in chapter 5 of the culture critics who have written about Nicaragua in the past fifteen or twenty years amply demonstrates this. Much of this interpretive discourse, notwithstanding substantive differences among authors, is imbued with a cultural nationalism that Aijaz Ahmad's (1992) succinct characterizations of post–World War II literary theory and its relationship to world-historical events critique.[1] In doing so, his analysis distinguishes "progressive and retrograde forms of nationalism with reference to particular histories . . . [and] the even more vexed question of how progressive and retrograde elements may be (and often are) combined within particular nationalist trajectories" (38). Ahmad's commentary helps to distinguish the role played by elite intellectuals in demarcating and enforcing hegemonic knowledge among Nicaraguan elites about class, ethnic, and national identities from the cultural politics of Sandinista Nicaragua, and how *El Güegüence* has been used in both discourses before, during, and since the revolutionary period. Doris Sommer (1991) has also underscored the construction of national identities through deployments of national literatures by Latin American states, working with feminist, Gramscian, and Foucauldian theories. Sommer links the romantic love between individuals of different classes and ethnic groups in important Latin American novels to state-led nation-building projects. Such novels, canonized as national literatures, establish "a metonymic association between romantic love that needs the state's blessing and a political legitimacy that needs to be founded on love" (41). Heterosexual romantic love thus becomes a cornerstone of the state and the nation, and intermarriage between social sectors weaves together a national identity sanctioned by the state.

Although I agree with Sommer's insights, it is then curious indeed that elite Nicaraguan intellectuals focused on *El Güegüence,* in which interethnic, interclass miscegenation between the governor's daughter Suche-Malinche and Güegüence's son Don Forsico is neither romantic nor necessarily (re)productive, but rather the result of chicanery and farce. Moreover, whereas Sommer understands the metonym between heterosexual romance, interclass and interethnic miscegenation, and the building of nation-states as allegorical, I understand *El Güegüence* as a parable. Yet Sommer's work constitutes a reminder to attend to the specifics of how novels and literary discourses become a part of national power structures. In the Nicaraguan case, although important elite literary intellectuals such as Pablo Antonio Cuadra and José Coronel Urtecho might have held only minor bureaucratic jobs under Somocismo, their published work performed enormously important roles in legitimizing the hegemony of Somocismo as a state and a social system, and thus the particular forms of knowledge about Nicaraguan culture and identity shaped by Somocismo.

This chapter consequently focuses on authors who best illustrate the way literature and its discourses, about *El Güegüence* in particular, build national culture and identity. I do not pretend to discuss all authors, Nicaraguan or foreign, who have written about *El Güegüence;* and I am hardly the first writer, by any means, to attempt a historiographical treatment of the *El Güegüence* literature. The principal contemporary historiographer of *El Güegüence,* Jorge Eduardo Arellano, a distinguished Nicaraguan man of letters through several decades of political and intellectual upheaval, has used his authority to elegantly and comprehensively reify the dominant interpretations of *El Güegüence.* I both use Arellano's work and turn around and analyze his work, for he offers a prime example of the relationship between an intellectual and the nation-building projects of successive states. By tracing the demarcation of Nicaraguan culture through the discourse about *El Güegüence* in a more or less chronological sequence of selected authors' treatments of the play, I show that the textual appearance of *El Güegüence* at the end of the nineteenth century was followed by the authoring of an interpretive literature composed of dominant and alternative modes of constructing cultural identity in Nicaragua, both of which contributed to the politics of culture and national identity during the twentieth century.

The dominant mode has functioned through the constant interweaving of elites' and outsiders' demarcations of Nicaraguan culture with a special focus on what all agreed was the heartland of cultural identity in the country: the Masaya-Carazo region. As twentieth-century Nicaraguan authors built cultural identity around *El Güegüence,* they legitimized each others' respective authority to demarcate Nicaraguan culture and cultural history in a reciprocally confirming manner, relying on the authority of metropolitan and colonial authors as the final word. The connection between Masaya as a cultural heartland, ceramics artisans, and *El Güegüence* provides an excellent illustration of this interconnection. In *Pottery of Nicaragua and Costa Rica* (1926), distinguished North American archaeologist Samuel K. Lothrop described pottery as a central, if not *the* central status commodity[2] among the pre-Columbian civilizations of western Nicaragua, and the Masaya-Carazo region in particular, using two main sources: actual archaeological remains of pre-Hispanic pots found in these two countries, and the early archives written by sixteenth-century Spanish explorer-scholars, predominantly those left by Captain Gonzalo Fernández de Oviedo y Valdes, as well as Gil Gonzáles Dávila and others. Focusing on the two pottery-producing indigenous civilizations in areas of what became western Nicaragua—the Mangue-speaking chiefdoms of Masaya-Carazo-Granada and of the Guanacaste region of Costa Rica, whom the Spaniards called the Chorotegas, and the Nahuatl-speaking Nicarao chiefdoms that occupied the Rivas isthmus, a narrow stretch of land between the Pacific Ocean and Lake Nicaragua[3]—Oviedo became the foundational authority not only for Lothrop but for subsequent authors whose writings demarcated Nicaraguan culture through the interpretation of *El Güegüence.* Lothrop mentioned *El Güegüence* in his description of Chorotega and Nicarao dance and drama, even if in a highly unflattering vein, as part of describing the cultural attributes of these peoples. In turn, Lothrop was subsequently cited by elite Nicaraguan authors in essays concerning pre-Hispanic cultures of western Nicaragua. Eduardo Zepeda-Henríquez's (1987) exposition of the Nicarao's supreme deity, **Tamagastad,** used Lothrop as an authority. Lothrop also appeared as a key citation in interpretive work concerning *El Güegüence*'s significance for Nicaraguan cultural identity and the essential role of the Masaya-Carazo region as the repository of that identity, which featured prominently in Pablo Antonio Cuadra's literary journal *El Pez y el Serpiente.* In the tightly bound in-group exchanges of mutually acknowledged authority in this journal, which featured prestigiously credentialed Nicaraguan and international authors, some key texts are almost entirely known through other texts, and the uses to which the latter put the former.

As previously noted, the dominant interpretation of *El Güegüence* elaborated by elite Nicaraguan authors, almost all of whom were either born or socialized into the elite intellectual circles of León and Granada, contended that it crystallizes the essential mestizo character of Nicaraguan national identity. For the mainstream circle of twentieth-century Nicaraguan intellectuals, including Cuadra, Francisco Pérez Estrada, and Jorge Eduardo Arellano, among others, certain unquestioned assumptions about the character of indigenous peoples in Nicaragua lay behind their contention that Nicaragua was and had been for a long time a nation whose character was inherently and overwhelmingly mestizo. Indigenous identities, for these authors, depend on certain unchanging and enduring traits that when present mark individuals and social groups as Indians. These traits cannot change, because the quality of Indianness is inextricably tied to the outmoded, the antiquated, the anachronistic holdovers of the pre-Hispanic era. Defining Indianness as equivalent to resisting change and innovation means that Indians are always tragic and doomed. These intellectuals' comprehension of indigenous identity denied Indians the possibility of dynamism after the Spaniards arrived. Change of any substantive nature spelled death for indigenous cultural identities. By contrast, twentieth-century Nicaraguan intellectuals ascribed precisely these qualities of cultural and technological dynamism to the mestizos, whose identity they viewed as still in formation, still acquiring traits and generating new and unique ones, and irrevocably linked to the rise of Nicaraguan national identity.

This narrative of national identity was legitimized by the authority of foreign scholarship, with the minor intervention of anthropology. After the heyday of Lothrop, the German linguists Berendt and Lehmann, North American linguist Marshall Elliott, the ethno-adventurers Squier and Brinton (all discussed below), and occasional archaeological nibblers (e.g., John Bransford, Doris Stone), serious ethnographic research in western Nicaragua no longer occurred. Richard Adams's chapter about Nicaragua in his *Cultural Surveys of Panama-Nicaragua-Guatemala-El Salvador-Honduras* (1957), discussed in the introduction, constituted an important exception to that generalization. Both Adams and Nicaraguan intellectuals understood *mestizaje* as triumphant or nearly so. The latter celebrated that inevitability; the former did not. Yet Adams, like most U.S. anthropologists of that era, probably did not take note of the local elite intellectual discourses, whose writing anthropologists at that time did not consider relevant to their work. During the 1950s, Adams likely would not have read Pablo Antonio Cuadra's *El Nicaragüense;* on the other hand, Nicaraguan intellectuals did not quote Adams to legitimize their views of *mestizaje.* The intertwining of dominant Nicaraguan intellectual interpretations of national culture and of *El Güegüence* with the authority of foreign scholarship therefore relied on quite old sources.

The alternative mode of interpretation among Nicaraguan intellectuals does not feature a single theme like the dominant mode. The dissenting and original interpretive approaches, those of Carlos Mántica Abaunza and Alejandro Dávila Bolaños, have had (and may yet have) important political implications, although they differ from one another in important ways. Both took the same verses and phrases from the play, and found different meanings therein. Mántica and Dávila Bolaños emphasized characters in the play, and different voices, phrases, and persona other than those in the purview of the dominant interpretation. In neither case, however, did their interpretations receive the stamp of legitimacy from prestigious foreign authors. The interpretations of Mántica and Dávila Bolaños thus remain confined and organic to intellectual discourses within Nicaragua, while their ideas, at least about *El Güegüence,* have been widely circulated within the country by the ultimate cultural bibliographer and arbiter, Jorge Eduardo Arellano, whose own political predilections are discussed later in this chapter.

One final analytic positioning may offer insight into the relationships among nation-building, national literatures, and metropolitan authority, given the radically different interpretations of *El Güegüence* and their ultimately diverging roles in constructing Nicaraguan national identity. Bakhtin (1953), who focused on novels and epics, elaborated the concepts of polyphony and heteroglossia, both of which describe written or oral narratives populated by multiple, nonhomogeneous, unintegrated voices. Many anthropologists have received his ideas via Clifford (1988: 46–47), who has understood Bakhtin's concepts as constructing a "utopian textual space" of multiple possibilities and imaginaries. In the case of the dominant interpretation of *El Güegüence,* the play became not a utopian space but a part of the conceptual cage in which elite intellectuals confined discourse about ethnic and national identity. On the other hand, alternative interpretations did create a rebellious space for double entendre and the resignification of indigenous words and names in the case of Mántica's work, and insurrectionary rebellion against colonialism, the Church, and whiteness in the work of Dávila Bolaños. All performances of this play do indeed foster a carnivalesque atmosphere, which is another application of Bakhtin's ideas by Clifford. My own vantage on *El Güegüence* sees the play as a carnival not of play but of power, and of the history of social and individual identities that dispute themselves and are disputed by others across time. As Verdery (1991: 320) suggests, it is impossible to understand Bakhtin's intentions except as construed through the brutalities of power's effects on language, performance, and interpretation in the nation-state, as he himself experienced those effects. Thus, we are brought back to the consideration of the lived subordination and domination of social groups under specific historical circumstances, which shape the performance and interpretation of nation-building narratives. In that light, this chapter lays out the parameters of an intellectual field in which Sandinista cultural policies formed, making clear the underlying complex assumptions, utopian or dystopian, depending on the social position of individuals and groups, that have sustained elite politics about Nicaraguan national culture and identity before and during Sandinismo. In a laconic sense, the interpretative literature about *El Güegüence,* and everything that went along with it, formed the soil out of which the Sandinista Ministry of Culture grew.

El Güegüence Is "Discovered"

The history of textual interpretation of *El Güegüence* began with Juan Eligio de la Rocha, a lawyer born in the city of Granada in 1815, who was also, it seems, the first Nicaraguan grammarian-philologist. Fluent in French, English, and Italian, he published *Los Elementos de Gramatica Castellana* in 1848 in León, where he taught French and later acted as mayor (1865) and as magistrate of the Supreme Court of Justice for the western region (1868). De la Rocha hand-copied two original manuscripts of *El Güegüence, o Macho Ratón* that he encountered in the city of Masaya or in the nearby vicinity after 1840, and he collected word lists and expressions from among the last fluent speakers of the Mangue language for his *Apuntamientos de la Lengua Mangue*. These aspects of de la Rocha's work remained unpublished until their rediscovery in 1874 by Karl Hermann Berendt, a German medical doctor and amateur linguist, who lived in Masaya during this period: "Living in 1842 in Masaya, [de la Rocha] wrote his observations concerning the language of the Mangues, about which I was informed by Dr. Gregorio Juarez of León. The brother of the deceased, Dr. Jesus de la Rocha of Granada, had the goodness to show me what he had found of these observations [in the former's notes], and this is what I have copied here" (4).

In compiling de la Rocha's own copies of the original *El Güegüence* manuscripts, Berendt, who called the drama "a comedy of the Mangue Indians," fused the two into a single version of the drama. Both the original manuscripts that de la Rocha worked from and his copies have since disappeared. Therefore, it is no longer possible to assess the nature of the transformations de la Rocha himself worked on the originals. I asked Flavio Gamboa about the linguistic transformations that had occurred during the textualization of the play by de la Rocha, Berendt, and others. He recalled that his grandfather had told him that *El Güegüence* had originally been performed in Mangue. According to written records left by his grandfather, the play was translated into pure Nahuatl, then later into the Nahuatl-Spanish dialect many years before the first manuscripts appeared and the transcription process began. Gamboa has shown me the writings left by his ancestors regarding this subject, and I have no reason to doubt their veracity. Unfortunately, Mangue is no longer spoken by anyone. But as Mangue was a tonal language, like Zapotec, Mixtec, and other idioms of the Oto-Manguean family (see Mason 1973), the true extent and complexity of homonymic punning and hidden double and triple meanings within the narrative structure of *El Güegüence,* a theme pursued by several Nicaraguan authors to be discussed, must undoubtedly remain vastly underrated.

Although Berendt stated that he did not alter or in any way attempt to translate what he found in de la Rocha's text (Brinton 1883: xli), this is a claim rendered dubious given that he must have made editorial decisions on what to include and exclude in deriving a single text out of two distinct versions of the drama. Berendt's version written in the Nahuatl-Spanish dialect remained unpublished. In 1883, North American medical doctor and folklorist-linguist Daniel Brinton for the first time published *El Güegüence,* subtitled "A Comedy-Ballet," as a Nahuatl-Spanish text, accompanied by an English translation that Brinton himself described as "a loose paraphrase" (1883: i). In several interpretive essays accompanying the text and translation in this volume, Brinton elaborated his knowledge of the Nahuatl-speaking Nicarao and Mangue-speaking peoples of the Pacific littoral. His understanding of the history of *El Güegüence* and explication of the characters and action of the play were thus accompanied by his assessment of traditional dramatic dances and musical instruments of this region.

Notwithstanding the tremendous impact of Brinton's publication of *El Güegüence* on the construction of twentieth-century Nicaraguan culture, Brinton, unlike Berendt, had never lived in or even visited Nicaragua. Brinton's reconstruction of pre-Hispanic western Nicaragua (like Lothrop's) depended primarily on the authoritative texts written by Oviedo and other Spanish explorer-scholars (e.g., Antonio de Herrera y Tordesillas, chronicler of the Indies, and Francisco de Bobadilla, a friar). Brinton also relied heavily on texts written by previous English-speaking authorities, the earliest of whom was Thomas Gage, a seventeenth-century English Dominican. His sources also included mid-nineteenth-century Smithsonian field-workers, such as the naturalist Thomas Belt (1911) and early archaeologist John Bransford (1881), but particularly the English adventurer, Ephraim Squier (1990). Squier's descriptions of the massive, dramatic stone statuary of the Mangue-Nicarao region in his 1853 article "Observations on the Archaeology and Ethnology of Nicaragua" became *the* essential nineteenth-century reference to archaeological sites in western Nicaragua; to this day, Squier's text retains a high profile as a primary citation. But according to Brinton, Squier actually misconstrued many linguistic and cultural aspects of contemporary society in the Masaya-Carazo region. In the essays that precede the text of *El Güegüence,* at least a part of Brinton's scholarly energies focus on his clarifications of the region's ethnography, thereby assembling his own unchallengeable authority concerning the actual state of affairs in the rich cultural geography of *El Güegüence.* Such authority was augmented by Brinton's retrieval of Berendt's confused, disorganized notes on the Mangue language, taken from de la Rocha's lost texts and published as "Notes on the Mangue; an extinct Dialect formerly spoken in Nicaragua" by the American Philosophical Society in 1885.

Brinton's *El Güegüence* essays focus on the linguistic affiliations between the Mangue and Nicarao peoples on the one hand, and the languages spoken in central and southern Mexico on the other, establishing the more ancient provenance of the former and the recent migration of and occupation of the Rivas isthmus by the latter, whom he refers to as an "Aztec band" fleeing the catastrophes afflicting the Valley of Mexico. Doting somewhat on the superior cultural level of the Nahuas, which he rated nearly as high as imperial Aztec society, he nonetheless did not downplay the Mangue, who, like their cultured neighbors, he claimed, also produced fine hieroglyphic books on parchment and lived in prosperous, socially stratified towns. This was but foreplay, because Brinton emphasized that both Mangue and Nahuatl language and culture had long since been dominated by Spanish customs and language, a situation underscored by the great difficulties Squier, Berendt, and others had encountered in soliciting Nahuatl and Mangue word lists from the locals after 1850. Brinton made clear that the last redoubt of these languages resided in the dances and dramatic representations of Masaya-Carazo. The *Loga del Niño Dios,*[4] a dramatic recitation recorded by Berendt in the village of Namotivá (which is none other than the Mangue name of San Juan de Oriente), was still at the end of the nineteenth century declaimed in a Mangue-Spanish jargon. The play *La Ollita/Cañahuate,* also cited by Brinton, was according to him still recited in Mangue "as late as 1822" (1883: xvii), although the source of this information is not given. Then there was *El Güegüence,* still performed and manifested textually in a Nahuatl-Spanish jargon that Berendt made clear was incompletely understood by the Nicaraguans of Masaya-Carazo by the mid-nineteenth century.

Brinton concluded that *El Güegüence* had been composed at the very latest during the early 1700s, and that an Indian or "half-caste" (not at all what Latin Americans mean by mestizo, a subject for much more consideration in chapter 4), fluent in Nahuatl-Spanish, had authored it. He interpreted Güegüence's name as a corruption of the pure Nahuatl **Huehuentzin,** or respected elder, a term of respect used for the **huehues** or elders who danced in important pre-Hispanic rituals and obviously intended by the play's author to satirically emphasize that Güegüence "is anything but a respectable person" (1883: xlv). Unlike later authors, Brinton shied away from interpreting the meaning of the drama's title as recorded by Berendt—*El Güegüence,* or *Macho Ratón*—and the implied relationship between these two characters. But Brinton did show that *El Güegüence*'s linguistic provenance derived from the Catholic Church's absorption of indigenous dramas into religious plays, in the post-1600 colonial period during which the Church used Nahuatl-Spanish as the language of catechism and the colonial authorities used it as the medium of government.[5] Notwithstanding the other dramatic representations performed in Masaya-Carazo, which Brinton acknowledged were declaimed in Mangue or Mangue-Spanish jargon during the nineteenth century, he indicated that the inhabitants of this zone had dropped their Mangue language, then adopted Nahuatl-Spanish, and then like other Nicaraguans eventually became monolingual Spanish speakers.

Thus, concluded Brinton, *El Güegüence*'s first textualized appearance in Nahuatl-Spanish reflects its composition during the early colonial era when that dialect dominated in Masaya-Carazo, an era ended by the victory of unadulterated Spanish and Hispanic cultural domination. Brinton suggested that several other details clue readers to the period of authorship: the use of early colonial monetary units in conversation (e.g., cuartillos, octavos, cuartos, maravedis) and the characterizations of the governor and the constable. Nonetheless, Brinton admonished his readers that the devices by which the action occurs in *El Güegüence,* and especially the way humor moves the action, are "strictly within the range of native thought and custom" (1883: xliii). Güegüence's chicanery and cunning, his feigned deafness and consequent gross misunderstandings of the words of "his betters," and his predilection for obscene, often phallic, humor are all signifiers, for Brinton, of the coarse attitudes and sensibilities of the indigenous mind in the Masaya-Carazo cultural heartland. Decades later, Lothrop laconically summarized a resonant view, calling *El Güegüence* "a drama distinguished by little plot but much coarse humor based largely on the play of words" (1926: 54).

How very ironic that all the subsequent elite Nicaraguan authorities about *El Güegüence* would quote Brinton and Lothrop only to prove the extraordinary literary merit and sophistication of this parable of their proud Nicaraguan identity!

Elite Intellectual Discourses

For elite Nicaraguan writers, however much they might interpret its significance differently, Brinton had discovered—or, via Berendt, rescued—*El Güegüence* from the obscurity of de la Rocha's private notes. That rescue, and the presence of diverse foreign adventurers like Squier in Nicaragua during the middle and late nineteenth century, coincided with the presence of other foreign interests and interlocutors with less benign intentions. The role of the centuries-long rivalry between the elite families of León and Granada in preventing a unified Nicaraguan state from coalescing after independence must be recalled. This rivalry found its expression in the Liberal-Conservative split familiar in Latin American history. In the Nicaraguan context, Liberals supported increased foreign investment, gearing production to new agricultural exports such as coffee, a broadly expanded state, and a reduced role for the Church, whereas the Conservatives tried to stave off the changes stimulated by new money, new crops, and any attacks on the Church. Continuous internecine warfare between the armed groups that elites inducted from among the rural folk, compounded by the geopolitical implications of Nicaragua's location, and the exigencies of nineteenth-century imperialist aspirations acted like an engraved invitation for foreign powers (Great Britain and the United States mostly), neighboring countries (Costa Rica in particular), and the weirder demagogical sort (William Walker, for example) to seize control of all or part of the national territory. Following the extended period of chaos caused by these various interventions, the emergence of a literary, intellectual, and scholarly community in Nicaragua more or less coincided with the first attempt to establish a strong central government, in other words a unified state, during the regime of José Santos Zelaya. Thus, it seems to me that the development of intellectual life in Nicaragua appears to have followed the contours of political history. In a weak, inchoate state over which rapacious elites sought the spoils, a foreigner rescued Nicaragua's national treasure, *El Güegüence,* just as foreign interventions acted as the stimulus for elites to close ranks around the integrity of the territory controlled by the putative state. When the Liberal dictator Zelaya at last formed a functioning state at the end of the nineteenth century, this created an environment in which elite intellectuals constructed a national identity, and in doing so reinterpreted Brinton's words to very different effects.

Nevertheless, the valorization of *El Güegüence* by authoritative foreign writers remained crucial to the development of the national elite's cultural work, which leaned heavily upon the scaffolding of authors such as José Martí, who called the play a "master comedy" (quoted in Arellano 1985), as well as the essays written on the play by many other authors that appeared elsewhere in Latin America, in Europe, and in the United States.[6] It was Martí's interpretation that sharply diverged from Brinton's and set in motion the dominant paradigm through which Nicaraguan intellectuals would come to perceive *El Güegüence*: "*El Güegüence* is not in any way an indigenous comedy masterpiece. In the first place, because the comedy genre did not exist in pre-Columbian times, at least not the way we would understand it. And in the second place, [the play] is completely and absolutely mestizo. As a product of full mestizaje, it achieves its mastery. [This is true] not only because of the language [in which it was written] but because of the issues with which it deals" (in Pérez Estrada 1992: 92).

During the 1890s, Nicaraguan intellectual life was transforming itself and its relationship with international intellectual discourses, especially in Latin America, with the entrance of a Nicaraguan poet of historical preeminence on the international stage. I refer of course to Rubén Darío, the founder of *modernista* poetry in the Spanish language, about whom so much has been written that any attempt to summarize his role in Hispanic literature would be foolhardy indeed. Darío's appearance provoked a vast interpretive literature written by virtually the same group of Nicaraguan authors who were writing about *El Güegüence*. The outpouring over "our Rubén," as he was called, initiated a discourse about Nicaragua's contribution to the Spanish language, to Spanish literature, and thus to world culture. For Nicaragua's literary elites Darío's literary triumph became an allegory that legitimized the entity called "Nicaraguan culture." Conversely, the essays by the same authors concerned with *El Güegüence* constituted a very different discourse about Nicaraguan national identity, primarily for local consumption, but legitimized by foreign authorities. Darío knew Brinton's volume, and occasionally referred to various lines from the play, although perhaps in a superficial sense (in Arellano 1985: 27). For the purposes at hand, Darío's work functioned as the springboard that launched the prestige, self-awareness, and aspirations of the national intellectual elite in its construction of Nicaraguan cultural identity. In the twentieth century, that construction orbited closely around the ever more engrossing project of interpreting *El Güegüence*.

Of the first generation of post-Darío literati poets, Salomón de la Selva left the most important impact upon the interpretive discourse relating *El Güegüence* to the demarcation of Nicaraguan culture. De la Selva was born in León, which at the turn of the century had produced Zelaya, the first nationalist president. Although many Nicaraguan intellectuals involved in the demarcation of national culture were shaped largely by the Conservative sensibilities of Granada, de la Selva's (1984) work was decidedly Liberal in orientation, championing Sandino in metaphorically romantic terms. Though his work was never favored under Somocismo, and was often published in anti-Somoza student publications, he also exercised "the most direct influence on the development of Nicaraguan political poetry" (Beverley and Zimmerman 1990: 59). Praising *El Güegüence* extravagantly, he characterized the play as "unique and precious," filled with "scenes of purest lyricism," and "as good as or better than what we know of Greek comedy before Aristophanes" (1931: 188). His exuberance also advanced efforts to annex *El Güegüence* into the chronicle of Spanish-language literature and its triumphs, notwithstanding its bilingual nature. Each subsequent author expended more effort on extolling the literary merits of the work, turning complex intellectual somersaults in the effort to understand its linguistic complexity. Interpretive authors working within the dominant school needed to control and narrow this linguistic and cultural complexity to enshrine the play as the original masterpiece of a literature defining Nicaraguanness as profoundly mestizo in nature.

Thus, when Nicaragua entered yet another period of internecine warfare during the first three decades of this century, defined by the political rivalries that followed the U.S.-sponsored fall of the Zelaya regime, literati of several kinds hallowed a place for *El Güegüence* in their constructions of Nicaraguan intellectual historiography. It was during this period as well that Nicaragua's political saint, Augusto César Sandino, fought the Yanqui intervention, established a liberated zone in the northern mountains, and was subsequently assassinated by Anastasio Somoza García, the founder of Somocismo, in a tableau to which only Greek tragedy could do justice. Sandino's rebellion nurtured the intellectual environment of the 1930s, and Nicaraguan intellectuals treasured the cultural legacies of two heroes: Darío and Sandino. In this ambience, Pablo Antonio Cuadra, born in Managua in 1912 and raised in Granada, cofounded with José Coronel Urtecho and others the anti-*modernista* Vanguard school of poetry, a group in which individual poets "defined themselves variously as nationalist, antiliberal, Catholic, ultrareactionary, futurist, pro-Sandinista, and fascist" (Beverley and Zimmerman 1990: 60).

Since the middle of this century and especially so during the era of Somocismo, Cuadra has been the most influential intellectual in the overall demarcation of Nicaraguan cultural identity. His influence was no doubt greatly abetted by the pro-Somoza turn in his sensibilities as early as the late 1930s, which earned him jobs in the Somocista bureaucracy (see Arellano 1969). In the 1960s, as publisher of the avant-garde journal *El Pez y la Serpiente,* Cuadra became more of an apolitical aesthete, publishing anti-Somoza poetry and prose as long as it conformed to his literary standards. Cuadra worked with another Nicaraguan intellectual, Emilio Alvarez Lejarza, with whom he republished *El Güegüence* in 1942 in his first literary journal, *Cuaderno del Taller San Lucas.* Lejarza had discovered another, fragmented manuscript in Catarina (the town located adjacently east of San Juan de Oriente) during the 1930s. Although this manuscript was not the text Lejarza translated and published with Cuadra's commentaries, Lejarza's discovery of another original version of the play undoubtedly contributed to the looming authority of Cuadra's interpretations. In anchoring the importance of *El Güegüence,* Cuadra identified the play and other folkloric tales as "the first original roots or traces that could give life and actual force to our literature, not to separate it but to distinguish and define it with acknowledged traits, as the Nicaraguan branch of the great tree of Hispanic literature" (1963: 21). In Cuadra's scheme of things it was impossible to underestimate the role of literature because "our national identity is still in the process of formation—a reality which is forgotten with excessive frequency—and our literature is one of the most important elements in that process" (13).

In one of Cuadra's most quoted commentaries, reprinted over fifteen times, in his collection of essays *El Nicaragüense* (1981), he was the first to associate features of Güegüence's character—disrespect for authority, satirical farce, sexual burlesque, a vagabond jack-of-all-trades lifestyle, facility with the spoken word—with a proto- and stereotypical Nicaraguan national character. Dating *El Güegüence*'s composition to the sixteenth century, at least a century earlier than Brinton's estimate, Cuadra described the play's appearance at "the initial moments of our cultural mestizaje, summarizing, in a caricatured and satirical form, all the characteristics that we have noted as belonging to the Nicaraguans" (1981: 91). By situating the play as far back as possible in post-Conquest history, reasserting Martí's revision of Brinton's jaundiced views to make the drama a literary triumph, and by identifying all of the main characters' personality traits with a national character, Cuadra anchored a new intellectualized construction of Nicaraguan identity. Without exaggeration, he entitled this essay "The First Character in Nicaraguan Literature: Güegüence."

Cuadra's meticulous attention to particular speeches and declamations by the characters in *El Güegüence* prefigured the explosion of text-based interpretations the play was to receive in the decades to come. In perhaps his favorite exchange, which unfortunately loses much of its lyrical cadence in translation, readers encounter a mixture of the poetic, sexual, and legal senses of the word "permission" (Spanish *licencia*):

Governor: So Güegüence, who has given you permission [*licencia*] to enter into the presence of the representative of the king in this province?

Güegüence: Lord have mercy, Lord Governor Tastuanes, what do you mean that I need permission?

Governor: You must have permission, Güegüence.

Güegüence: Lord have mercy, Lord Governor Tastuanes. When I was traveling into the country, on the roads to Mexico, through Veracruz, Verapaz, Tecuantepec, riding my mule, taking my boys with me, Don Forsico ran into an innkeeper and asked him to bring us a dozen eggs; so we were going ahead and eating and unloading our stuff and loading it back up again, and just kept going along like that; and nobody has to give me permission for this, Lord Governor Tastuanes.

Governor: Well, here you must have permission, Güegüence.

Güegüence: Lord have mercy, Lord Governor Tastuanes, as I was coming down a straight street a seated girl in a window of gold sighted me, and she said to me: "How gallant you are Güegüence, what a wild guy you are, Güegüence, here is a shop, Güegüence, come in, Güegüence, sit down, Güegüence, here are some sweets, Güegüence, here is some lemon." And since I am such a witty guy, I jumped from the street with a riding coat which was so dressed up that no one could tell what it was, so full of silver and gold down to the ground; and this is how a girl gave me permission, Lord Governor Tastuanes!

Governor: Well, a girl isn't going to give you permission now, Güegüence.

(In Lejarza 1993: 28–29)[7]

Güegüence's mastery of satire, subtlety, and cadence in this speech gave Cuadra extraordinary pleasure, and his attentiveness to the literary qualities in the text once again led him to radically depart from Brinton's assertion that an Indian had authored the play. With his own stereotypes of Indian brutishness in mind, Cuadra mused contrarily, imagining an author who "seems to me a bit like a literary romantic [*un soplo de romancero*] . . . a sweet apparition of pre-classical Spanish theater" (Cuadra and Lejarza 1942: 89).

Attending to the language and lyricism of *El Güegüence,* and drawing interpretive deductions from both literary analysis and research concerning the historical contexts that shaped the play and its performance, became if anything even more pronounced in the work of subsequent scholars. Francisco Pérez Estrada, Leonese anthropologist and poet born in 1912 and a member of Cuadra's literary Vanguard movement, republished *El Güegüence* using the Catarina manuscript in 1946 and wrote interpretive essays concerning the play. He never worked directly for the Somocista state, which was perhaps threatened by the kind of independent research Pérez Estrada undertook, but his work was supported and published by the Banco Central, which, as we will see, maintained autonomous interests in supporting Nicaraguan cultural endeavors, including the artisans of the Masaya region. Early on, Pérez Estrada's work led him to exalt *El Güegüence* in literary terms, again in the context of Spanish-language literature, claiming that the play's existence meant that for Nicaraguans there "is nothing to envy from the best Castillian writers" (1954: 39). But he was even more concerned to show the historical and ethnographic relationships between *El Güegüence* and whatever he could discover about pre-Hispanic indigenous theater in order to conclusively demonstrate the profoundly hispanified, mestizo nature of the play.

For example, Pérez Estrada explained that although the use of masks certainly characterized pre-Columbian performances, the colonial authorities had outlawed the making and use of masks as part of their overall suppression of indigenous religious observance in which masks played a part. He concluded that the masks of the *machos* were entirely Spanish in origin, arguing that *El Güegüence* and other dramas enacted on the streets of towns in Masaya-Carazo form part of the celebration of patron saints and thus reinforce the overall domination of Catholicism. Likewise, Pérez Estrada contended that the perfection of the Spanish syntax in which the play was written fundamentally obviated the importance of the Nahuatl words and expressions spoken by the characters, insofar as the literary quality of the text is concerned. He was, however, curious to know the unknowable: to what extent, if any, Berendt had altered the original manuscript, and the importance, if any, of the Mangue language in the composition of the originals. But Pérez Estrada ultimately concluded that the author of *El Güegüence* had actually been a *criollo* Spaniard and, moreover, a Spaniard concerned to publicly air an incipient anticolonial critique of the economic structures and moral strictures extant in the 1700s.

Pérez Estrada's ethnographic description of Nicaraguan culture thus stressed the predominance of the Spanish language, its infiltration into and total transformation of indigenous thought, and the binding of popular tradition with the celebration of Catholic rituals, especially those focused on the patron saints adopted by each locality. "Nicaraguan material culture, of the popular and traditional variety," he wrote, "has been completely mestizoized, such that all of the new Spanish techniques of production have completely dominated the older Indian ones. The countryside has endured a profound Hispanic influence, the repercussions of which extend into all areas of life, especially in the area of belief-systems" (1992: 126).

In the closing lines of *El Güegüence*, Pérez Estrada found the words that appropriately eulogized his own interpretation of Nicaraguan history, words that so embodied the play that he entitled an essay "El hilo azul: La frase del Güegüence" ("The Blue Thread: *The* Phrase of *El Güegüence*") (1968). As Güegüence mournfully contemplates the marriage of Don Forsico to Suche-Malinche, he moans: "Ah, in my time, when I was a boy, in the time of the blue thread, when you could see in the fields of the Diriomos, lifting up those packs of guavas, isn't that right, boys?" (in Lejarza 1993: 49).[8] This speech is indeed rich in allusion and allegory, and has been debated, particularly the phrase "en el tiempo del hilo azul," by many of the authors cited here. Brinton wrote: "This [phrase] has foiled all whom I have consulted. Dr. Valentine thinks it refers to the season of the year when the verdure reappears after the drouth. F. Diego Duran states that the village conjurors were accustomed to suspend charms to the necks of boys by blue and green threads . . . Thus understood, the time of the blue thread would be equivalent to boyhood." (1883: 82). For Pérez Estrada, "en el tiempo del hilo azul" clearly connoted a bygone age, the age of indigenous culture, now long and irrevocably over, superseded by a hispanified, mestizo popular culture that can only be called "Nicaraguan."

Pérez Estrada's decisive characterizations of *El Güegüence* further elaborated the discourse of national identity presided over by Cuadra. By contrast, the interpretations proposed by his contemporary, Carlos Mántica Abaunza, a linguist from León (b. 1935), opened the door to more complex views of the play, its anonymous author, and the history of its textualization. His independent work was much too sophisticated and offbeat to be supported by the state, and was published by foreign sources, such as the U.S.-funded Revista Interamericana de Bibliografía, or avant-garde journals such as *El Pez y el Serpiente*. Mántica, whom Arellano called a "nahualist" (in Lejarza 1993: 57), focused his research and interpretation on the Nahuatl-Spanish idiom in which *El Güegüence* was written. He concentrated on the indeterminacy of signification due to the double, triple, and quadruple punning possibilities that tumble forth from a text written in two languages simultaneously: Nahuatl-Nahuatl puns, Spanish-Spanish puns, Spanish-Nahuatl puns, and Nahuatl-Spanish puns, all based on homophonies built into the prose of the text. Mántica disparaged the conventional translation of Güegüence's name, which since Brinton had been viewed as a satiric deployment of the Hispanified version of **Huehuentzin** (honored elder) for the ill-reputed Güegüence. He proposed several possible Nahuatl origins for Güegüence's name, including **huehuenche** (masked, dancing performer) and **güegüecho** (screaming, crazy turkey). Without ruling out the relevance of any of these etymological histories, he favored a derivation of **cuecuentzin** (great buffoon). Mántica also took up the translation of "Macho Ratón," probably being the first to do so. The literal Spanish translation, as Brinton noted (1883: xlviii), is "male mouse," although he believed its colloquial connotation in this context was "masker," or "masquerader." By contrast, Mántica explored the Nahuatl-Spanish and Nahuatl-Nahuatl homophonies of Macho-Ráton, finding that the term mixed hispanified Nahuatl words for "deceiver" (**tentlamachito**), "comedy" (**machiotlatolli**), and "dancer" (**macehuaton**).

Using the evidence he assembled, Mántica explained why Brinton had named his textualization of the original manuscripts "*El Güegüence;* A Comedy Ballet," because the name Macho Ráton apparently connotes both comedy and dance. It is unclear whether Brinton was aware of this connection, as he commented very little upon the meaning of Macho Ráton. On the other hand, he did change the name of the play in recopying Berendt's notes. Mántica, however, had larger fish to fry. In the original title, "*El Güegüence, o Macho Ráton,*" he detected the historical fusion of two distinct performance pieces. The *machos* do not appear until very near the end of the play as it has been performed for the past two hundred years, and Mántica asserted that their dance was added to the performance of *El Güegüence* long after the author had already composed the play. The title recorded by Berendt, which we would like to assume he got from de la Rocha, stemmed from a historical decision by the performers to join together two dramatic performances, for reasons that must remain unknown.

Mántica's essays thus feature unconventional analyses based on innovative research, which seem to repeatedly indicate that *El Güegüence* represents a very long-term accretion of oral, textual, and performance-based transformations, all of which remain within the manuscripts at hand. In recalling many characteristics of the play's dialogue, which indicated to him that the author lived in the seventeenth century, he underlined the cultural complexity of a population that for hundreds of years was bilingual and rooted in both Iberian and indigenous historical consciousness as shaped by the political economy of the Conquest. For example, when Güegüence lists the commodities he would sell to Governor Tastuanes from his traveling shop, he says, "Oh Lord have mercy, Lord Governor Tastuanes! Let's not be fools. Let's be friends and bargain over this merchandise and clothing. In the first place, I've got chests of gold, chests of silver, clothing from Castille, smuggled clothing, regular huipiles, feather huipiles, silk socks, golden shoes, beaver hats, stirrups with straps made of gold and silver, all for the pleasure and satisfaction of Lord Governor Tastuanes" (in Lejarza 1993: 29–30).[9] A huipil is a shirt or blouse without sleeves, still woven and worn in Guatemala;

and clothing made from feathers were among the high-status goods wielded only by the powerful ruling elites of pre-Hispanic Meso-america. When grouped with gold, silver, and silk, items of obsessive interest to Spanish elites, and beaver hats, a prestige item characteristic of the colonial economies of the seventeenth century, Güegüence's collection of items for sale seems like one of Borges's surrealistically heterogeneous lists that can only evoke indeterminacy.[10] Attention to such apparent confusion is the only way, Mántica argued, to discuss the meaning of the play and its allusions, such as "el hilo azul," which have bemused the elite intellectuals and their discourse of Nicaraguan culture. In other words, Güegüence need not be identified as either an Indian or a mestizo, and the play does not narrate a decisive sociocultural victory of one group over another.

Other intellectuals writing after Mántica returned to interpret *El Güegüence* with the far more focused agenda promoted by Cuadra, his publications, and his semiofficial position as intellectual apologist for Somocismo; that is, that *El Güegüence* was an allegory for *mestizaje* and the first document of Nicaraguan national identity. In the case of Eduardo Zepeda-Henríquez, poet, folklorist, and literary critic of the mid-twentieth century, there is an explicit distancing from the multiple indeterminacies of Mántica, and perhaps an even narrower elaboration of Cuadra's project. Zepeda-Henríquez, born in Granada in 1930, was a younger participant in the poetry movement of the 1950s that descended from the Vanguardist movement dominated by Cuadra, Urtecho, and others (see Llopesa 1988). For him, the personality of Güegüence "is the symbol—and as such, an undignified one—of the manner of existence for the Nicaraguan people, the people of the most perfect mestizaje in Hispano-America" (Zepeda-Henríquez 1987: 133). Not content with the image of a post-Conquest "perfect mestizaje," Zepeda-Henríquez argued that a "primitive mestizaje" had also characterized pre-Columbian Nicaragua, given the presence of several distinctive civilizations, of Meso-american and South American provenance, in the area that is now the national territory. Moreover, Zepeda-Henríquez's description of *mestizaje* went even further than Cuadra's in erasing any lingering indigenous traits present in Nicaraguan identity. His prose, always poetic and romantic, relies on playful homophonies that are lost in translation from Spanish to English; but the message remains no less forceful, perhaps even vehement:

In the roots of Nicaraguan identity, there is, then, a vernacular agony that, in the coming of the Hispanic component, has become a struggle of a universal sort, but especially a most excellent mixture. From this, Nicaragua achieved an anguished, but complete assimilation of distinct clashing forces and a complete and no less anguished assimilation of Spanish. And I do not put the emphasis, as Pablo Antonio Cuadra does, upon the "duality" [of this outcome], which is, in the end, the uniformity of mestizaje. I insist, on the contrary, upon the true "unity" which distinguishes what is ours; from a painful crossroads, comes only one cross: the Nicaraguan being, a total integration, and by the same token, integral and without duplicity. (134)

For Zepeda-Henríquez, Güegüence himself is an old rebellious mestizo or ladino, but really a rebel without a cause; an articulate but filthy-minded cynic who can spin a tale and dance with equal facility.

In this light, Zepeda-Henríquez explicitly rejected much of the complex analysis other authors have made of *El Güegüence,* and particularly the etymological work of Mántica, who was not even named in the following denunciation, which as usual involves clever wordplay:

Not translating in a timely fashion, and above all, doing so in a risky and inopportune manner, could have caused a certain nahualist of ours to have wanted to see indigenous traits in the sub-title "Macho Ratón" displayed by the comedy *El Güegüence.* And while we recognize that etymological scaffoldings could turn out well if done cleverly, the fact is that looking for the Nahuatl origins of two extremely Spanish words such as "macho ratón" is, at once, foolishness. Because in this case, "macho" is a metaphor of ladino origin applied to Indians, or if one prefers, a disguise of the same; for we should not forget that for this ladino that is in all senses Güegüence, the Indian has to be a "beast of burden" . . . So that is how one can explain the cruel insults that Güegüence makes against the Machos. This is precisely the negative characteristic that Nicaraguans have formed of this hybrid animal . . . As for "ratón," this is also an insult . . . From here then, if we were to imitate the aforementioned translators, "macho ratón" would also be "sick mule," or "tumor" of [a horse's] tail. (141)

Zepeda-Henríquez's scorn of other interpretations of *El Güegüence* may have derived from a narrower sort of nationalism not inconsistent with some of the intellectual activity going on in circles inspired by the Vanguardists. Yet such views remained within the mainstream construction of Nicaraguan cultural identity by elite authors in the mid-twentieth century, and his book on Nicaraguan mythology was widely circulated during the last years of Somocismo.

The long heyday of Somocismo that spanned the 1930s to the 1970s witnessed, as we shall see later, a steady degradation of artisan-crafts in the Masaya-Carazo region and unrelenting attacks upon remaining indigenous communities all over western Nicaragua. Ironically, given these realities, some of the intellectual elite during this time engaged in a nostalgia for indigenous culture and its legacies, which they identified as "folkloric" and which they recognized as concentrated in the cultural heartland of *El Güegüence,* the Masaya-Carazo region. During the 1950s, the journal *Nicaragua Indígena* published articles characterized by this kind of *indigenismo,* akin to but less highbrow than the literary discourse of *El Pez y el Serpiente,* certainly more openly Somocista and patronizing of indigenous peoples than the latter (see Whisnant 1995: 118–19). One author, Enrique Peña Hernández (originally a lawyer), published a volume entitled *Folklore de Nicaragua* (1986) that reflected this *indigenismo,* characterizing *El Güegüence* as a pinnacle of Nicaraguan folk culture. Unlike the literati, Peña Hernández was a native of Masaya (b. 1922) who first published his work with a tiny press in his hometown in 1968. He paid no homage to the victory of *mestizaje,* but instead emphatically affirmed the Indianness of Masaya-Carazo, and especially of the people from the Monimbó barrio of Masaya and of Diriamba, the last sites where by mid-century *El Güegüence* was still performed. Although Peña Hernández's accounts are adorned by lists of common racist epithets (cited in his "refranero del indio de Monimbó") and celebrations of brutal machismo among the *indios,* he also consulted with local historians and patrons of the arts, recovering the manner in which *El Güegüence* had survived Somocismo. In fact, his descriptions do not really depart much from Pérez Estrada's ethnographic detailing of the alliance between popular street performances, such as *El Güegüence,* and Catholic ritual; yet Peña Hernández's purpose was to celebrate local instead of national culture:

Nicaraguans must unavoidably recognize that Diriamba fulfills the high and noble cultural function of conserving in its pristine and genuine expression the principal works of our folkloric theater, especially *El Güegüence,* which has a unique and honorable place in the [Latin American] continental region . . . The illustrious folklorist of Diriamba, Dr. Leopoldo Serrano Gutiérrez, in his valuable and interesting work *Folklore Nicaragüense,* has given a detailed description of the festivities of San Sebastian of Diriamba, explaining to us the manner and form of the play's performance. Dr. Serrano Gutiérrez reports: "To perform the piece, the Machos are placed so as to form a circle; at the head goes the dancer who plays Macho Viejo who is carrying a chest, and they say 'chests of gold, chest of silver' in the story. The Machos dance and tap dance, a few times with the music of San Martin, as Güegüence says . . . Those who are masqueraded as Machos have a mask that represents the head of a mule; they wear normal pants and shirts and waistcoats, and their shirtfronts bear rings and shiny chains and they carry a rattle in one hand and [pull] a flour mill in the other. In the center of the circle that the Machos form, are placed the characters, and to the side is the group of musicians. The dialogue goes through its comic development as each character comes on. All the characters wear masks, with the exception of the Ladies and Suche Malinche. The Governor, Güegüence, the Royal Scribe, the Constable, wear an apron covered with coins and golden adornments. It is notable that each character wears a different costume, but all feature an abundance of adornments and flowers, especially on their hats, which are high, and look more like scepters than a hat. Also notable is the tendency towards showy and gaudy colors, similar to the brilliant adornments. (1986: 140)

Peña Hernández also contributed an ethnographic footnote to the debate over the meaning of Macho Ratón's name, in describing his appearance during the month-long bacchanalian San Jerónimo festival in Monimbó: "Afterward, Macho Ratón appears, a masquerading Indian with the head of a mule with its mouth wide open, its teeth ready to bite, [a mask] made of wood, painted black, and [wearing the costume] of a mouse with a long tail that almost touches the ground" (1986: 70).

This somewhat refreshing reminder of street performers' interpretations of *El Güegüence* in the Masaya of the 1960s, the midday of Somocista domination, seems to have made little difference to the ongoing literary debates. Cuadra, and later Arellano, either were not aware of possible contradictions between a discourse of national (and nationalist) Nicaraguan *mestizaje* and a celebration of regionalism. More likely, they simply assumed that all intellectual activity in Nicaragua, especially interpretations of *El Güegüence,* contributed to the overall project of elaborating Nicaraguan national identity, a project inevitably led by poets and other literary types. Arellano has been particularly adept at reconciling mutually hostile interpretive work, a task that took some doing after the appearance of Alejandro Dávila Bolaños's edition of *El Güegüence* in 1974.

A Marxist Reinterpretation

The career of Alejandro Dávila Bolaños provides a radical contrast to all the preceding authors' lives, in terms of his personal formation, politics, and mode of contributing to intellectual discourse. It is not so much that Dávila Bolaños presents a real anomaly in the scheme of Nicaraguan intellectual production, because by the early and mid-1970s his political perspectives were shared by a growing sector of Nicaraguan intellectuals who were already or later became aligned with the armed struggle of the Sandinista Front. Rather, Dávila Bolaños's cultural outlook, or better said, his interests and emphases concerning Nicaraguan identity singled out his work, even compared to other leftist and critical thinking in Nicaragua at that time. Born in Masaya in 1922, trained as a medical doctor in León, he wrote extensively about pre-Hispanic Mangue and Nicarao mythology (see Dávila Bolaños 1977). Indeed, on one book's jacket he described himself as a "descendent on the paternal side of Mangue/Chorotega Indians." Dávila Bolaños clearly identified as a socialist and a revolutionary, having spent extensive amounts of time in socialist countries before the triumph of the Sandinista Front; he was imprisoned countless times by the Guardia, and was assassinated by them in 1979, just four months before the Sandinista triumph. His contribution to the revolutionary process was unique: he spent most of his last years organizing and helping to administer the National Center for Traditional Popular Medicine, and his most widely read work is concerned with pre-Columbian herbal medicine (1974a). In 1948 Dávila Bolaños chose to leave León and Granada, the intellectual centers of western Nicaragua, as well as his native Masaya, for the northern mountain town of Estelí, where he wrote and published his work. Using small local printing houses, such as Editorial La Imprenta and Tipografía Geminís, Dávila Bolaños published his books in quantities typically between five hundred and one thousand copies. These publications were paid for by his wife, Merceditas, a woman of apparently independent means. The influence of this work, particularly his interpretation of *El Güegüence* elaborated in the "Introducción Dialectica" to his translation of Brinton's text (1974b), far exceeded the necessarily limited circulation of his books.[11]

In this introductory essay, Dávila Bolaños assumed the widest possible historical overview, starting with the arrival of Paleo-Indians in what is now Nicaragua some thirty thousand years ago, he claimed. With sweeping generalizations, he portrayed a diverse pre-Columbian population in western Nicaragua, dominated by the Mangue and Nicarao, whose civilizations he described in the most splendid terms. He even asserted that the philosophies of these peoples had reached a dialectical form of reasoning. By contrast, Dávila Bolaños described the Spanish Conquest in the most unequivocally bitter and cynical terms, previously unknown among Nicaraguan intellectuals:

Very Spanish were the figures of these Christian barbarians, who, in the name of their Catholic kings and of their humble "god" who died to redeem mankind, destroyed the chiefdoms of peoples who never knew them or offended them in any way, assassinating their chiefs, burning their sacred temples, overthrowing the indigenous Gods they worshipped, killing their respected Priests, and in the same places where their cities had been they [the Spanish] raised up military fortresses bristling with soldiers armed with iron and fire, who demanded blind and absolute obedience to the new masters, who were themselves. (1974b: 11–12)

To the events of this unprecedented cataclysm, Dávila Bolaños applied "the scientific conception of historical materialism, the only method for correctly interpreting the socio-economic problems of oppressed peoples, and hence, their cultural manifestations" (1974b: 23). Thereby he reached the conclusion that the racial antagonism between the Spanish overlords and indigenous peoples was actually a class struggle between "two races that held opposite social interests, derivative of antithetical political, economic and religious concepts" (16). From this perspective, Dávila Bolaños viewed *El Güegüence* as "popular revolutionary theater" of the colonial era (19), with "revolutionary anti-Spanish, anti-Catholic intentions" (22). These contentions he set out to prove using etymology, history, and a withering scorn for the previous interpretive work written by "our reactionary intellectuals." Although this epithet specifically excluded only Carlos Mántica, the "nahualist" whose interpretive work also departed from the mainstream, it is worth remembering that Pérez Estrada, apostle of *mestizaje,* also imbued his interpretation of *El Güegüence* with anticolonialist overtones.[12]

As a Marxist, Dávila Bolaños observed that the victory of "reactionary" interpretations of *El Güegüence* had been conditioned by two aspects of nineteenth-century historical transformation. On the one hand, Nicaragua's national independence and the advent of capitalism had shaped a different perception of the play, allowing elite intellectuals to label it folklore, erasing its radical role during the colonial epoch. More important, from his perspective, the shift from a multilingual colonial environment, in which Spanish, Mangue, Nahuatl-Spanish, and other tongues were spoken, to the unidimensionality of Spanish dominance during the nineteenth century facilitated the intellectuals' treatment of the play as a dance-comedy. Much of Dávila Bolaños's argument rests upon showing that the significance of *El Güegüence* varies radically depending on whether one interprets a Spanish or a Nahuatl-Spanish version. Through such politicized etymological inquiry, Dávila Bolaños reinterpreted the meaning of particular characters' names and declamations and thereby the intentionality of the play's author.

For example, like the "reactionaries," Dávila Bolaños concluded that Güegüence's name signifies "respected elder." But for Dávila Bolaños, the term was not ironically deployed, because according to his analysis Güegüence represented a revolutionary leader, not a dirty old man. In a similar vein, Dávila Bolaños interpreted Macho Ratón as "the cloaked one," whose role was to clandestinely communicate information about insurrectionary activity against the Spanish authorities buried within the dialogue by the author. According to Dávila Bolaños, the play's author was

without a doubt: an Indian. Born in the old **Manqueza** (Masaya, Granada, Carazo) [the Mangue homeland]. He translated from Nahuatl and Mangue, and knew Spanish at the same time. This person was surely a translator of [colonial] laws between Indians and Spaniards, with respect to tributes, tithes, fines, forced labor, etc. that the white men, creoles and non-creoles, demanded from and imposed upon the natives. It's possible that he had been clerk and secretary for the Police, in activities related to Indians. There he observed the antagonisms, the violent struggle, the coarse encounters, the fight between the two races that was the social [milieu] characteristic of the colonial period. (1974b: 31–32)[13]

Dávila Bolaños argued that the play's author had belonged to an extremely secret, esoteric, exclusively Indian sect, called **Los Naguales,** analogous to the Freemasons, which acted as the base of operations for indigenous uprisings and plots to permanently overthrow the colonial order.[14] As such, the actions and words of the characters in *El Güegüence* operated as a revolutionary code which analyzed the contradictions of colonial society in order to motivate those viewing the play to organize the undoing of that society. Thus, Governor Tastuanes, the constable, and the royal scribe are archetypes of colonial authority and caricatures of the same, whose behavior in the play was meant to produce contempt and loathing from the audience, impelling them to political action. Dávila Bolaños interpreted the meaning of Güegüence's sons' names in this politically strategic light. Don Forsico's name, derivative of Nahuatl homonyms, signifies "large goad," or the force behind his father's revolutionary leadership, and Don Ambrosio's name, from Spanish homonyms, makes clear that he is an untrustworthy mestizo. In a less clear-cut case, Dávila Bolaños, like the "reactionaries" and Brinton before them, noted that Suche-Malinche's name connotes the historical role of La Malinche, the Mexican Indian woman who helped Cortés defeat the Aztecs and became his mistress. Beyond this commonplace, he declined further comment. The Machos, he deduced, clearly symbolize the diverse indigenous ethnic groups whose continuous rebellions would eventually force the Spaniards and their progeny out of Nicaragua.

Because *El Güegüence* is a "bi-lingual work, with two completely different, antithetical interpretations" (1974b: 34), depending on whether it is read for its Spanish or its Nahuatl syntax, Dávila Bolaños admitted to the comic aspect of the play without conceding much to the "reactionary" intellectuals. Unlike the latter, for whom this comedy-ballet is a farce by means of which the victory of *mestizaje* is artfully expressed, Dávila Bolaños identified comedy in the play as another rejection of Spanish colonialism:

When the indigenous masses on the streets laugh with boisterous chorusing at Güegüence in his struggle against Governor Tastuanes, they are strengthening their own social conscience, developing their collective personality, giving life to their hatred, consolidating their trust in their leaders, supporting the decisions issuing from their revolutionary councils, maintaining the implacable contempt they feel against the white men. Because laughter was the people's condemnation, the applause of the crowd [was] the Indian's revenge against the monarchist-Catholic regime, and its cruelties, lies, injustices, and abuses . . . [L]aughter, mockery, and satire are powerful means to potentiate the peoples' self-confidence, especially when they have been roused by the dishonor of the abhorred enemy. (48–49)

Through the analysis of several key declamations, Dávila Bolaños underscored the use of humor and bilingual coding as a revolutionary weapon and means to conspiracy. For example, in the opening words of the play, the constable greets the governor in Nahuatl-Spanish: "**Matateco Dio mispiales**, *Señor Gobernador Tastuanes*." Brinton and the Nicaraguan intellectual community, including Dávila Bolaños, have customarily translated this line in Spanish as "El Señor Dios Misericordioso lo guarde, Señor Gobernador Tastuanes," or, in English, "I pray God protect you, Lord Governor Tastuanes." But under the gaze of Dávila Bolaños, and supposedly the colonial audience as well, this line is transformed through Nahuatl-Spanish homonyms and becomes "Mi Dios te mate. Tu Dios te guarde en la tumba, Señor Gobernador Tastuanes," or, in English, "My God will kill you, your God will watch over you in your grave, Lord Governor Tastuanes." Reviewing many other declamations, Dávila Bolaños arrived at similarly shocking revisions, all of them coded but resounding denunciations of the Spaniards. Perhaps Dávila Bolaños's most important revision concerns the enigmatic phrase "en el tiempo del hilo azul": "This speech, the most esteemed by our intellectuals because of the phrase "hilo azul," mnemonically evokes the "Azul" of our Rubén, as well as our [national] topography: blue lakes, blue mountains, blue skies, etc. How different was the real intention of the rebel author [of the play]. [The phrase] actually refers to the movement of [political] agitation that the Indians of Granada-Masaya-Carazo carried out among the black slaves, brought from the Antilles" (1974b: 61–62).[15]

Here, Dávila Bolaños referred to the slaves that had been brought to work the rich agricultural lands around the village of Nandaime in Carazo, a mini-region still inhabited by many Afro-Nicaraguans, and identified by Arellano, as we shall see below, as one of the most important locations where *El Güegüence* was originally composed and performed. Instead of "fardos de guayabas," translated by Brinton as "packs of guavas," Dávila Bolaños revised the phrase as "pardos de guayaberas," or "black slaves dressed in guayaberas." The latter term refers to a simple sort of shirt, which Dávila Bolaños supposes was spun out of the "hilo azul" produced in primitive factories, dyed blue by the indigo that Spanish taskmasters wrung out of Indian and black slaves with blood and sweat. Thus Dávila Bolaños transformed the supposed referent to utopian pre-Hispanic times into a symbol of the unity of the oppressed against the colonial system.

Dávila Bolaños's version of Nicaraguan history as seen through his interpretation of *El Güegüence* becomes the subtext, I argue, for the most influential Sandinista historical overview of colonialism's transformation of indigenous peoples in western Nicaragua, elaborated in Jaime Wheelock's *Las raíces indígenas de la lucha anti-colonialista.* Both books were published in the same year: 1974. Wheelock's text, in turn, helped to shape Sandinista policies toward the Masaya-Carazo region, heartland of indigenous traditions such as artisanry and *El Güegüence*. But it is equally true that the policies of the Ministry of Culture under Sandinismo maintained the influence of the other intellectual tradition elaborated in the *El Güegüence* literature, the tradition presided over by Pablo Antonio Cuadra, elaborated in the revolutionary era by Jorge Eduardo Arellano, and developed into an official cultural politics by a third Granadino intellectual, Ernesto Cardenal.

A Bibliographer's Work

Born in Granada in 1946, Jorge Eduardo Arellano is a historian of Nicaraguan literature and the bibliographer par excellence of *El Güegüence*. Educated in Spain, and fabulously well published, his career spans the eras of Somocismo, Sandinismo, and the uncertainties of the post-Sandinista era, and straddles the horses ridden by Nicaragua's three cultural icons. If, in the historical panorama of the twentieth century, Rubén Darío and the swirl of intellectual activity concerned with his work represents the allegorical high road to Nicaragua's national cultural identity, and *El Güegüence* and its interpretive literature the unruly parable of the same, then the person of Augusto César Sandino and the reams of interpretive literature published about his legacy from 1979 to 1990, constitute the political road to national identity.[16] As a member of the Granadino avant-garde during late Somocismo, a publishing powerhouse and limelight of the revolutionary intelligentsia under Sandinismo, and now ostentatiously independent of the Frente through his position in the Academia Nicaragüense de la Lengua, Arellano's intellectual fortitude has enabled his survival through the earthquakes, real and figurative, that have moved Nicaraguan history during the past five decades. His transformations in fact derive from a fairly consistent view of Nicaraguan identity and destiny, whether he is writing about Darío, Sandino, or Macho Ratón. His celebration of Nicaraguan *mestizaje,* it seems, puts up a big enough tent to include all Nicaraguan intellectuals, whom Arellano, in turn, reconciles with one another in his analytic and bibliographic prose. Perhaps nowhere is that more evident than in his treatment of *El Güegüence.*

During extensive research at the Iberoamerican Institute in (formerly West) Berlin in 1981, Arellano encountered a previously unknown manuscript of *El Güegüence,* copied by German linguist-ethnographer Walter Lehmann in 1908. The famous author of *Zentral Amerika* (1920) was already known to have copied a manuscript of the play that originated in Masaya; Lehmann found the second text, rediscovered by Arellano, in Nandaime. And although Dávila Bolaños ridiculed the fetishism over *El Güegüence* manuscripts, claiming that "in reality, [the other versions] are no more than mutilated paraphrases of [Brinton's] text published by [Cuadra's] *Taller San Lucas*" (1974a: 21), there is no doubt that such research helped to build Arellano's special relationship with the play and his ability to make interpretive conclusions about it with authority and legitimacy. Thus, in his most fully realized interpretive essay, "El Güegüence o la Esencia Mestiza de Nicaragua," Arellano can assert, without citing any supporting evidence, that Nandaime "was the original, real geographical cradle of *El Güegüence*" (1985: 68) rather than Masaya, or even Diriamba. He makes this claim notwithstanding his own admission, like Peña Henríquez before him, that the play is performed most frequently and faithfully to the old manuscripts in Diriamba alone. Arellano also revises other authors' intentions and the significance of their work when it suits his own interpretations. For example, Arellano quotes a passage by José Coronel Urtecho, Vanguardist, contemporary of Cuadra, and apologist for both Somocismo and Sandinismo: "Now *El Güegüence* is a rural dance that seems to celebrate the first mule-drivers, symbolized by the macho-ratónes [*sic*], which seemed to be a question of taking the place of the **tlamenes** or Indian stevedores, the same types as the Indians who traveled the roads of Nicaragua selling their ware, where they still spoke in Spanish and Nahuatl" (in Arellano 1985: 56).

When Arellano notes that "[i]f we substitute for Indian mestizo, for Nicaragua Mesoamerica, and for Nahuatl and Spanish the Spanish-Nahuatl lingua franca, the quote [becomes] more precise and correct" (1985: 56), he can assume the mantle of Urtecho's prestige and legitimacy while simultaneously changing the meaning of what the old man originally intended. In somewhat less egregious fashion, Arellano makes note of authors whose views clearly diverge from his own in such a way as to not pick fights with them; but neither does he necessarily take their views very seriously. Thus Dávila Bolaños's theories are "based upon a very personal and *sui generis* re-creation" (Arellano 1985: 69), rather than upon Marxist scholarship. Similarly, Arellano chooses *not* to contrast Cuadra's identification of *El Güegüence* as the manifesto of Nicaraguan mestizo identity with Mántica's open-ended etymological analysis. Instead, he treats Mántica's insights as chronologically later refinements of Cuadra's earlier interpretations, preserving the authority of the latter, his mentor. These graceful maneuverings reach their zenith in Arellano's expositions regarding the significance of the "hilo azul" and the authorship of the play.

Versatile literary figure that he is, Arellano duly notes the subtle and pervasive connotations of "el hilo azul" which have reverberated in the realm of Nicaraguan intellectual culture for decades. But Arellano is not merely interested in name-dropping choice morsels like the title of Darío's most famous work, "Azul," to mark the effects of the phrase upon Nicaraguan literature. Rather, in his methodical way, he seeks to marshal hundreds of years of the most authoritative texts to unquestionably establish the truth of his own multilayered interpretation. First, Arellano documents beyond the shadow of a doubt that pre-Hispanic indigenous peoples of western Nicaragua knew about and used the marine mollusk *Murex purpureus* to dye cotton thread and cloth purple. This shellfish, the very same that the Mediterranean civilizations of antiquity valued so dearly, was immediately recognized by the Spaniards.[17] Subsequently, the colonial administration demanded purple (sometimes called blue) cloth as part of the tribute of the Indians of Masaya-Carazo, woven and dyed in primitive factories (*obrajes*) in which workers labored under slave-like conditions. Such production continued after independence, Arellano shows, quoting the ever-dependable authority Ephraim Squier, who reported on the techniques of extracting the dye from the mollusks in 1852. Although Squier specified that the people who wove and dyed this precious cloth in Masaya were Indians, Arellano pays little attention to that detail, because he must show that the reference to "hilo azul" in *El Güegüence* figures in the nature of mestizo national identity that for him characterizes the play. It may be helpful to repeat Güegüence's declamation at this juncture: "Ah, in my time, when I was a boy, in the time of the blue thread [*el hilo azul*], when you could see in the fields of the Diriomos, lifting up those packs of guavas [*fardos de guayabas*], isn't that right, boys?" (in Lejarza 1993: 49). In Arellano's hands, the evocation suddenly and seamlessly refers to the tasks of a "young mestizo boy," laboring perhaps on the family farm, who had to carry the dyed textiles, product of his family's labors, to market. Perhaps, Arellano suggests, "lifting up" might refer to childish pranks of swiping guavas, a distinctive-tasting tropical fruit, during the course of the daily chores. Güegüence's speech thus recalls his youth nostalgically, through a colloquialism, "en el tiempo del hilo azul," which Arellano again documents as a mnemonic common among folk and literati alike during this century. The slippage between identities in western Nicaragua and in Masaya-Carazo specifically, whereby Indian becomes mestizo when that suits Arellano's purposes, again occurs unproblematically.

As he turns his attention to the question of the play's authorship, Arellano summarizes previous theories, particularly Pérez Estrada's insistence, based on Cuadra's authority, that the author must have been a Spaniard. Arellano returns to the arguments over the author's obvious competence with the Spanish language, and his agile management of homonyms and double entendres (the idea that the author might have been a woman never occurs to any of these Nicaraguan intellectuals). The author could not have been an Indian nor even a common mestizo, Arellano argues, as neither social stratum could possibly have attained the evident literary sophistication of the author during the seventeenth century. Neither could a creole businessman nor a colonial functionary have written the play, as others have suggested, for both groups are harshly criticized, ridiculed, or satirized at various points during *El Güegüence*. Instead, Arellano reintroduces another Vanguardist poet's theory, Joaquín Pasos's claim that a priest wrote the play, whom Arellano qualifies as a worldly, literary priest, probably from Granada. To Dávila Bolaños's observation that *El Güegüence* is profoundly anti-Catholic, Arellano responds that the play's character is actually agnostic, which he claims was a common enough attribute of the Spanish clergy during the seventeenth century. It is difficult to concede to his logic, however, since this period was, after all, the era of the Inquisition.

One might empathize with Dávila Bolaños, who registered a certain degree of sardonic incredulity at the self-aggrandizing theories of so learned a man as Arellano, theories that not only reinscribe the dominance of elite interpretations and demarcations of Nicaraguan culture, but specifically lionize the Granadino perspective. In that light, it is ironically important that Arellano's two-volume republication of *El Güegüence* (1985) included an old essay by a North American philologist that contradicts much of Arellano's theorizing concerning the authorship and character of the play. Marshall Elliott's (1884) analysis showed that characterizing the prose in which *El Güegüence* was written as literary Spanish did not do justice to the syntactic complexity of the mixing of Nahuatl and Spanish in Brinton's text. Moreover, Elliott detected a linguistic shift in the manuscript, one that Dávila Bolaños also observed some ninety years later, although the latter drew less radical conclusions. "I think," wrote Elliott,

that here is strong internal evidence for believing that the whole comedy is not by one and the same author, but rather made up of two comedies or parts of comedies that bore the names respectively of Güegüence and El Macho-raton [*sic*] . . . My suspicions in this direction were first aroused by the change of language that takes place about the point where El Macho-raton is first mentioned, that is from about the fiftieth page of the text onward . . . The proportion of Nahuatl words is smaller from this point forward than in the first part of the work, especially in the speeches of the Governor and the [Constable]. The language of Güegüence and his sons, in a majority of cases, is almost pure Spanish in character and composition, whereas towards the beginning of the work they are often understood with difficulty by one who does not know the native idiom . . . I think the conclusion may be drawn with a certain degree of probability that the Macho-raton part of the work is of an epoch different from the Güegüence proper. (1884: 66–67)

Elliott's essay leaves questions of cultural identity wide open and throws the question of authorship into a new kind of uncertainty. Mántica drew almost identical conclusions about the play's composition, or better said, its split (linguistic) personality. Arellano's essay is not concerned with the uses to which either Mántica or Dávila Bolaños put such hypothesizing. He is therefore catholic in his bibliographic tastes but orthodox in his theoretical orientation. Perhaps Arellano's inclusion of Elliott's essay in his own edition of *El Güegüence* serves to underline several themes that Nicaraguan intellectual history has featured repeatedly: the interweaving of foreign and national authority in demarcating Nicaraguan culture; an emphasis on language and etymology in reviewing Masaya-Carazo, the zone of cultural origination; and, Arellano's own predilection toward inclusive bibliography, notwithstanding substantive internal differences. Arellano's successful intellectual reincarnations over the last half-century and his mastery over the open-ended incongruities in the interpretive literature concerned with *El Güegüence* thereby reify the circuits by which particular intellectuals and their interpretations of national culture have maintained control over Nicaraguan national identity.

Operationalizing Tropes from *El Güegüence*

All of the intellectuals who have interpreted the significance of *El Güegüence* have essentialized this play, with the exception of Carlos Mántica. Mántica's analysis of multiple disjunctured meanings most closely resembles my own interpretation. *El Güegüence,* I would argue, is not about the closure of national identity and its characteristics among Nicaraguans: it is not about the nation at all. It is a tale told by the locals in one part of Nicaragua, that purposely and purposefully leaves questions of their identity open-ended, and celebrates subversion, disorder, and confusion. The alliance between poor thieves and rich officials of the state at the end of the tale is meant to leave listeners and readers wondering, rather than sure or reassured. I believe the tale has been performed for hundreds of years because, as a parable for and a paradigm of local discourses in Masaya-Carazo, it has helped to confound the totalizing discourses of nation. Heard and understood as confounding boundedness, the significance of the play's tropes is not confined to the Masaya-Carazo region but has relevance elsewhere in Nicaragua, without symbolizing any essential Nicaraguanness.

In using *El Güegüence* in the coming chapters, my task is twofold. First, I must show how the mainstream, dominant interpretive discourses concerned with *El Güegüence* and the alternative interpretation elaborated by Dávila Bolaños provided intellectual raw material out of which cultural policy was spun under Sandinismo. In particular, the interpretation of historical transformations of national, indigenous, and mestizo identities found in the *El Güegüence* literature form a conceptual trunk out of which policymaking toward the artisans of western Nicaragua grew. At the same time, my own interpretation of the play, inspired by Mántica's polysemic interpretive work, illuminates disjunctures over class, gender, and ethnic identities I witnessed during fieldwork. I use several key images from the parable of *El Güegüence* and its interpretive literature explored in this chapter to descriptively unfold the ethnographic material and illuminate its significance.

The next chapter describes the politics of the Ministry of Culture toward the artisans, the artisans' formation of their own union in reaction to and against the Ministry, and the manner in which this conflict played out in the actions taken by the revolutionary state, and the underlying analysis of class and nation by the intellectuals of the Sandinista Front. I use the image of Güegüence's conflict with the authorities, and his protest against the idea that he must have their permission to do what he already does, to argue against mainstream essentialist interpretations of the play. Instead, I see Güegüence's relationship to authority as an anti-essentialist parable that illuminates the artisans' resistance to and accommodation of the power of the authorities, a power riddled by contradictions about identity and the paradoxical ability to give permission.

In chapter 3, I abandon mainstream interpretations of the play altogether, and struggle to find the parable in the silence of Suche-Malinche with respect to the lives and ideas of artisan women. The character and role of Suche-Malinche and the way (the lack of) women's presence in the play shaped elite demarcations of women's subordinate and mute place in national cultural identity are underlying themes in this chapter. If the Sandinista revolution empowered subaltern and silenced social sectors, that empowerment did not affect artisan women directly. During the 1980s, many of the women with whom we worked both in San Juan and among the families who make *cerámica negra* expressed themselves primarily as artisans and secondarily as women. The 1990s have seen a new feminist discourse growing in Nicaragua, but that discourse has not necessarily connected with artisan women in this decade. The effects of the silence of Suche-Malinche thus remain powerful, but I read this silence as underscoring the sterility of men's alliances both in *El Güegüence* and in the construction of the Nicaraguan nation and the state. As a feminist parable, then, the play warns of the dangers of women's silence and, as an unfinished story, opens the possibility for new subversions of certainties and hierarchies.

In chapter 4, I use "the time of the blue thread," the paradigmatic phrase from *El Güegüence,* to discuss the new indigenous movement in western Nicaragua. The indigenous movement, I argue, has constructed a counternarrative of Nicaraguan history, in which indigenous peoples survived rather than disappeared, as elite intellectuals have asserted. But this counternarrative, of continuity rather than submission, reifies the rigid boundary between indigenous and mestizo identities that elite intellectuals also assumed. Alternatively, I consider the time of the blue thread to embody identities that are not ethnically bounded nor decisively won or lost but linked to the daily experiences of artisanal work. The contrast between the blue thread as anti-essentialist parable and as essentialist counternarrative opens up a series of tensions between my analyses and those of Flavio Gamboa, and shapes a discussion of various forms of Indianness and mestizoness in light of the contemporary indigenous movement and its possible effects on Nicaraguan national identity.

Although my aim is not just to tell parables, it becomes difficult to separate the parables from the ethnographic exegesis as this volume progresses.

Chapter 2

Nobody has to give me permission for this, Lord Governor Tastuanes,

or, Why the Artisans Did Not Become a

Revolutionary Class 1979–1990

A Meeting in Masaya

At the end of March, 1985, the artisans' union UNADI (Unión Nacional de Artesanos–Diriangén, or National Union of Artisans–Diriangén[1]) held a regional meeting in the ruins of the old open-air marketplace in Masaya, which had been destroyed by Somoza's jets during the final Sandinista uprising of 1979. I attended the meeting with the San Juanero potters from the Co-op, who had taken the opportunity afforded by the bus ride from San Juan to Masaya to drink a few shots of Flor de Caña. At the meeting, I recognized the president of UNADI and several delegates to the union whom I knew, including María Esthela Rodríguez, one of the *cerámica negra* women from Matagalpa. Two officials from the Ministry of Culture with whom I had worked were there, and several others from the Ministry's marketing arm ENIARTE (Empresa Nacional de Industrias Artesanales, or National Enterprise of Artisans). Victor Tirado, one of the nine *comandantes* ruling the country, gave the keynote address. "We must all make great sacrifices," he said, "in the struggle against the aggression waged by imperialism against our country . . . Your social sector can make an important contribution to the popular movement for national liberation and development of the people." I noticed that he never specifically mentioned artisans or artisanal production, while at the same time he made clear that his presence signified the Sandinista Front's recognition of the existence and value of "your social sector." "It was like being lectured to, like we were children at the party of adults," commented Bladimir Nororís, a San Juanero potter with whom I worked closely, "and we were allowed to attend."

At the end of 1984, President Daniel Ortega attended UNADI's second national meeting, where he even more explicitly gave approval to the activities of the union. As reported by *Barricada,* the official paper of the Sandinista Front, Ortega seemed cognizant of the actual demands of the union and the problems besetting the artisanal sector. These problems had become distinct from those affecting other sectors, although all were linked by the larger crisis caused by the violence and economic blockade sponsored by the United States. In the *Barricada* article, and apparently in the mind of Ortega, the artisans' cause was legitimated by the linkage made by both the Frente and UNADI between the artisans and certain maxims Sandino himself had uttered: "I am an urban worker, an artisan as we say in this country, but my surpassing dreams live on the horizon of internationalism, in the right to be free and to demand justice; but to reach this state of perfection it will be necessary to spill our own blood" (UNADI 1985: n.p.).

For important leaders in the Frente, then, the artisans were a social sector that formed part of the masses and should be considered a revolutionary constituency. The presence of powerful individuals at UNADI meetings might be seen, I think now, as an act of giving permission to artisans to do what they were doing, to continue to be artisans, and to marry their cause with the greater cause of Sandinismo, much like Governor Tastuanes's eventual approval of Güegüence and his son's betrothal to the governor's daughter. But during the 1980s, the Frente and its leadership were not the only force working to legitimate artisans. The Ministry of Culture and several of the bureaucracies within the Ministry acted upon very different ideas about artisans, their identities and histories, and their role in the revolutionary transformation of Nicaraguan society. In a nutshell, the artisans chose permission from the Frente to organize themselves as a class officially part of the revolutionary coalition, and thus to seek through their union the patronage of state ministries to secure raw materials, access to national and international markets, and new technologies. Through UNADI, artisans simultaneously opted to reject the programs promoted by the Ministry, which involved both lionizing the artisans as torchbearers of cultural revolution as well as oversight by Ministry officials on all matters of technological development, marketing, and relations of production in artisanal workshops. Yet the roots of policy toward artisans in western Nicaragua[2] made by both the Frente and the Ministry grew out of the same intellectual soil of cultural discourse: Minister of Culture Ernesto Cardenal inherited the elite Granadino traditions of poetry and literary critique from Pablo Antonio Cuadra and José Coronel Urtecho, and Jaime Wheelock, Daniel Ortega, Tomás Borge, and others elaborated a theory of Sandinista class struggle whose views of Nicaraguan history had been unleashed on Nicaragua's cultural discourse by Alejandro Dávila Bolaños. This intellectual soil also provided the medium for artisans to contest the cultural policies that affected them. Ultimately, this led to the breakdown of both the Ministry and the Union and the victory of an elitist version of cultural policy that simply elided the possibility for contestation.

To trace the conflicts over cultural policy and the artisans' navigation of them, I will detail two distinctive interpretive views of artisans and artisanal production in the Nicaraguan past and during the Sandinista Revolution, represented by the figures of Cardenal and Wheelock and the tropes of cultural revolution and class struggle, respectively. In this chapter, the coexistence of these two different interpretations of national cultural identity within the overall politics of Sandinismo forms the backdrop for describing the varied and varying responses of the artisans to state policies. To trace that interaction between elite discourse on the nation, Sandinista state policy, and the active role of the artisans in defining and then refusing a class identity, I have provided a great deal of historical foregrounding of various sorts regarding the emergence of Nicaraguan artisans into the twentieth century, artisans' participation in the overthrow of Somoza, and the ideologies behind the two different interpretations of artisans operating within the ministries of the Sandinista state. This foregrounding frames "the action": artisans' attempts to define themselves during the events of 1984 to 1990, during which time the San Juaneros and other artisans rejected the Ministry, created UNADI, and then found themselves without either the Ministry or their union. Both the foregrounding and "the action" are composed of descriptions in several registers. My analytic voice will alternate with academic and Sandinista sources, essays written by Orlando Gallegos and Roberto Potosme, and the spoken words of potters from San Juan and from the families who make *cerámica negra*. These registers are juxtaposed in each section, but remain distinct.

In the end, the artisans neither helped to lead the cultural transformation of Nicaragua nor became a revolutionary class, even though they had gained the permission of different authorities to do both. But during these processes, their notions of themselves and their work did indeed change.

The Artisans in Nicaraguan History:
Academic and Intervening Sandinista Narratives

It would indeed be reassuring, to academically trained minds at least, to insert at this point a summary of the Nicaraguan historical background shaping the situations that confronted artisans after 1979. An anthropologist might preface the discussion of the various currents in Sandinista cultural policy that derived from different interpretive views in elite discourse by reviewing an objective historical literature. But no such literature exists; all contributions to the historical discourse are positioned, shaped by conscious and unconscious a priori perspectives on Nicaraguan history that are related to Nicaraguan politics, and in the case of non-Nicaraguans, the political relationships between authors' home countries and Nicaragua extant during whatever period an author may have been writing. One can review literature that is not directly related to debates over Sandinista cultural policy and their effects on artisans—literature not written by Ernesto Cardenal and others working for the Ministry of Culture, not written by Jaime Wheelock and other leading lights within the Frente—as well as use contemporary theory in anthropology to help frame a discussion of the contestation over cultural politics during Sandinismo. Such a review, however, always and inevitably leads back to and entwines with Sandinista discourses. Before undertaking this historical recounting, let me muse briefly about assumptions and interpretations that have been woven into this endeavor.

In March of 1984, I attended two weekends of dancing and celebration in San Juan, preparatory exercises, Agustín Amador told me, for the big fiesta in June. During the course of the day, a procession of about two hundred people traveled in a roughly circular path around the streets of the village; to those in the procession, people in doorways passed refreshments consisting of *chicha,* a weakly fermented corn beverage, and baked corn cakes called *rosquillas.* As a part of the procession, men fought *chilillo* duels, ritualized battles between men wearing horsehead masks and armed with sticks the tips of which were covered by the skin from bull's penises. The masked men, called *chinegros,* pranced around like crazed horses, but Agustín told me that the men were never supposed to hurt each other in the battle. In fact, he said, even though *chilillo* battles told the story of the Spanish Conquest, only best friends could be *chinegros,* to ensure that no one would get hurt. I was watching the dancing to determine if he was right. After a few glasses of *chicha,* I tried to engage the oldest person in sight, the father of Gregorio Bracamonte, in my opinion the finest potter in San Juan, in a conversation about the history of *chilillo* and of San Juan. I asked him for how long he thought San Juaneros had engaged in *chilillo* duels.

"This is a very, very old dance," he said. "It really is very old. This is how things have always been done here."

"How old, do you think?" I persisted.

"More than a hundred years," he replied and turned back to watch the battle.

Years later, I remembered the *chilillo* procession I saw and connected it to the larger culture of public performance in Masaya-Carazo, linking the mock battles that recall the Conquest and the grimacing horses' heads of the *chinegros* to the parable of *El Güegüence;* certainly my constant reframing of memory and experience over the past fifteen years yields as capricious a quality of historical recall as that which I frequently encountered among San Juaneros. When I asked about the pre-Columbian history of the village, Agustín and Bladimir showed me Lothrop's book, *Pottery of Nicaragua and Costa Rica* (1926), a copy of which the Co-op owned and which they used to design and paint the so-called *vasos mayas,* or Mayan vases, one of their main products. As an academic, I felt comfortable with such a dependable and solid reference, especially because it seemed to me that the San Juaneros themselves had very little to say about that history. That assumption was unfounded.

I also persisted in thinking that the Co-op itself constituted one of the developments that had come to San Juan after the Sandinista triumph, when actually its history began during the final years of Somocismo and owed its existence to certain individuals in the Technical Services Department of the Banco Central. It took me a long time to understand the importance of the pre-Sandinista origins of the Co-op in terms of what occurred later, and that it was possible, as Orlando Gallegos admonished me repeatedly, that honest and socially aware people had worked in the Banco Central even under Somocismo. Orlando told me that "the Banco Central was the only institution under Somocismo which was not corrupt" (in Field 1987:63), an opinion reiterated by many people who worked in the Ministry of Culture. I do not know if they were right; however, the description of economically and culturally decadent artisan communities found in the Banco Central's study of *artesanía*[3] was accepted by all the players who worked in the field of artisanal development in Sandinista Nicaragua. My historical reconstructions, it seemed, were always tinged by the horror of Somoza's private army, the Guardia Nacional, and the typical *internacionalista*'s solidarity with the revolution. These vignettes about historical memory and its assumptions illustrate the difficulties in bringing ethnographic experiences to bear upon the origins of twentieth-century artisans in western Nicaragua, and how artisans related to Sandinista views of class and class struggle, during the revolutionary period. We must settle instead for partial, situated analyses (Haraway 1991).

At the end of the twentieth century, the artisan communities of western Nicaragua remain, as they have been historically, a heterogeneous lot. Their heterogeneity — some groups of artisans constitute small populations in isolated rural agricultural villages in the coastal region, the northern highlands, and the central plateau of western Nicaragua, but the largest artisan community in the country is an urban barrio, Monimbó, located in the city of Masaya — clearly derives from the character of the Spanish Conquest in this part of Central America. Newson (1987), Stanislawski (1983), and others have documented the demographic collapse of the linguistically diverse indigenous chiefdoms extant in the territory of contemporary Nicaragua at the time of contact with Europeans. This collapse, remarkable even in the context of many similar contemporaneous devastations, resulted from both the cycle of plagues that ravaged the "New World" after the Spaniards and other Europeans arrived, as well as from Spanish military domination of the populous Nicaraguan Pacific coast. This region featured few apparent precious metals, but the lands that became Nicaragua served a purpose in the early colonial precious metals economy. The Spaniards who founded the city of León in the sixteenth century rounded up and exported tens of thousands of indigenous peoples to use as slaves in the mines of Peru.

Slaving, and the associated shipbuilding industry, built the fortunes of the Leonese elites, whose city was located not far from the good harbor at Corinto (Newson 1987). In the increasingly depopulated interior region, a second elite stratum of landowning cattle barons coalesced around the colonial city of Granada (ibid.). The military and political competition between the elites of the two cities, noted in the previous chapter, commenced almost immediately and continued throughout the colonial period (Romero Vargas 1988).

As Ralph Woodward (1985: 89–91) has implied, Nicaraguan independence within a flimsily united Central America was something of a political fait accompli that occurred more as a by-product of Mexican independence than through the political agitation of the deeply divided elites. Since the nineteenth century, foreign and (more recently) Nicaraguan authors have attempted to describe the kind of people who inhabited Nicaragua following the Conquest and into the period of independence, and I review these authors to shed light upon the ancestry of contemporary artisans. This very issue also, of course, underlies the entire *El Güegüence* literature with respect to the identity of all western Nicaraguans. The comments of European observers (Boyle 1868 in Burns 1991; Squier 1860) make clear that midway through the nineteenth century the largest communities identified by outsiders and Nicaraguans as "Indian," Monimbó and Sutiava, were composed of Spanish speakers living mainly in towns built during the Spanish colonial administration. In the 1850s, Squier complained that he could find barely a handful of fluent speakers of native languages, and noted that among "the Indians" the practice of Catholic rituals did not greatly differ from the practice of Catholicism in communities Nicaraguans called mestizo. Yet Squier exulted in the richness of artisanal production he found in Masaya. However, Nicaraguan historian Julian Guerrero described Indian rebellions occurring in the northern highlands (Matagalpa-Jinotega area) at the end of the nineteenth century, conducted by peoples still speaking indigenous languages and wearing "Indian clothing" (Guerrero and Soriano de Guerrero 1982); but this region has never been the central or even much of a peripheral area of artisanal production, notwithstanding the presence of the makers of *cerámica negra* there. Then too, as we shall see, the origins of *cerámica negra* are hardly indigenous.

Recently, Bradford Burns (1991) has discussed the disunity among Nicaraguan elites, the lack of national identity during the long period of internecine conflict, and the relatively weak economic position of Nicaragua's elites as the condition for the emergence of what he identifies as a village- and town-based "folk" society in western Nicaragua during the eighteenth and nineteenth centuries. The economy of the Nicaraguan folk depended, according to Burns, on subsistence agriculture and the artisanal production of basic commodities. Burns's analysis highlights the creation of numerous local, basically self-sufficient economies throughout the western region and the key importance of artisanal production in sustaining those economies, but his account does not clarify how the "folk" themselves conceived of their ethnic identity, nor why outside observers named certain communities Indian and others mestizo. By contrast, in Nicaraguan historian German Romero Vargas's (1988) exhaustive treatment of eighteenth-century historical transformations in the western region, he details shifting ethnic boundaries differentiating the masses of Nicaraguans, the people whom Burns called the "folk." In other words, although certain communities were called Indian and others mestizo by both Nicaraguans and others, the characteristics marking these identities were not stable, and over time the Indian ethnic category was less and less marked by distinctive cultural practices, language, and presentations of self. Like Burns, Romero Vargas described artisanal production as a characteristic trait of western Nicaraguan society, yet the latter's analysis makes especially clear that artisanal production per se did not constitute, at least by the eighteenth century, a marker for either Indian or mestizo identity.

Romero Vargas's approach coincides with Sandinista historians' analyses, which, like Romero Vargas's work, emphasize changes affecting rural communities, particularly the transformation of the Indian communities that were reconstituted after the population collapse that followed the Conquest. By Sandinista historians, I mean Jaime Wheelock and those who worked in research institutes connected to MIDINRA, the Ministry of Agrarian Reform, particularly CIERA (Centro de Investigaciones y Estudios sobre la Reforma Agraria), which have elaborated on his work. One of their primary historical foci has been on the latter part of the nineteenth century, when foreign interventions succeeded in creating a temporary and fragile alliance between different sectors of Nicaragua's elite social stratum, stimulating the formation of the first unified state under José Santos Zelaya, and inserting the first major presence of capitalist development, based as elsewhere in Central America (see R. G. Williams 1986) on plantation agriculture. As part of an effort to anchor the Sandinista Revolution in the waters of Nicaraguan history, Wheelock's book *Las raíces indígenas de la lucha anti-colonialista en Nicaragua* (The Indigenous Roots of the Anti-Colonialist Struggle in Nicaragua) (1981) elaborated the fate of indigenous populations and their struggles particularly after the introduction of the first plantation crop, coffee, in the northern highlands during the nineteenth century. Wheelock detailed the connections between a historic series of Indian rebellions in the seventeenth, eighteenth, and nineteenth centuries, and the early twentieth-century Nicaraguan class struggle led by Sandino and his followers, the first Sandinistas.[4] Whereas Indians all over Nicaragua had for centuries struggled to defend their language, culture, and religion from the brutality of Spanish rule, by the mid-nineteenth century "The Indian in Nicaragua was slowly experiencing a progressive transformation towards becoming a *campesino* of the small peasant type, acquiring the consciousness and concerns of the small proprietors, and from this engendering a struggle of a more economic and class nature in what had been an ethnic and religious [struggle]" (Wheelock 1981: 89).

The seizure of communal lands previously owned by indigenous communities for coffee plantations contributed heavily to the declining fortunes of agricultural indigenous communities. Indigenous cultural identity, in Wheelock's view, did not really exist in Nicaragua after the end of the nineteenth century, but the indigenous political legacy survived in the form of an insurrectionary class consciousness among rural campesinos and certain urban populations. In other words, indigenous ethnicity in contemporary western Nicaragua had been transformed into subaltern class status. The battle for ethnic and cultural autonomy transformed into a class struggle, and thus the dynamics of ethnic identity described by Romero Vargas were laid to rest once and for all, but in a manner identical to Dávila Bolaños's dialectical analysis of *El Güegüence*. For both Wheelock and Dávila Bolaños, the narrative of Nicaraguan history had led to the class struggle, and the identity of the Nicaraguan people had been and would continue to be decided by the dynamics of class. Thus, Dávila Bolaños' radically alternative approach to the *El Güegüence* discourse resonated with Wheelock's revolutionary revision of Nicaraguan history.

Wheelock's view was further elaborated in CIERA's (CIERA-MIDINRA 1984b) impressively documented and detailed history of the Segovias, a northern mountain region. The authors trace the destruction of communal land and collective social relations within indigenous communities to the new plantation economy and the brutal domination of the rural north by the coffee planter class; but they also remark upon the scorn that the coffee owners evinced for local, artisanally produced commodities (297), a scorn that, in combination with the heavy demands placed upon plantation laborers, eventually led rural folk to abandon artisanal production as they also abandoned their old language and ways of dressing and relating to one another. For the CIERA authors, indigenous identity and artisanal production were laid to rest in a tomb that became the crucible of class struggles in the north, the struggles that the Sandinista Front were later to lead.

But if the theme of class struggle dominates the Sandinista view of Nicaraguan history, and if that view mirrors Dávila Bolaños's interpretation of *El Güegüence,* we may also note that the history of the Masaya-Carazo region from whence the parable originates does not exactly fit the Sandinista narrative. Artisanal production of basic personal and household commodities continued in the Masaya-Carazo region notwithstanding the social convulsions in the north, a historical phenomenon analyzed in Sandinista literature only in the context of artisans' participation in the insurrections that overthrew Somoza, as I will relate shortly. Artisans in this region were not affected by the intrusion of plantation agriculture to any great extent, although some coffee came to be grown in the highland areas in Masaya. Coffee, like edible crops, was grown by farmers owning relatively small plots, a feature that distinguished this region from any other in the country during the many decades prior to the Sandinista period: "A noteworthy piece of information which must be related is that the department of Masaya is one of the very few in the country where the land has not been idled [under the control of large landowners], and the great majority of it is in the hands of numerous small property owners" (Guerrero and Soriano de Guerrero 1965: 57).

Perhaps in the case of the artisans of Masaya, Nash's (1993) work with Mayan potters in Chiapas may be relevant, hinting that people make subsistence decisions based on the ideational understandings of life and experience anthropologists have called "cultural": "The preservation of small-plot, semi-subsistence household production supplemented by artisanal production in the context of growing economic crisis is a cultural preference that cannot be explained in economic terms alone" (148). The Mexican case is actually quite relevant, because the experience of government management of artisanal development in Mexico significantly influenced the Ministry of Culture's policies in San Juan and elsewhere in western Nicaragua. Yet economic and political crises in late-nineteenth- and early-twentieth-century Nicaragua shaped the transformation of artisanal production and of a form of indigenous identity in Masaya-Carazo in ways different from what occurred in Chiapas and elsewhere in Mesoamerica where easily recognizable "Indians" remained (both to national and international observers). Dunkerly's (1988) description of early plantation economies in Central America indicates that artisanal production functioned as a subsidy for capitalist accumulation by keeping low the costs of reproducing the labor force among the "semiproletariat." Kaimowitz (1986: 16) defined Nicaraguan semiproletarians as "any rural family which engages in both self-employed agricultural activities and wage labor." The economic position of artisans in Masaya-Carazo, in villages and towns, elaborates these discussions: since the recovery from the demographic collapse of the Conquest, most families in the region own small parcels of land from which family members derive a portion of their subsistence, and at least one member of the family earns income from the sale of artisanally produced commodities. Capitalist development of plantation agriculture in the north likely fed off the cheap supply of artisanally produced goods from Masaya-Carazo, practically ensuring the survival of artisan communities in this region until the establishment of the dynastic Somoza dictatorship in the 1930s.

The violent breakdown of the alliance between León and Granada that occurred during the first three decades of the twentieth century shaped the creation of a new state in Nicaragua run by the Somoza dynasty and a new situation for the artisan communities of Masaya-Carazo. The new Somocista state arranged an uneasy standoff between elite factions that allowed the Somocista state to administer the spoils. As Robert Williams (1986) has shown, the "modernization" of agriculture during the Somoza era swelled the urban informal sector, as the introduction of cotton and beef agro-export production forced thousands of peasants off their lands. The Somozas persecuted artisans in many ways. Flavio Gamboa remembers that Monimbó, the largest community, was stripped of the areas of communal land that had belonged to it, making the Monimboseños for the first time completely dependent upon their earnings from artisanal production. Economic policies favored imported consumer goods over those produced nationally, which led to a decline in the quantity and quality of goods produced over the four decades of Somocismo.

This did not go unnoticed by one organ of the Somocista state, the Banco Central, which commissioned a study of Nicaraguan *artesanía* in the mid-1970s. The Industrial Division of the Department of Technical Services of the Banco Central Nicaragüense published its study *La Situacíon de la Artesanía Nicaragüense* in 1976, documenting the places where artisans lived in the country, what they produced, and the problems affecting the production and sale of artisanally produced goods. Although it was this study, and not the Sandinista triumph, that led to the creation of the Co-op, the bank's report does not appear to have entered into early Sandinista analysis of Somocista Nicaragua (see El Programa Sandinista 1969, and El Programa Historico del FSLN 1981 both in Gilbert and Block 1990), which focused, and not incorrectly, on the havoc wreaked upon the country by the domination of several agro-industrial complexes (cotton and cattle, as well as coffee) and the country's utter prostration to the will of the United States in all matters.

Thus, neither the persistent presence of *artesanía,* particularly in Masaya, nor the form that indigenous ethnicity had come to take in the region—an identity not clearly marked by cultural practices, language, or presentation of self—played a role in the overall Sandinista analysis of Nicaraguan society. Yet the Frente's victory over Somoza in 1979 depended on a strategic alliance with artisan communities, particularly the proudly indigenous Monimboseños. The utopian ideology of Ernesto Cardenal offered the Sandinistas a way to incorporate the complex identities of the artisans into the revolutionary process, because Cardenal proposed to include the artisans in the project of constructing a national culture. Thus, the systemic failings of Cardenal's analysis, which identified both the San Juaneros and the *cerámica negra* women as Indian artisans, could slide because of the useful exigencies of ideological alliance.

Indians and Artisans: The Fables of Ernesto Cardenal

The character of Cardenal's leadership of the Ministry of Culture derived from the combination of several seemingly incongruous philosophical and cultural currents that he had brought together in his own life, and the ways his creative synthesis dovetailed with both the ideologies and practical necessities of the Sandinista leadership. Combined in Cardenal were: the poet who inherited the worldviews of the Vanguard masters José Colonel Urtecho and Pablo Antonio Cuadra, their summations of *El Güegüence* and thus of Nicaraguan identity, and a consequent opposition to Somocismo based on Granadino conservatism; the religious ascetic, the follower of Thomas Merton, who had preached and lived a very ancient, contemplative ethic of Christianity that idealized material poverty and spiritual richness; the Marxist, the acolyte of Castro's Cuba, whose interpretation of class struggle focused on the cultural derangement of the bourgeoisie and the cultural impoverishment of the working masses; and finally, the government minister, who set out to enfranchise the working masses through a program of cultural democratization. Cardenal declared: "Cultural liberation in Nicaragua has been part of the struggle for national liberation . . . Our revolution is of the present, and especially of the future, but it is also of the past . . . our patrimony, which could not be seen before the Revolution, is now alive. National traditions now flourish. All of that which is our national culture has always been part of our national liberation, but liberation was the condition under which our culture could be converted into the common good" (in Rosset and Vandermeer 1986: 412).

The ceramics contests that the Ministry of Culture held in San Juan de Oriente from 1980 until 1982, in which many current and former Co-op *socios* (members) entered their finest pieces, embodied some of the finest moments for Cardenal's ideas and policies about artisans. Both *Barricada,* the official Sandinista newspaper, and *La Prensa,* the voice of the opposition parties and the conservative Catholic clergy, described "the Indian blood" of the San Juaneros, their hard-working nature, their ceramics tradition, and in *Barricada,* their devotion to the revolutionary process. *Barricada* also emphasized Minister Cardenal's attendance at the ceramics competitions, often accompanied by large photographs that showed Cardenal hugging a San Juanero (e.g., Gregorio Bracamonte) or inspecting the pottery.

But by 1984, the *socios* at the San Juan Co-op were thoroughly dis-illusioned by the policies, programs, and projects the Ministry had instituted at the Co-op. The Co-op became one of the most important sponsors of the artisans' union, UNADI, and many individuals elabo-rated particularly caustic critiques of the Ministry's work. I wanted to love Ernesto Cardenal like every other *internacionalista* and like every author who had then written or was in the next few years to write about Nicaragua's cultural politics. Roberto Potosme's sum-mary comments reflect the way that the San Juaneros experienced the actualization of Cardenal's dreams, goading me to begin a seri-ous critical analysis of the Ministry's policies. "Look, Les," he began, "people in the Ministry, they get involved with us, because our work has a 'cultural' [in a sarcastic tone] aspect . . . but after all these years, what we've seen is that they are more busy with their own projects than with those of the artisans. What the Ministry of Culture would like is that we become their workers, and that is something we will never do" (in Field 1987: 228).

The manner in which Cardenal's experiences and analysis of Nica-raguan culture and society applied to the artisans of Masaya-Carazo and all of western Nicaragua derived from his vision of a theoretical and practical unity between, on the one hand, the legacies of pre-Columbian civilizations and indigenous arts in Nicaragua and, on the other hand, the construction of a revolutionary culture, for which the political and economic transformation of the country would lay the basis. In many ways, Cardenal's program for cultural revolu-tion resembled the mass campaigns for literacy and health that the Sandinista Front deployed immediately following their victory. Car-denal advocated training thousands of disempowered Nicaraguans to paint, write poetry and fiction, weave, and make music. By ren-dering the means of cultural production accessible to the Nicaraguan masses, Cardenal intended to "democratize" Nicaraguan culture and to enfranchise the intellects and creativities of the impoverished ma-jority. As for Nicaraguan *artesanía,* the move by Cardenal's Ministry of Culture to "rescue" folk arts and communities of artisans under-scored his view of artisans as the survivors of pre-Columbian cul-tures and indigenous populations, respectively. According to Carde-nal: "Folk art had been decaying more and more during the long era of *Somocismo,* and in the end Nicaragua was already a country very poor in folk art. It was thought to be irretrievably lost. The Revolution came to rescue it, and in a very short time ancient lost popular arts have reappeared in many parts of the country . . . [such arts] are an expression of our identity as Nicaraguans" (in Rosset and Vandermeer 1986: 412).

This vision of the democratization of culture and Cardenal's convictions about western Nicaraguan artisans grew out of three specific episodes in his life: the Solentiname commune, his "discovery" of Cuba, and his alliance with the FSLN. In 1965, Cardenal bought the island of Mancarrón in the Solentiname Archipelago of Lake Nicaragua, where he constructed his own church, founded a commune, and initiated a cultural experiment among the isolated and impoverished residents of the island. The experiment consisted of distributing paints, brushes, art books, clay, kickwheels, and looms to a large number of individuals on the island and encouraging them to paint, weave, and make ceramics. Some years later, Cardenal sponsored a series of poetry-writing workshops among the population of barely literate adults. He successfully gave the tools of creativity to the people of a community who had not believed in their capacity to create anything in excess of their own means of subsistence. For the artisans of Masaya-Carazo, the price of Solentiname's success, I would say, was tallied in a pervasive paternalism among the employees of the Ministry of Culture and their orientation toward their own plans for developing artisan-craft rather than a concern to consult with already existing artisan communities. The Ministry seems to have found the already existing artisan communities more difficult to incorporate into the democratization of culture programs than the introduction of creative, artistic, and artisanal programs into areas of Nicaragua (like Solentiname) where such phenomena had shriveled away under Somocismo.

Another factor to consider in foregrounding the actual experiences of artisans like the San Juaneros and the women who made *cerámica negra* during the years when the Ministry basically mandated cultural policy was Cardenal's *indigenismo*. This term has been used from Mexico to Argentina to connote reverence, usually heavily romanticized, for the pre-Columbian civilizations of Latin America. Inspired both by the rich array of sophisticated pre-Columbian ceramics Solentiname's farmers found in their fields, and by romantic notions about Indians, Cardenal's poetry described indigenous cultures as classless, spiritually and environmentally harmonious, and unaggressive. His *indigenismo* celebrated the technological backwardness of pre-Columbian civilizations, in comparison with European technologies, and linked that very backwardness with a spiritual and cultural superiority that permitted him to characterize the people of ancient Nicaragua as true Christians (Cardenal 1973). This form of *indigenismo* resonated with the sentiments expressed in *Nicaragua Indígena,* the Somocista journal described in the previous chapter, at the same time reaffirming the inevitable victory of *mestizaje* celebrated by Pablo Antonio Cuadra in his interpretation of *El Güegüence.* By glorifying an indigenous past that was already lost, and identifying the artisans as a "last of their kind" holdover, Cardenal isolated the artisans in a cultural dead end. Only his politics of cultural transformation could rescue the artisans by incorporating them into his project of revolutionary national identity, an identity that again reified *mestizaje.*

Cardenal's *indigenismo* had direct consequences for the artisans that resonate with how other Latin American states have utilized *indigenista* appropriations of indigenous culture to build a national identity. In all cases, national identities that glorify pre-Columbian Indian civilizations have not necessarily moved to remedy or even recognize the economic exploitation of subaltern social groups, groups that in many cases identify themselves as indigenous (see Stephen 1991, 1993a). For Cardenal and the Ministry, the *indigenismo* deployed by intellectuals constructing the new Mexican national identity in the wake of the Mexican Revolution was most influential. In Mexico, *indigenismo* became an official development policy aimed at indigenous communities across the nation, whereby specific artisan-crafts were appropriated, re-formed, and promoted in both their production and marketing spheres by a state bureaucratic organ, the Fondo Nacional de Artesanías, or FONART (see Novelo 1976; García Canclini 1981). The officials in the Ministry were aware of both the documentation of artisan-craft's decline by the Banco Central—I read the report in the Ministry's Managua offices—and of FONART's success with developing artisanal production. The latter heavily influenced Cardenal's Ministry from 1979 to 1983, and some of the Ministry's projects in the San Juan ceramics cooperative involved consultants brought in from Mexico (Field 1987).

Cardenal's visits to Cuba in 1970 and 1971 facilitated the fusion between his utopian experimentation with the use of culture and creativity in Solentiname and his *indigenismo*. He returned to Solentiname convinced that revolutionary socialism combined egalitarian Christianity with a return to the social order of pre-Columbian civilizations: "I had discovered that now, in Latin America, to practice religion was to make revolution . . . In Cuba, I had also seen that socialism makes it possible to live out the Gospels in society. Fidel has reconciled us [Christians] with Communism. And I also saw that this island returned to what it had been before because Pedro Martír [Spanish explorer] tells us that for the Indians of Cuba, the earth was held in common just like the sun and water, and there was no 'mine' or 'yours,' the seed of all evil" (Cardenal 1974: 324).

The Cuban epiphany brought Cardenal to the attention of the Frente Sandinista. Cardenal had met with Tomás Borge, one of the FSLN's founders, as early as 1968. The basis for alliance between the two was clear. Cardenal's potent mixture of Christianity and Marxism made him a powerful ally in the Frente's attempt to win over at least a part of the Catholic clergy to the revolution, which was part of the Sandinistas' overall strategy of fusing their political and economic goals to the religious values of the vast majority of Nicaraguans. That aspect of Sandinista politics, which formed a key component of the construction of national cultural identity during the revolutionary period, has been documented extensively by non-Nicaraguan authors (see Randall 1985) in popular and accessible works (see Zwerling and Martin 1985), by historians (e.g., P. Williams 1989), and by anthropologist Roger Lancaster (1988). Some have claimed that the Sandinistas interpreted the Solentiname commune as "a living counterculture to the world of Somoza; an anticipation of what Nicaragua could be after Somoza" (Zwerling and Martin 1985: 45); by the same token, others recall that "the Sandinistas sometimes criticized it [Solentiname] as a dangerously illusory alternative to the brutal realities of power in Nicaragua" (Beverley and Zimmerman 1990: 68). In either case, by 1976 the Solentiname communards had abandoned nonviolence for guerrilla warfare, in alliance with the Frente Sandinista. Cardenal wrote: "Culture for us can not be separated from social development. Also, one might say that in Nicaragua, it is inconceivable to consider economic development without cultural development . . . we attend to the needs of the artisan for cultural, political and economic reasons" (in Rosset and Vandermeer 1986: 413). Sandinista intellectual Ricardo Morales Avilés had elaborated on this topic in 1974, years before the Frente's victory:

Intellectuals either produce and renew culture according to the taste and acceptance of the bourgeoisie and in the service of its domination, or they use the forms and means of culture as a revolutionary weapon in the service of the people. The question is this: will the intellectual perform a cultural function directed toward the people, or concede his position to the bourgeoisie and imperialism? For the revolutionary intellectual, the cultural battle is the battle for a new society . . . free from bourgeois domination . . . the cultural struggle cannot rest above the revolutionary struggle, nor lie parallel to it; the cultural struggle is an integral part, one front of the revolutionary struggle. How can one talk about culture, national culture, creativity and development, goods and human cultural values, and personal realizations, when we face the everyday, concrete struggle in the streets, the countryside, the factories, the haciendas, the universities, and high schools? Given the current situation of the people, the fact that a prodigious literature can exist, esthetically speaking, in no way changes the reality of exploitation, hunger, illiteracy, and misery. (In White 1986: 92)

In other words, there was agreement all around about the use of cultural policy as a tool for revolutionary change. If Cardenal's programmatic found a place for the artisans and assigned them a particular role in cultural transformation of the whole country, the Frente, at least initially, gave the Ministry carte blanche to unfold this aspect of the democratization of culture.

Artisans, Class, and the Overthrow of Somoza: Sandinista Interpretations and Policies

The complexities and contradictions of Sandinista class analysis and class politics were one additional factor shaping cultural policy toward artisans, blending with Cardenal's revolutionary utopianism in ways molded by the events leading up to and culminating in the Sandinista victory. In a nutshell, the triumph against Somoza led the Sandinistas to conceive of the artisans as a revolutionary class. However, by allocating Cardenal's Ministry of Culture much of the responsibility for the construction of national culture, the Sandinistas initiated cultural policies that the artisans interpreted as marking them as a subaltern ethnic group. The artisans opted for a class identity that appeared to offer a way out of that undesirable classification. In this section, I discuss the Frente's analysis of the artisan "class," which derived from an eclectic mixture of Marxist historiography, macroeconomic analysis, and the politics of coalition building.

I learned a great deal about the relationship between the Frente Sandinista and the artisans of San Juan from Roberto Potosme, a Co-op *socio*. Among all the people in San Juan, I think we have the most intellectual relationship, even though Roberto's formal education has been stunted by lack of access and the rural poverty typical of San Juaneros. Very soon after I began working at the Co-op, Roberto began confronting me with questions. "Les," he said to me several weeks into my fieldwork, "come here and talk to me while I throw pots." I went over and watched him turn out a dozen mugs in a few minutes. He said, "On the radio yesterday, they were calling the government of Pinochet in Chile fascist." Yes, I replied. "Well," he continued, "I have also heard that Germany under the Nazis was a fascist state." Yes, I repeated. "Well," he said, "there are many differences between Germany then and Chile now. How can they both be called fascist?"

We became close friends and discussed Marxist concepts frequently. Roberto was the only person I knew in San Juan who talked about class. When he became the delegate to UNADI from Region VI, he told me that "artisans were the most exploited class in the Somoza times . . . Besides, Somoza did the most to persecute artisans and damage their ability to produce . . . Since the Revolution, this class is going up, because this is an important class." Some weeks later, we spoke about the individualism of artisans in San Juan especially; I asked him whether that trait would make it difficult to organize artisans and to stimulate their class consciousness. He responded, "The individualism of the artisans here is not a huge problem, because it originates in their bad experiences under Somocismo, and can be rectified by clarifying the situation. This will not obligate us to be fanatic Sandinistas either." Roberto's analysis of class was shaped by his own experiences, of course, but also by his involvement in UNADI, itself a product of the class analysis at large in Sandinista Nicaragua.

Sandinista concepts about and analysis of class in Nicaragua, elaborated by FSLN founders Carlos Fonseca and Tomás Borge, as well as major figures such as Jaime Wheelock, Ricardo Morales, Carlos Nuñez Tellez, and others, derive from a reading of Marx's historical work, particularly *The Poverty of Philosophy* (1847), *The Eighteenth*

Brumaire of Louis Bonaparte (1852), and *Class Struggles in France* (1895). Early documents released by the Frente during the struggle against Somoza, the first few years of programmatic statements produced by the Junta of National Reconstruction, and articles from *Barricada* and other media provide evidence for much of the thinking about class among the Sandinista leadership. In addition, the work of Carlos Vilas, a political scientist who worked within the Ministry of Planning and later for a semi-independent research consortium on the Atlantic Coast, provides a unique insider's critique particularly with respect to the politics of class struggle and alliance under Sandinismo.

Vilas (1986) identifies a primary contradiction in socialist and revolutionary socialist states like Sandinista Nicaragua. Such states operationalize concepts of class consciousness and class identities informed by Marxist thought, while at the same time such states attempt to construct national identities. In Nicaragua and elsewhere this contradiction results from incorporation into the capitalist world-system and the poverty and disempowerment of the vast majority of people (13–23). Sandinista analysis combined several concepts (domination, oppression, exploitation) that are distinct in Marx's analysis of class (see Wright 1985: 56–57) to describe a situation unfamiliar in Marx's time. Marx predicted that the daily experience of oppression among workers in the most advanced industrial states would eventually act as a precondition for a growing consciousness on the part of the workers. This consciousness would culminate in their understanding of the inherently exploitative nature of capitalist production, leading them to throw off the domination of the capitalist class. In classical Marxism, the workers are the revolutionary subject, and their victory is society's victory. In Sandinista analysis, the oppressive domination of society exercised by the tiny Somocista elite stimulated a growing consciousness on the part of the entire Nicaraguan people, including the working class, the peasants, the semiproletarianized rural people, artisans, and a variety of other social groups such as students, women, and the urban unemployed. The revolutionary subject elaborated by Sandinista social theorist Orlando Nuñez Soto (see 1987) was a multiclass, multisector alliance. As the Planning Ministry's "Plan de Reactivación Economica en Beneficio del Pueblo" (1980) put it: "The Working People (industrial workers, peasants, small producers and wage workers in general) are the principal subject of the liberation of Nicaragua and its transformation" (Solórzano 1993, vol. 5: 101).

Revolutionary consciousness, in this view, was constituted by a specific understanding among each of these distinct social classes and sectors of their exploitation under the Somocista economic system and a common understanding among all of these groups of their country's domination by the capitalist world-system. This consciousness, in turn, impelled the revolutionary movement that overthrew the oppression of Somocismo. The successful revolution thus inherently addressed both the exploitation of the Nicaraguan people in their own country by the tiny class of Somocista capitalists, as well as the country's domination under the capitalist world-system for which Somocismo acted as the warden.

Having removed the oppression of Somocismo by overthrowing the Somocista elite, expropriating its vast properties and vanquishing its control over the state, the Sandinistas' national project of ending Nicaragua's domination also initiated a variety of projects aimed at resolving economic exploitation—at least that was the idea. Sandinismo promoted and relied upon mass movements among the diverse social classes and sectors considered the revolutionary masses. But early policies seemed to gloss over the potential for conflicts of interest between the groups considered "the people." Nuñez Tellez wrote a pamphlet for the mass organizations that aggressively promoted the following agenda:

First, to bring together all social sectors.

Second, to repeatedly express your demands in the political, economic and social realms.

Third, to have proposed ways to reach economic goals.

Fourth, to have participated in the transformations of the State.

Fifth, to strengthen the work of creating the militias.

Sixth, to have oriented the content of your mobilization around combating the positions of the enemies of the Revolution and around the essential tasks of production.

Seventh, to participate actively in the work of literacy.

Eighth, to raise the levels of consciousness and education in your ranks.
(In Gilbert and Block 1990, document 13: 12)

Notwithstanding the broadness of these guidelines, Nuñez Tellez also insisted: "We would like to generate consciousness in the mass organizations, although if this were to be true, we must work so that the political revolutionary project is kept safe at the same time [the mass organizations] are the instruments capable of autonomously expressing the demands of the social sectors they represent" (16). At least theoretically, the Frente asserted that diverse social sectors could simultaneously unite around the project of nation-building and autonomously pursue the distinctive goals of their sector. This view continued even into the crises of the mid- and late 1980s, when the economic base of many social sectors began to dissolve and tens of thousands of people crowded into Managua to eke out a living in the byzantine mercantilism of the scarcity-based informal economy: "In the very roots of the popular classes' overlapping and complementary interests can be found one of the most important bases of the Sandinista policy of national unity and mixed economy. Furthermore, this lack of polarization of the economic structures of the popular classes is buttressed by a growing nationalism which unites the Nicaraguan people in the face of foreign aggression" ("Managua's Economic Crisis" 1986: 46–47).

In this deeply problematic reconciliation of diverse class interests with nation-building in the face of an economic blockade that tended to exacerbate the problems confronting each social sector, Sandinista analysis of the role the artisans had played in overthrowing Somoza unfolded in particular ways. Sandinista authors adapted Wheelock's portrait of class struggle and class consciousness to analyze the actual events of the Nicaraguan Revolution, in which the artisans took up arms against Somoza. Vilas (1986: 112) has statistically demonstrated "the predominance of artisans and self-employed" persons within the ranks of participants in the insurrections that overthrew Somoza. Yet in the most salient case, that of the Monimboseños who participated in all three insurrections against Somoza, artisans did not rise up as a revolutionary class but as a rebellious community. Monimboseños experienced the Somocista construction of the nation as both a rebellious subaltern ethnic community as well as an economic sector that Somocista development policies systematically undermined, and that combination led to the uprising against Somocismo in 1978, the first in the whole country. This uprising was organized and carried out without the aid or leadership of the Sandinistas.

Sandinista leaders, including Minister of Defense Humberto Ortega, acknowledged the spontaneous character of the Monimbó uprising: the Monimboseños "began to work as a Sandinista unit when they still lacked the organized leadership of the Sandinista movement" (in Hodges 1986: 247–48). Given the Sandinista understanding of artisans as producers with particular relations to means of production, combined with Wheelock's widely accepted summation of the fate of indigenous peoples in western Nicaragua, Sandinista analysts managed to discuss the Monimbó uprising as a conjugation of artisanal economy, rebellion, and indigenous identity crystallized through the language of revolutionary class consciousness: "The spontaneous behavior of the masses is an incipient expression of revolutionary consciousness. That is, the spontaneity of the masses is relative, such that while actions appear undisciplined, they exist objectively as a class institution" (Institute for the Study of Sandinismo 1981: 54). Authors writing for the Institute emphasized the importance of the Monimboseños as artisanal producers in relation to the uprising: "In a practical sense, the artisans of Masaya demonstrated their talents once again through the domestic production of arts—guns, bombs, mortars and pistols" (131).

The National Guard suppressed the Monimbó uprising with the fierce brutality that characterized Somoza's reaction to the period of revolutionary insurrections. Monimbó and Masaya played a key role during the rest of the period leading up to the Frente's triumph and contributed to the iconography of the revolution in at least two important ways. First, the image of the Monimboseños disguised in makeshift masks reminiscent of those worn during the patronal celebration of San Jerónimo, hurling homemade bombs (called *naranjas,* or oranges) at the Guard's tanks, became indelible; a picture of this scene taken by renowned photographer Susan Meiselas was mass-replicated on posters that were hung everywhere in Nicaragua in the mid-1980s. Nicaraguan artisans were consequently enshrined as an important national class in the revolutionary coalition that overthrew Somoza, notwithstanding Sandinista ambiguity concerning the ethnic identity of Monimbó and the Masaya-Carazo region. Second, the Sandinistas' acceptance of the significance of artisans not only as the producers of goods but as the producers of culture only strengthened the hand of Cardenal in general and assured the Ministry of Culture a leading role in policies affecting artisans. Culture, artisans, and the artisanal region (Masaya) became integral faces of the revolution.

Within the first few years following the Frente's victory, the central political symbol of Sandino was joined to the symbolisms of Darío, and also of *El Güegüence* (see Whisnant 1995 for an in-depth exploration of the connection between Sandino and Darío in Sandinista iconography). One *Barricada* reporter quoted a poet saying that Rubén Darío "represented the voice of indigenous America, Latin America" ("Darío" 1983). In an article entitled "The Anti-imperialist Darío" (1986), Cardenal's elite Grandino mentor, José Coronél Urtecho, who soon became the grand old man of Sandinista literati, admonished: "the cult and cultivation of Rubén Darío and Augosto C. Sandino, the great forefathers of our cultural and national history, are indispensable to maintain faith in ourselves and to encourage us to continue the same paths for the good of the country, of Nicaraguan culture, of our language, and Latin American environs." In this schema *El Güegüence* became the distant forerunner of Darío, the street theater of the machos, a first evolutionary step to modernist poetry and anti-imperialist politics (see Solórzano vol. 8: 473). This also further enshrined artisans and Masaya-Carazo in the centerpiece role cultural policy was to play under Sandinismo. But the patronage that artisans in Monimbó and elsewhere expected as a result of their role in the revolutionary insurrections and their importance as revolutionary icons was complicated by the successive and shifting political strategies and economic models deployed by the revolutionary state.

Early macroeconomic studies conducted by the Ministry of Industry, which showed that "small industries" (those employing fewer than thirty workers) accounted for 37 percent of industrial employment, attracted the attention of state planners. Moreover, 54 percent of all industrial establishments employed fewer than five people, which defined them as "artisans." The revolutionary state acknowledged that such industries, far from being marginal, "satisfy the demand of broad sectors of the market, especially in the production of basic consumer goods such as shoes, clothing, baked goods, and wood products" (Vilas 1986: 74). Moreover, government statistics showed that the small industrial sector actively contributed to exports, at the same time relying heavily on imported raw materials. By 1982, the Ministry of Culture and the offices in the Ministry of Industry dealing with small industries were promoting the accelerated production of basic consumer goods by small industrial enterprises as the best opportunity to improve the supply of those goods for the majority of Nicaraguans (Brundenius 1987). Influenced by FONART's deployment of artisanal development in rural and semiurbanized areas of Mexico (see Canclini 1982: 69–70), the Ministry of Culture also advised the state that the initiation of artisanal projects under the rubric of the democratization of culture could stimulate the small industrial sector to soak up the persistently high percentage of unemployed persons located in urban areas, particularly Managua (Field 1987).

Even though the Ministries of Industry and Culture agreed in a fundamental way about the importance of artisans for revolutionary economic development, the differences between the relationships each bureaucracy established with the artisans facilitated the manner in which the artisans' union formed and functioned. Beyond the artisan case, however, the fundamental contradictions engendered by Sandinista political alliances with different social constituencies, each with competing interests, in the context of building a unified revolutionary state was the foundation for a persistent lack of coordination between the planning ministries of the revolutionary state. Mutually incompatible economic policies and pronounced shifts in overall planning within the macrocontext of agricultural and agroexport development resulted, documented by Baumeister and Cuadra (1986) and Coraggio (1986) and reiterated in a slim volume written by a real insider, Alejandro Martínez Cuenca (1992), former Minister of Foreign Trade (1979–88) and Minister of Planning and the Budget (1988–90). By no means am I implying that it was wrong for the Sandinistas to concentrate their scarce financial resources and planning apparatus on the agro-industrial sector and on the various sectors composing the agricultural workforce. Probably, they had very little choice, precisely because of Nicaragua's dominated position in the capitalist world economy and the Somocista state's wholesale conversion of the economy to agro-exports. However, the result of using a rhetoric of class alliance that included the artisans in the context of building the national economy produced a confusing situation for the artisans, forming the broader backdrop for the stillborn formation of the artisan class.

The ambiguity of Sandinista economic policy toward artisans was thus part and parcel of the most problematic aspects of revolutionary economic planning. During the first five years of revolutionary transformation, the state seized control of foreign exchange to direct a capital-accumulation process aimed at building a mechanized, capitalized modern agricultural-export sector on the state farms created through the expropriation of Somocista holdings—some 20 percent of the arable lands in the country (Irvin 1983; Fitzgerald 1985). Early on, state planners declared that the amount of land belonging to and the percentage of production coming from the small and medium-size farm sectors would decline relative to the state farms as a result of the revolutionary transformation of the economy (Fitzgerald 1985). The rural proletariat, organized into its own mass organization, would grow in size and power, according to these plans, and eventually supply labor for the new agriculturally based industries that would lead the overall modernization of the economy (Fitzgerald 1985; Kaimowitz 1986). These macropolicies implied that the state, notwithstanding many public statements to the contrary, undervalued the worthiness of small industries, such as those characteristic of artisanal production, as sites for significant investment.

Assigning responsibility for defining cultural and economic policies in artisan communities to the Ministry of Culture certainly fit with the Frente's early tendency to control small and medium-size producers through the revolutionary state bureaucracy, but more so with the Sandinistas' understanding of artisans as producers of culture. Even before the start of the contra war, resources for artisanal development were scarce and artisanal production was confined to a lonely corner in an overall scheme emphasizing agro-export-based industrialization. Ernesto Cardenal's proposed construction of national culture, if successful, would reward the artisans, perhaps ideologically more than materially, by giving them a key role in the Sandinistas' project of nation-building. Under these circumstances, the Frente's understanding of the artisans as a revolutionary national class was compatible with the program for artisanal development based on Cardenal's depiction of artisans as carriers of Nicaragua's surviving indigenous culture and as one of the torchbearers of the new revolutionary culture. Unfortunately, during the period when the Ministry's control over artisans went unchallenged, the artisan communities' experienced the Ministry's programs as oppressive rather than liberating.

Permission from Governor Tastuanes:
The Heyday of the Ministry of Culture

In this section, "the action" that occurred as a result of opposition to the Ministry of Culture on the part of the San Juaneros, the *cerámica negra* potters, and other artisans finally begins to unfold. The essay written by Orlando Gallegos initiates this discussion.

Les and Gia

Dearest Friends:

I delayed for a long time in writing and preparing the information which you had requested. Actually, I got lazy but one day I decided to start and finished this little piece of work which I hope serves in terms of the ideas which you expressed to me.

I only hope that you will write to me and give me your comments in case there is something more to add or if it is necessary to include something else which interests you.

For myself, I wish you luck in your work and in your research, which I hope this will help to complete.

At present, I am not working at all in anything even resembling artisan-craft, as I am an administrator of a hospital located in the city of Jinotepe.

So long and I await your comments.

Regards,
    Orlando

SHORT OUTLINE CONCERNING
THE HISTORY OF ARTESANÍA IN NICARAGUA

Historical Context

In 1976, the Banco Central of Nicaragua, through the Department of Technical Investigation of the National Artesanía Program, conducted and published an investigation about the state of artesanía in Nicaragua which took shape in the book *La situación de la artesanía nicaragüense* (The state of artisan-craft in Nicaragua). It was by way of this study that in 1977 the Banco Central of Nicaragua founded the first Ceramics Studio-School in San Juan de Oriente, a town located 40 kilometers south of the capital city Managua, with the purpose of upgrading the technology artisans used to make both utilitarian and decorative pottery, in order to rescue the art of pre-Columbian ceramics. In this effort, the first instructor was a Mexican (Pedro Tecayehualt), followed by a German (Wolfgang Heyne) and finally by a Spaniard (Arturo Margalló), all of whom taught the uses of the kick-wheel, of glazes, and of molds.

At the beginning of 1979, a Colombian began to give classes about co-operative production, and thus the first Ceramics Producers' Cooperative was founded. This process was delayed when war broke out in the middle of 1979.

Development

After the war, the support of the Banco Central continued the same as before through the National Artesanía Program. In 1980, the Dirección de Artesanía came under the control of the Ministry of Culture, continuing to support the Ceramics Studio-School; but at the same time, the Cooperative began functioning, which was promoted at first with loans from the National Development Bank. In 1982, the Arahuac Stoneware project was started with loans from the Banco Popular and with technical aid from FONART in Mexico. One San Juanero artisan was sent to study in Mexico City with the invaluable aid of FONART.

This project was essential for the development of the Cooperative, for it provisioned the Cooperative with a high-temperature kiln and different kinds of heavy machinery such as mills of various kinds.

This cooperative became the principal supplier of utilitarian pottery on the national level, deriving from the scarcity of this commodity in the country caused by the blockade imposed by the government of the United States.

At the national level, the Dirección de Artesanía established better relationships with artisans of all kinds, who were the main support of the economy at that moment in time, as their products substituted for imported goods made of leather, as well as shoes, clothing, foods, etc.

The Cooperative grew and become stronger economically; production was absorbed entirely by demand from the government alone, which subsequently distributed products on a national level. There were laws which regulated the creation and growth of the Cooperative; the Cooperative was relieved of tax burdens based upon a law regulating cooperatives passed in 1963. Until 1986, it functioned in this way; after that year, they began passing a series of progressive taxes, the most important of which was the tax on revenues, from which began the collapse of many cooperatives, with the added weight of the scarcity of raw materials, the sale of which was under the centralized control of the Ministry of Industries. (The Ministry of Labor was then charged with giving seminars to the cooperatives concerned with finance, costs, organization, regulations, etc.)

Orlando's letter to us with the enclosed essay, most of which I have cited above, arrived a year after I last saw him in 1995. Working in the administration of a hospital in the small city of Jinotepe, only 20 or so kilometers from San Juan but a world away in terms of his daily life and concerns, Orlando had not promised that he would write anything soon. The friendship we had developed in the 1980s led me to place a great deal of trust in Orlando and his intention to help in the making of this book. When I visited him in 1993, he had been unemployed, and our friendship and the loyalty I felt toward him had cheered him up somewhat. He introduced me to Flavio Gamboa at that time, through some of his friends in Monimbó, so he was also very well aware of where my interests were turning in the post-Sandinista era. In reading his essay, I am sharply struck by how deeply Orlando's views have influenced mine, how so much of what I wrote in my dissertation derived from our conversations, and even by the similarities in the ways we both refer to events and what influenced events. Thus, it seems that rather than using Orlando's essay to substantiate my own analysis, I am mostly filling in the details in Orlando's reconstruction and trying to substantiate his already formed observations with some of the resources to which I have had access. We do not disagree with one another over the past; where we have diverged is over perspectives for the future, as I will make clear in the last section of this chapter.

Clearly, the Banco Central's report was an essential source of information for the Ministry of Culture, which created a bureaucracy specifically to pursue the restoration and revival of folkloric *artesanía*. Unlike the Banco Central, however, the Ministry pursued the development of artisan-craft with a dual agenda shaped by the Sandinista triumph: creating the foundation for a revolutionary national culture, and producing consumer goods for the majority of Nicaraguans. To accomplish these tasks, a Ministry document identified three problems to overcome:

a) Nicaraguan artisans depend upon imported products from "rich countries," both raw materials and tools. Therefore, artisanal production is vulnerable to the international economics of trade.

b) Artisans depend upon middle-men for the transportation and sale of their goods. This leads to speculation and profiteering among the middle-men who exploit the artisans' weakness.

c) Artisans are victims of an ideological-cultural mentality imposed upon us for centuries which says that "what is made here does not function and is ugly." At the same time, this contempt for nationally produced goods is matched by an exaggerated admiration for imported goods. (Dirección de Artesanía 1985: 2)

The Dirección de Artesanía was the bureaucratic organ created by the Ministry to facilitate and regulate the flow of raw materials to artisanal workshops, as well as to plan specific development projects. ENIARTE, another Ministry bureau, opened a chain of retail outlets called Casas de Cultura (Culture Houses), which attempted to secure monopoly access to the manufactures of artisans all over the country and to encourage artisans to mass-produce items that sold well. Both the Dirección and ENIARTE tried to increase the production of artisanal goods, in quantity and in kind, and to increase Nicaraguan consumers' access to these goods. At the same time, the leadership of these bureaucracies pursued their political-cultural agenda, the significance of which revealed itself in time.

This agenda, shaped by Cardenal's commitment to the "democratization" of culture, paradoxically authorized the Ministry to define the indigenous, the authentic, and the marketable in a way that seemed quite arbitrary to many artisans in the two communities where I worked in 1984. The top-down operational procedures of the Ministry of Culture's bureaucracy were not, I would argue, inescapable consequences of Ernesto Cardenal's cultural politics; the Solentiname experiment seemed to promise otherwise. The dynamic that shaped the relationship between the artisans and the Ministry revolved around the meaning of the concept "Indian" for Cardenal and other high-level administrators, on the one hand, and for the lower-level bureaucrats implementing policy, on the other. Cardenal's conceptualization of Indian and artisan had been crystallized in his contact with the Mexican cultural bureaucracy, especially FONART, which since the 1940s had promoted "arte popular," the folk art of rural peoples that FONART considered the expression of their ethnic identities. To FONART policymakers, the artistic expressions of Indian ethnicity could be transformed into material culture for sale, promoting "an elevated sense of race and a national conscience that was previously missing" (Novelo 1976); promoting the production of material culture also provided gainful employment to rural masses without very much investment by the state (García Canclini 1981). These were the FONART perspectives that appealed to Cardenal's administrators. But Nicaraguan artisans experienced Ministry policy primarily as interpreted by the urban, educated, middle-class functionaries of ENIARTE and the Dirección, who lived and worked in Managua and made only brief sojourns to the houses and workshops of artisans. The Ministry's employees saw the artisans as Indians in another sense: as a rural, impoverished, and marginal social category that should be managed by the Ministry. For the most part, it was the artisans' experience of the latter attitude that led them to reject Cardenal's characterization of them as the folkloric carriers of indigenous culture; but contact with FONART had also left its mark on the San Juaneros, and new concepts of "arte popular" accompanied their rejection of the Ministry, as Orlando hinted.

After the Sandinista victory, the Ministry of Culture took responsibility for the San Juan cooperative, an arrangement the *socios* found agreeable at first. From the Ministry's point of view, the San Juaneros seemed like archetypes of the Cardenalian ideal of indigenous artisan. The Banco Central study of Nicaraguan *artesanía* that the Ministry relied on noted that pottery had been made by Indians in San Juan "since Neolithic times" (Industrial Division of the Banco Central 1976). Initially, the *socios* in the cooperative did not hide or exaggerate their indigenous ancestry; Agustín Amador said: "We are Indians [*indígenas*] because we have always lived here, and because we have always made pottery, like our ancestors." Early on, people told me that San Juaneros called themselves *indígenas* because "our blood is pure Indian," in the words of Gregorio Bracamonte. With an indigenous identity defined mainly by the persistence of artisanal production, San Juan's attractiveness to the Ministry was magnified by the existence of the cooperative and its dedication to raising the technical and artistic levels of ceramics production. The San Juaneros, in turn, initially felt flattered by the Ministry's praise and attention.

The Dirección de Artesanía initially decided to transform the kind of ceramics the cooperative produced. Before the overthrow of Somoza, the *socios* had made ceramics mostly of an ornamental nature, using designs and shapes reproduced from pre-Columbian ceramics San Juaneros frequently encountered digging in their fields; particularly gifted individuals, such as Gregorio Bracamonte and Ezekiel Membraño (an autodidact artisan and artist from Masaya), led the way in systematically finding the best-preserved pre-Columbian artifacts, copying their designs and adapting them to contemporary pottery production techniques. In 1982, the Ministry proposed the training of a large cohort of new *socios* to facilitate the introduction of a new production technology and a new product line: a utilitarian stoneware table service, featuring a durable vitreous glaze fired at high temperatures in a propane-fueled kiln, to be designed for home use and sold in the Casas de Cultura. FONART provided funds, as Orlando noted, and Evaristo Bracamonte, Gregorio's brother and Co-op *socio,* traveled to FONART studios in Coyoacan and Guanajuato. FONART sent a consultant, Hector Lopéz, to work on the project. His report, which I read at the Ministry of Culture in Managua two years later, reveals the resonance between the Ministry and FONART in their analyses of the San Juaneros' craft and its potential:

The population of San Juan is traditionally known as a producer of clay goods that satisfy the needs of a sector of the population that requires utilitarian goods at an acceptable cost, [goods] which cannot be advantageously substituted by products made of materials other than clay . . .

. . . [The Co-op *socios*] have assimilated . . . the use of manual tools and implements that have boosted production—which could facilitate the introduction of technological changes to be used to develop a line of products more in accord with real [national-level] needs. (N.d.: 1)

The Proyecto Vajilla, or stoneware project, failed both as a new production strategy and as a marketing venture during 1982. On the one hand, the *socios* acknowledged that many of the project's problems stemmed from the serious economic and military crises afflicting Nicaragua around the time the project was initiated. Although the Ministry's plan did not require the importation of raw materials, it did depend on the long-distance transport of many key materials, such as clay and glazing substances, from other regions of the country to San Juan. After 1982, the onset of the contra war meant that shipments of petroleum and its derivative propane to Nicaragua became increasingly irregular, vulnerable to sabotage and unstable pricing. Nevertheless, the *socios* assigned much of the blame for the project's failure to the Ministry's inability to plan realistically. The temperature range of the new kiln built to fire the stoneware did not correspond to the temperatures needed to fuse the glazes on the pots. The kickwheels were shoddy and built too large for the diminutive San Juaneros. Moreover, the Ministry's marketing study had misjudged the capacity of the new product to satisfy consumer preferences, because the planners had not completely understood that most Nicaraguan homes made use of glass and plastic tableware. The disappointing sales of the stoneware they did manage to turn out convinced the *socios* that utilitarian ceramics had almost no market;

instead, the Co-op, with Orlando's coordination, set out to carve out a niche where no existing consumer preferences existed.

▪ By mid-1984, the Co-op had succeeded where the Ministry had failed. One aspect of that success originated in the *socios'* enhanced production of unique, sophisticated, ornamental vases derived from their study of pre-Columbian art. The Banco Central provisioned the cooperative with Lothrop's aforementioned classic, *Pottery of Nicaragua and Costa Rica* (1926), earlier, which exercised a strong influence on the development of artistic styles in the cooperative. After six months of working at the cooperative, Agustín, Bladimir, and other *socios* who designed or aspired to design pre-Columbian-style pottery made clear their hope that I would bring books about pre-Columbian art back from the United States for their use. The market for these vases always exceeded the supply the *socios* could turn out. Moreover, the *socios* discovered local sources for most of the pigments used to paint the vases, and successfully designed a high-temperature kiln that used locally plentiful wood. Then in 1983, and by 1984 on a significant scale, the cooperative mapped out and executed the mass production of beer and coffee mugs targeted toward commercial enterprises rather than the market for household goods. Restaurants, cafés, bars, banks, resorts, and the Sandinista Front itself purchased these mugs by the thousands. The Co-op's mugs became ubiquitous in Nicaragua, but bottlenecks frequently threatened their production, as the war and the economic crisis of the 1980s deepened. Both the nonleaded glaze and the propane fuel necessary for producing these mugs were imported, and only the consistent ingenuity of the cooperative's administration prevented the collapse of production.

The result of the Ministry's blunders and the Co-op's independent success led the *socios* to ridicule ENIARTE and the Dirección, especially the idea that Ministry bureaucrats knew anything about improving artisanal techniques, training new artisans, or reviving indigenous culture. Although the subject of indigenous identity was not one I especially pursued during the mid-1980s, it was by the same token not a subject that ever came up in the Co-op or in their communication with the Ministry people by late 1984. Instead, Orlando increasingly worked through the Ministry of Industry to secure raw materials for the Co-op, arrange the shipment of mugs to customers all over western Nicaragua, and to settle the Co-op's tax predicaments, which Orlando mentioned in his essay. At the time, Orlando told me that "the future of this cooperative is located in the production of utilitarian objects through artisanal means" (Field 1987: 166).

During the final months of 1984, when the Co-op decisively cut its ties to the Ministry of Culture, I increasingly heard talk among the *socios* and other San Juaneros about "we artisans" (*nosotros los artesanos*) and the need for a new relationship with the government. In an effort to gain perspective on these emotionally and politically intense events in San Juan, Gia and I began traveling to the northern mountain region to work with the producers of the ornamental black ceramics, *cerámica negra,* in the towns of Matagalpa and Jinotega. The practitioners of this craft, three generations of women in the extended Pineda de Castro and Rodríguez de Pineda family, were experiencing the Ministry's policies as even more patronizing than had the *socios* of the San Juan cooperative. These women's experience of the inappropriate development plans that had become familiar to many artisans dealing with the Ministry in the mid-1980s plays an important role in recounting the decline of the Ministry's influence over artisans and the exploration of a class identity for the artisans in UNADI.

Following the Sandinista victory, the market for *cerámica negra* expanded because the Ministry began selling it in the Casas de Cultura. Through restrictive agreements, which the women did not entirely understand at first, the Dirección de Artesanía succeeded in monopolizing the production of two of the artisan women, Benita Pineda in Matagalpa and María Dolores Castro Pineda in Jinotega. Later, ENIARTE convinced several *artesanas* to produce thousands of replicas of miniature *cerámica negra* figurines that were selling well in the Casas. Doña Benita told us: "They wanted thousands of these little birds, and I didn't think I would have any time to make other things. It takes all my time to fulfill the agreement with them, and there just isn't any time to make other things."

In 1981 and 1982, the Dirección formulated several proposals for "improving" the craft. In Matagalpa, the Dirección decided to build a *cerámica negra* cooperative. Doña Carmen Rodríguez Pineda and Doña Benita Pineda inspected the plans for this cooperative and criticized the scale of production the plan envisaged, noting that the amount of time and money the Dirección expected the women to invest was incompatible with raising children and performing other household responsibilities. Soon thereafter, Doña Carmen and her daughter María Esthela formulated and submitted a counterproposal to the Ministry that called for the construction of a training workshop next to their houses. After two sessions of training, the women figured they would be able to assess how much production could be increased and how much responsibility they could delegate to new producers. Notwithstanding Cardenal's long-standing commitment to train new artisans, the Dirección refused to consider the women's plan, calling it "impractical." In Jinotega, the Dirección proposed that Doña Silvia Pineda de Castro and her daughters María Dolores and Ramona adopt the use of kickwheels and electric kilns to replace their manual, wood-kiln production techniques. The women turned these proposals down on several grounds. There were probably not enough people working the craft in their extended household, María Dolores observed, to justify such a drastic change. More to the point, Ramona noted, such a change would completely alter the appearance and character of the final product. This reasoning led the personnel in the Dirección to conclude that the *artesanas* were technophobic. Comments circulating in the Dirección office in Managua, and clearly meant for my ears, characterized the *cerámica negra* women as "secretive" and "suspicious."

By the mid-1980s, the *cerámica negra* women had rejected the technical and technological advice of the Ministry, but had nonetheless become dependent on the Dirección for the transport of raw materials to their homes and finished products to markets. In both Matagalpa and Jinotega, the *cerámica negra* women insisted that they were interested in using new techniques and technologies to improve the quality of their craft, but that they had given up trying to explain their perspectives to the Ministry bureaucrats. Doña Benita in particular felt that the mass production of figurines ordained by ENIARTE diminished their craft, but that she at least had little choice but to comply as so much of her income depended on sales through the Casas de Cultura. The final straw came in 1985, when the women in both towns learned that the Ministry had decided to call *cerámica negra* an indigenous craft. In retrospect, this decision signaled how far Cardenal's Ministry was willing to stray from conventional Sandinista historiography of northern Nicaragua to extend the geographical scope of Cardenal's fable about the relationship between artisans and Indians in the nation's history. Once the *artesanas* got wind of the Ministry's plan to publish a pamphlet about the indigenous origins of *cerámica negra,* they sat down with Gia and me and plotted a counterstrategy. Doña Carmen suggested that we obtain the draft of the pamphlet, or other documents relating to this counterfeit history, to assess just how serious the Ministry's misconceptions were. She insisted that their craft had nothing to do with indigenous civilizations, but had been invented by their female ancestors a few generations ago. María Esthela agreed to accompany Gia and me on a trip to La Trinidad, to interview Doña Carmela, the oldest living woman of the extended family, who both Doña Carmen and Doña Silvia agreed was the one person who could set the record straight. Her story is in the next chapter.

As far as the Ministry documents were concerned, they traced the development of *cerámica negra* from a pre-Columbian culture called Castillo Esgrafiado, that had evidently left ceramic remains in the northern mountains from A.D. 1200 to 1550. One document stated: "Cerámica negra is characterized by the velvety, jet-black finish, and engraved complex designs achieved with Indian techniques from the pre-colonial epoch . . . the themes have advanced [since then], losing the religious character that inspired them in Indian times" (Ministry of Culture 1985a: 5). María Esthela, with whom we began to work closely, was infuriated by this official history. In neither Matagalpa nor Jinotega had any of the artisans been consulted by anyone in the Ministry about the history of their craft or the writing of the official version. On the one hand, the *artesanas* reacted to the Ministry's counterfeit history of their craft as evidence of discrimination against them because of their gender. Doña Carmen said: "They [the Ministry] didn't respect us. We are women and they think we are uneducated and ignorant—they don't take our ideas seriously."

On the other hand, in Matagalpa and Jinotega, just as in San Juan, artisans decided on the basis of blunders made by Ministry personnel to entirely reject the Ministry's analysis of *artesanía* and its programs for reviving crafts. Many of the artisans in San Juan and the northern towns concluded that the economic projects the Ministry had unsuccessfully carried out stemmed from deeply flawed conceptions about artisans and how artisanal production should be developed. These artisans concluded that further collaboration with the Ministry was a dead end. When UNADI formed at the very end of 1983, several of its most articulate leaders came from San Juan and the *cerámica negra* families. María Esthela summarized this for us: "*Artesanía* is the work of the hand, the trained hand. Only we can decide what machines are useful. We have to develop things ourselves, because we know the techniques. How can people in the Ministry of Culture know these things?"

Permission Given, Permission Denied, or, Why the Union and Why Its Demise?

It seemed providential to me at the time that the San Juan Co-op became so instrumental in the founding of UNADI, and that Roberto Potosme, one of my best friends in the Co-op, had been chosen as a delegate from his region. Thus I felt that it was natural that Roberto contribute an essay about UNADI to this book, and he thought so as well. As far as evaluating his reconstruction of events, both in the essay and in our conversations in the 1990s, my view of the mid-1980s intertwines with Roberto's in a way similar to what I have noticed in Orlando's analysis. By contrast, because I was not in Nicaragua when the union fell apart, Roberto's explanations of those events make him a more conventional primary informant for me. The fact is that his explanations concur with what other academic authors, such as Beverley and Zimmerman (1990) and Dawes (1993), have written. Roberto's essay therefore constitutes an informed insider's discussion of UNADI's history.

What Was UNADI?
The Union of Nicaraguan Artisans Diriangen was founded on the 18th of November 1981.

This was the first time in the history of Nicaragua that all the different branches of artesanía congregated at the national level. In our first meeting we spent three days expounding upon the different necessities and problems affecting this sector. In order to address these issues we agreed to form a National Directorate, composed of artisans, for we believed that only the artisans themselves could hear us and help us in our problems. And so the Directorate was composed of one artisan from each region.

In 1983, we approved a Steering Committee, with the following members:

Gerardo Avendaña, president (Estelí)
Francisco Montiel, vice president (Granada)

María Esthela Rodríguez, secretary (Matagalpa)
Roberto Potosme, first assembly (Masaya)
Elsa Guevara, second assembly (Camoapa)

Then in 1983, we began working more directly. We were working on many problems. We organized 70 percent of the regions, we replaced raw materials, supplies, and we strengthened our cooperative society. Five thousand artisans affiliated at the national level. The artisans trusted the union and thus the union grew into new areas, such as provisioning, sales, technical services, and organizational work.

We were able to purchase a truck which served to supply all the raw materials which the artisans were asking for.

We were able to hold public expositions, and the raw materials were sold at cost prices.

In summary, I consider that our work was very useful and that we were able to develop ourselves, achieving an improved standard of life. Then, with this development, came problems on the part of the leaders of the A S T C (Association of Sandinista Cultural Workers). I personally consider and want to make it known that what brought about the downfall of our union were the jealous professionals, actually Rosario Murillo, who was the one leading the A S T C. I saw that we had more authority and credibility with the artisans than they as a governmental entity did. Then she proposed that a single entity be formed, and U N A D I became a charge of the A S T C and she ran all over the Directorate, and spoiled everything we had achieved. Well, she always maintained that we the artisans had to work in and not direct this sector, so important to the country, that this was the task assigned to them. And after becoming their charge, the Union completely disappeared, and the artisans were left without much representation. Today at present, the Ministry of Culture is not interested in anything having to do with artisans, and we are really going nowhere in a hurry.

Just as Roberto deeply influenced my thinking about the development of the Co-op in San Juan and the failures of the Ministry of Culture, María Esthela Rodríguez Pineda of Matagalpa also was instrumental in shaping my views about U N A D I. In witnessing the unwitting arrogance of E N I A R T E bureaucrats, among whom I counted a few friends, I saw them work to monopolize the sale of products from some artisans, buying products from artisans for low prices and selling them for inflated prices in the Casas de Cultura, using their privileged access to transportation to create relationships of dependency among artisans struggling to reach markets and buy raw materials, and demanding mass production from artisans that clearly impacted their lives negatively. After seeing ENIARTE's tactics backfire, Gia and I were enthusiastic about UNADI's program. We agreed with Roberto and María Esthela that only artisans could legitimately set aesthetic standards for individual crafts. UNADI bought artisans' products without imposing restrictions on their other sales, and resold these products at a 20 percent markup in UNADI's own sales outlets. The profit from sales were reinvested in the purchase of raw materials and resold to UNADI affiliates at wholesale prices. UNADI also initiated a variety of artisanal training workshops organized and instructed by artisans. Through its regional delegates, UNADI purchased new technologies specifically requested by particular artisans. In practical terms, UNADI's regional delegates were charged with establishing aesthetic criteria for *arte popular* to guide its purchase of artisanal products from individual artisans. At the same time, UNADI's training programs sponsored the upgrading of aesthetic standards within each community of producers. In this, the union worked directly against the mass production of artisanal commodities promoted by ENIARTE and the Dirección de Artesanía. UNADI had seemingly addressed all the major issues confronting artisans.

UNADI appeared to receive the unequivocal support of the Frente from its founding in late 1981 until 1986. Soon after the first national meeting of UNADI delegates, the union was granted legal and juridical status by the National Constituent Assembly, which meant that the union's bylaws and statutes were held admissible by the state. The government granted UNADI the right to import machinery using some of the dollar-credits that were in extremely short supply in the country. At the end of 1984, *Barricada* showcased President Daniel Ortega's appearance at UNADI's Second National Assembly. *Barricada*'s reporter drew attention to Ortega's recognition of the artisans as a "fundamental part of" and a "revolutionary class" within Nicaraguan society, much as Victor Tirado did the next year at UNADI's regional meeting in Masaya. Ortega also criticized "the interference of both private and state intermediaries" who had exacerbated artisans' difficulties in obtaining raw materials ("Los artesanos" 1984), clearly a reference to the artisans' resentments against ENIARTE and the Dirección de Artesanía. Highlighting UNADI's agenda, the reporter wrote: "The artisans demand direct accords with the producers of these [raw] materials, and request the establishment of

Artisans' Houses where these materials will be sold at a fair price; UNADI also plans to increase the exportation of *artesanía* to generate income so that UNADI can become the channel through which raw materials and artisanal goods are bought and sold." UNADI's ability to garner favor and gain recognition from the Sandinista Front contributed to the decline of the Ministry of Culture's influence in artisanal development. But the ultimate downfall of the Ministry depended on factors outside of the world of artisans.

UNADI's successes took place during a period when the political influence of small and medium-size economic sectors and their mass organizations was increasing, even though the economic contraction due to the war made resources scarcer than ever. The state was forced to admit that small and medium-size farmers were continuing to produce food and export crops efficiently and profitably while the state farms languished (Kaimowitz 1986). Political factors also played a role in changing Sandinista alliances. To secure the northern frontier against the contras, the state moved to distribute land to the land-hungry rural semiproletariat in 1984 (Vilas 1991). The Sandinistas may also have deployed agrarian reform to solidify its support, especially in the northern region, because of the Frente's poor electoral performance in rural areas during the first national elections held in that year. Thus, notwithstanding the fact that in 1986 the state was still investing resources with a preference for large, capital-intensive agro-export projects located mostly on state-owned enterprises (Kaimowitz 1986), the Frente also recognized the need to promote mass organizations representing the interests of the small and medium-size producers. As the war effort consumed increasingly vast amounts of resources and foreign exchange, the revolutionary state attempted to devalue the currency, slash state subsidies of basic commodities, and downsize the bureaucracy, but was unable to fully implement this program because of its alliances with vulnerable small and medium-size producers, including the vast informal sector centered in Managua (Vilas 1991; Oquist 1992). UNADI's characterization of the artisans not as indigenous culture carriers but as a class of small producers among the Frente's revolutionary constituencies hinged the economic development of *artesanía* on a self-managed solution to artisans' raw material and marketing problems. This program fit well with the Sandinistas' political alliances and economic limitations as the 1980s wore on.

Reframing the discourse of artisanal development as a question of stimulating small industries through self-reliance and cooperation with the Ministry of Industry was accompanied by UNADI's response to the ideological-cultural issues that the Ministry of Culture had prioritized. The analyses published by the union worked within aesthetic and artistic rather than ethnic or indigenous parameters, which radically redefined the concept of *arte popular*. Their interpretation had been influenced by FONART, but also by the union's networking with cultural ministries in Spain and Bulgaria (Field 1987). UNADI's "Governing Memoranda of Our Commercial Activity" (1985) stated: "We cannot commercialize artesanía in the same way that the usual markets and other sales centers have done. This is because our objectives are other than the mere seeking of profit. We are interested in the promotion of *arte popular*."

The Sandinistas' favoring of UNADI's alternative conceptualization of *arte popular* was facilitated by the interventions of Marta Zamora, a politically influential person who had founded the Dirección de Artesanía, resigned from it when it strayed from her original intentions, and ended up working in the Casa del Gobierno (Government House), the Sandinistas' power center in Managua. In an article she wrote for *Barricada*'s literary supplement (1985), Zamora wrote about the artistic-creative nature of *artesanía* as *arte popular*, the relationship between artisan-craft and industry, and the political and historical reasons for maintaining an artisanal sector in revolutionary Nicaragua: "Artesanía that lacks artistic intentions that justify and enrich it is simply a primitive form of production condemned to disappear under the advance of industrial development. Artesanía with artistic intentions, that is arte popular in the field of manufacture, augments its value all the time, thus raises its standard of creativity and individual skill, which distinguishes it from the anonymous and standardized character of assembly-line industrial production." By defining *arte popular* as "utilitarian and decorative objects made with artistic intent using artisanal means," Zamora implied that as far as production of commodities alone was concerned, industrial means were superior and preferable for ideological reasons: "The artistic content of artesanía and arte popular should be themes for debate in the cultural tasks of our Revolution, the results of which will contribute to the wholesale enrichment of our culture."

Artesanía's proper field of endeavor, for Zamora, was autonomous production of revolutionary culture, not the mass production of items for either utilitarian or ornamental use, which ENIARTE had decreed. Zamora's article legitimated UNADI's agenda but only part of the San Juan Co-op's production. That is, the Co-op's revival of pre-Columbian motifs individually designed and painted by potters working collectively under the sponsorship of the Frente fit the description of *arte popular;* on the other hand, the mass production of utilitarian mugs did not. Although this contradiction was mediated by the Co-op's dual affiliations with UNADI and the Ministry of Industry, the Co-op on the whole seemed to model UNADI's concepts of artisanal production and the role of *arte popular* and *artesanía* in revolutionary society. Its autonomy and the ability of Orlando and the *socios* to negotiate their way through the various bureaucracies fit the artisans' self-conception as independent producers, as expressed by articulate individuals such as Roberto and María Esthela. The Frente found UNADI's definitions ultimately less ambiguous than Cardenal's and, more important, they appeared to actually function effectively, rendering the artisans a social class ideologically and economically allied to the Frente's overall goals. But that situation did not last long.

Years after I left Nicaragua I learned that UNADI's ability to gain the favor of the Frente had reflected not only the political opportunities afforded by the Sandinistas' attempt to ally with organizations of small and medium-size enterprises, or the ideological alignment between UNADI, its friends in the Frente, and the Frente itself: a feud within the state's cultural bureaucracy was at least as potent a factor in UNADI's ascent, as Orlando related to me in 1993. Rosario Murillo, the head of the Association of Sandinista Cultural Workers (ASTC) and spouse of President Ortega, was attempting to wrench control of the politics of national cultural construction away from Cardenal and his Ministry as early as 1983. Beverley and Zimmerman (1990: 103) explain that "the Sandinista leadership was reluctant to take a firm stand one way or another on cultural policy, for fear of making the mistake of the Cubans in the late 1960s of favoring one cultural 'line' over others."

Whisnant (1995) too has detailed Murillo's and the ASTC's attacks on Cardenal's democratization of culture from a platform denouncing the Solentiname-derived poetry workshops, which Cardenal was promoting for the entire country. ASTC critics wrote in a number of publications that the workshops were producing "an official poetry," with a single politically correct format. This was only the opening salvo in Murillo's campaign to assume control over Sandinista cultural policy. In the mid-1980s, the ASTC competed with the Ministry of Culture for state and international funding, became an important patron of the arts, and began staging song, dance, mural-painting, and other artistic forums, and contests and outreach programs, particularly in the war zones (Beverley and Zimmerman 1990).

UNADI therefore took shape during the interregnum between Cardenal's decline and the decisive shift to Murillo's control over cultural policy. By 1986, the Ministry of Culture had become almost powerless, at which point Murillo's ASTC annexed UNADI. The union's leadership was relieved of effective control over policy, and resigned en masse. Roberto put it bluntly: "UNADI died on the spot"; its demise coincided with the decline of the political influence of and membership in all forms of mass organizations throughout the country (Vilas 1991; Oquist 1992; LaRamée and Polakoff 1990). The Ministry of Culture was abolished in the drastic monetarist reforms and bureaucratic hemorrhaging of 1988. With the demise of the institutional basis for the alliance between the artisans and the Frente the support of most artisans for the Frente also diminished. Roberto testified that a plurality of artisans voted for the anti-Sandinista alliance, UNO, in the 1990 elections, a claim substantiated in Oquist's (1992) exhaustive analysis of the elections.

The End of the Artisan Class?
The End of Revolutionary Culture?

When I returned to Nicaragua in 1993, Roberto, Orlando, Agustín, and María Esthela filled me in on the events leading to the demise of the Ministry and UNADI and the Frente's electoral loss. Even Roberto had stopped talking about the artisans as a class; instead, he had helped to organize a new cooperative in San Juan very different from the older one. Whereas the old Co-op employed full-time workers to produce ceramics collectively, the new cooperative was a group of independent producers, who made pottery in their homes and sold it in a central building. San Juanero potters contracted to sell their ceramics at the new cooperative if their products met the standards set by the cooperative's coordinating board. I noticed that most of the ceramics sold in the new Co-op resembled products that the *socios* of the old Co-op had made in the mid-1980s.

Agustín had resigned from the old Co-op years ago. I visited him for many days during my stay in the area, and watched him work. He, like Gregorio and many other former members of the Co-op, owned his own kickwheel, had built his own kiln, and had gathered a quite impressive number of oxides and glazes for his use. Both Gregorio and Agustín, perhaps the most innovative potters in San Juan, had stopped making pre-Columbian style ceramics in any quantity several years earlier. Both had branched out to explore new uses for their pots and new motifs with which to ornament them. Agustín was making very large lamp bases, floral vases, and amphora-like pots, decorated with brilliantly colored tropical birds, frogs, and flora. Gregorio showed me a number of planters he was preparing to glaze, the likes of which I had never seen. They were free-form, with many different levels and places for putting small plants, and the bodies of these vessels had been inscribed with zodiacal symbols, runes, and other abstractions.

Perhaps I had never wanted to face the fact that for years Gregorio had been an alcoholic, but I probably knew it on some level. After 1990, he had given up rum and converted to a Protestant sect. In 1993, he was a much livelier person than the one I had known, still immensely gifted as an artist, but now prone to warning friends, including myself, about the moral decline of the wealthy nations due to homosexuality and premarital sex, and the signs that showed the apocalypse was approaching. Gregorio had always had tremendous success in selling his pots, not only because of their superior technical and aesthetic qualities, but because of his facility in securing wealthy and foreign patrons. During Sandinismo, he had sold pieces to European embassies; now he was affiliated with a Central American artisans' consortium, ERCAC. Now it was Agustín who sold pots to European diplomats. At the old Co-op, the *socios* reminded me that they had lost both their old markets—various branches of the Sandinista government apparatus and the flow of *internacionalistas* that had invariably passed through San Juan—and were now reaching for others. Indeed, I had already seen pots made at the Co-op for sale in The Nature Company in California and at Third World craft stores. Roberto informed me that a chain of folk art stores based in Italy had contracted with the new cooperative recently. As I talked to all the artisans I knew, it became apparent that the San Juanero pottery scene had become completely individualized, that prices, clientele, design, and technique had exploded into myriad different forms. In this competitive post-Sandinista market, Roberto had once again nudged me to understanding: the concept of the artisans as a class or a social sector was no longer a relevant one in the daily lives and experiences of artisans. In the last section of Orlando's letter, he summarized his view of the end of UNADI and his pessimism about the future.

UNADI was created, and it was the union defending the interests of the artisans at the national level, in addition to promoting exhibitions and trade-fairs all over the country. They tried to obtain imported materials due to the scarcities in local commercial activity.

Following the change of government in 1990, the artisans are now defenseless; there is no policy of supporting artisans. Many cooperatives— more than 60 percent—have shut down, and there are hundreds of unemployed artisans, many of whom are pursuing other activities, such as the informal economy. Later on, the government founded PAMIC, an aid program to small businesses, which has among its goals financing and stimulating the production and sale of artisan-crafts in local, national, and international trade fairs.

Other small groups exist which provide finance to artisans with tiny funds; these loans are short-term and with rather low interest are accessible to artisans in order to finance their production.

I personally consider that the situation for artisans will weaken with the signing of the [U.S.] free trade agreement with Mexico which will occur in the next few months, due to the high costs under which Nicaraguan artisans work and the fact that they are not equipped with modern technology.

With this post-Sandinista retrospective, I conclude that the contra war and the exigencies of class alliance that conditioned the revolutionary state's inability to pursue consistent economic and political programs during wartime probably doomed the Ministry of Culture's attempts to construct a national culture in which artisanal development would have figured prominently. This became true at least after 1982. Then too, the Ministry of Culture failed to create a constituency among the artisans, who perceived that Cardenal's *indigenista* discourse had ranked them as subaltern ethnics. The artisans understood all too well that all of Nicaragua's ruling elites, including the

Sandinistas, considered the status of "Indian" as either subordinate or marginal or simply nonexistent. The artisans' rejection of *indigenista* stereotypes has occurred elsewhere, even among artisans who are far more "Indian" than the San Juaneros; Stephen (1993a: 49–50) has shown this in the case of the Zapotec weavers of highland Oaxaca, who speak their Zapotec language, dress distinctively, and feature other clearly recognizable markers of indigenous identity. In Nicaragua, the rejection of official *indigenismo* coupled with the emphasis the Sandinistas had placed on the oppositional history of the artisans as a class conspired to temporarily generate meaning and purpose for a class discourse among a group of individuals who became the leaders of the artisans' union. The rise of a mass organization among artisans was facilitated by a common realization among artisans throughout western Nicaragua that they did face the same shortages of equipment and raw materials, the same lack of access to markets, and the same depressed prices for finished products—in other words, that they experienced the same relationships to production and distribution. The revolutionary state's engagement with small and medium-level producers during the mid-1980s provided the forum for the artisans' class identity as enunciated by UNADI. Economic collapse and the disintegration of the still formative revolutionary political process at the end of the 1980s meant that this class-based identity became an unsustainable path toward the development of artisanal industries and the empowerment of the artisan communities. In effect, the war broke the back of the revolutionary nation-building project and of nascent revolutionary classes that, like the artisans, had attempted to navigate the contradictions of the revolutionary process.

For the artisans of the Masaya-Carazo region, the fall of the Sandinistas also meant that cultural discourse based upon the interpretation of *El Güegüence* as national parable again had failed to create a viable place for them, this time in a revolutionary Nicaraguan identity. The breakup of the artisans' involvement with the project of revolutionary culture and the failure of the artisan class together suggest that Masaya-Carazo ought not to be construed as the crucible of Nicaraguan cultural identity—whether as mestizo identity, as asserted by Pablo Antonio Cuadra and other intellectual limelights; as indigenous identity, as Ernesto Cardenal believed; or as various combinations thereof attached to a revolutionary political agenda, as assumed by both Cardenal and many in the Frente. Neither can the tale of the Indian revolutionaries (of Monimbó and elsewhere) be taken as a parable for the historical trajectory of class struggle in western Nicaragua, a tale told by Dávila Bolaños, inscribed in Wheelock's work, and retold in various ways by other Sandinista historians and Ernesto Cardenal. In the shambles of these interpretations of Masaya-Carazo, the historical role of the artisans, and the meaning of *El Güegüence,* the artisans of San Juan currently look like a diverse community of distinctive, individual producers, each with her or his own production and sales strategies. Yet these various strategies do not entirely obscure a still common set of demands and desires for the improvement of conditions for artisanal production. Their demands remain the same: government support for improved access to raw materials, domestic and foreign markets, and favorable prices for finished products, as Orlando, María Esthela, Roberto, and others insisted. Thus, the individualization of the artisans may only obscure the extent to which artisans still compose a social sector, albeit an inchoate one, but one that could coalesce again, perhaps under new signposts of identity.

Since the electoral defeat of the Sandinistas in 1990 and the election of first one and then another government, neither of which have demonstrated interest in artisans or artisanal production, such new configurations of identity have indeed appeared in western Nicaragua. These new configurations touch upon and intersect with but do not completely embody the demands I have consistently heard among the diverse artisan communities of western Nicaragua during and after Sandinismo. The appearance of new identity movements in Nicaragua is an unanticipated by-product of the mass organizations and unions sponsored by the Frente during the Sandinista era, which empowered many thousands of people to voice their opinions and to utilize their thoughts and experiences as raw materials for more profound analysis of the country and its predicaments. In the next chapters, I consider two identity movements, the feminist or women's movement and the indigenous movement, relating these social and cultural movements to the artisans with whom we worked in Jinotega and Matagalpa and in San Juan, respectively. In these discussions I revisit *El Güegüence* repeatedly, not as a parable that provides certainties about Nicaraguan history and identity, but rather as a parable rich in tropes for addressing and attempting to understand disjunctures and contradictions in the new social and cultural manifestations of the post-Sandinista era. This means that although I disagree with the central premise of elite discourse about the play—that it tells us important details about who the Nicaraguans are—I am convinced that the multiply positioned readings of *El Güegüence* remain intrinsic to both Nicaraguans' and outsiders' analyses of the Nicaraguan past, present, and future.

Approaching the original Ceramics Cooperative in San Juan de Oriente in 1983, from the village's single paved street. This street also passes by the school and the church, and leads up to the Pan-American Highway. (Photo by Les Field)

The kickwheels alongside the west side of the San Juan Co-op in 1983. Various kinds of mugs are seen, thrown that morning. (Photo by Les Field)

Juanita Bracamonte working at the kickwheel in the Co-op in 1983. Patricia Gallegos is resting to her left, and Mario Nororís looks on. (Photo by Les Field)

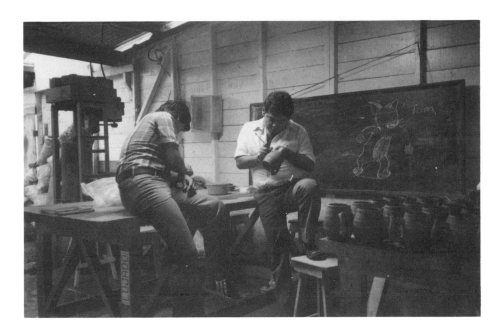

Orlando Gallegos, coordinator of the Co-op, in 1983. He is applying the final
touches to a batch of mugs before they are sent to the propane-fired kiln.
(Photo by Les Field)

Digna Gallegos sanding and finishing mugs in 1984, before they are fired in
the propane kiln. (Photo by Les Field)

Agustín Amador in his mother-in-law's house in 1985. (Photo by Gia Scarpetta)

Catalina Bracamonte, her sister Ester, and their cousin Ena in Orlando Gallegos's office at the San Juan Co-op in 1985. (Photo by Gia Scarpetta)

Ester Bracamonte and cousins Ena and Patricia standing in front of the Co-op with Gia Scarpetta in 1985. (Photo by Les Field)

Juanita Bracamonte throwing pots on her own wheel at home in 1985. (Photo by Gia Scarpetta)

Josefa Nicoya fashioning pottery by hand outside her home in San Juan. (Photo by Gia Scarpetta)

The interview with Aunt Carmela in 1985 regarding the history of *cerámica negra*. María Esthela Rodríguez Pineda, delegate to the artisans' union UNADI during the mid-1980s, stands at the extreme right of the picture next to Aunt Carmela. (Photo by Gia Scarpetta)

María Dolores inscribing designs on a *cerámica negra*
pot inside her mother Doña Silvia's house in 1985.
(Photo by Gia Scarpetta)

Large *cerámica negra* pots in the *solar* of Doña Silvia's house in
Jinotega in 1985. (Photo by Gia Scarpetta)

María Dolores tending *cerámica negra* pots being blackened in a bed of burning pine needles in her mother's house. (Photo by Gia Scarpetta)

Doña Silvia of Jinotega polishing pieces of pottery with smooth rocks in 1985. (Photo by Gia Scarpetta)

Gregorio Bracamonte holding up an example of his new line of pottery in 1993. (Photo by Les Field)

Astrological symbols on free-form pottery made by Gregorio Bracamonte in 1993. (Photo by Les Field)

Gregorio Bracamonte, holding a large pot he is selling to European
collectors, in 1995. Gregorio still utilizes pre-Columbian motifs, but
now employs oxide colorants that were unavailable during the 1980s
and did not appear on the actual pre-Columbian pots. (Photo by Les Field)

Flavio Gamboa talking about *mestizaje* just before finding a large
field containing broken pre-Columbian pottery in 1995.
(Photo by Les Field)

Chapter 3

Breaking the Silence

Suche-Malinche, Artisan Women, and

Nicaraguan Feminism

Problematizing the Category "Artisan"
on the Grounds of Gender

The previous chapter's discussion of the rise and demise of the artisan class during Sandinismo assumed an unproblematic social category: "the artisan." Although I made clear that, for example, the individuals who make *cerámica negra* are women, and that among the San Juanero potters both women and men work as *socios* at the Co-op, I have not so far addressed how gender has played a role in either the organization of work or formations of collective and individual identity among pottery producers. Of course, it has.

My willingness to hold the question of gender in abeyance for the purposes of discussing the issue of class reminds me of the manner in which the Frente Sandinista understood what Tomás Borge (perhaps the second most powerful comandante during Sandinismo) called "the woman question." Immediately following the triumph of the Sandinista Front in 1979, Sandinista discourse about women focused on the personal heroism and strategic brilliance of an impressive group of individual women, such as Dora María Téllez, Doris Tijerino, Gladys Báez, Nora Astorga, Monica Baltodano, and many others, whose participation in the guerrilla warfare of the early Sandinista years and the later insurrectionary phase brought the Frente to triumph and ensconced these women in the new revolutionary state as comandantes. The positioning of these women in the highest circles of the Frente no doubt brought to the fore the goal of incorporating a vast cadre of women into the revolutionary process, both politically and economically. This project was initiated and led by

the Sandinista women's organization A M N L A E (Asociación de Mujeres Nicaragüences Luisa Amanda Espinosa) and elaborated by the
women comandantes and a group of women of affluent backgrounds
and internationally recognized intellectual and artistic achievements.
This group included Daisy Zamora, Milú Vargas, Giaconda Belli,
Michele Najlis, Vidaluz Meneses, and Sofía Montenegro. It would
be artificial to separate, on the one hand, the influence these women
exercised over A M N L A E and their capacity to bring their feminist
perspectives into the innermost circles of the Sandinista Front, from,
on the other hand, the overall prestige and influence of Nicaragua's
artistic and literary intelligentsia, both male and female. That prestige predates the Sandinistas' victory to be sure, as detailed in the
discussion of the elite discourse concerned with *El Güegüence* and
Nicaraguan national identity. But the more or less direct access to the
halls of power enjoyed by the literati, including prominent women
among the intelligentsia, became especially pronounced under Sandinismo. The international acclaim that accrued to several women (in
particular, see Daisy Zamora 1981, 1988, 1992, and Giaconda Belli
1987, 1988, 1990) put them on a par, at least in terms of cultural
capital, with the literary men, who included Sergio Ramírez, Ernesto
Cardenal, and Omar Cabezas, men who nevertheless achieved positions of far greater power in the Sandinista government than any of
the women ever did.

A M N L A E occupied a proximate position with respect to the Frente
Sandinista, as did the many other mass organizations, all of them
delegated to organize support for Sandinista policies among the various revolutionary constituencies considered by the Frente to be "the
Nicaraguan people." Sandinista proclamations about women offered
the model of revolutionary heroism among the women comandantes
in order to inspire the participation of women in the revolutionary
project through A M N L A E. The specification of women's rights in the
Sandinista state's proclamations made broad assumptions about the
capacity of the revolutionary state to arbitrate and change gender relations as a part of the overall transformation of Nicaraguan society.
Such assumptions were necessarily linked to the Sandinista Front's
class analysis of Nicaraguan society and history, and to long-standing
political practice in socialist countries and revolutionary movements,
that is, to their overall understanding of social contradiction, which
assumed that by redressing economically based social inequalities,

other forms of oppression based on gender, race, ethnicity, and so on would also ultimately achieve resolution (see Stephens 1988). It is also true that many men in the Frente's leadership came to understand the ideological dimensions of women's oppression as distinct from class struggle and class identities. Analysis of those aspects of women's oppression expressed in the practices of machismo, such as male abandonment of wives and children, male violence against women, and, of particular interest to the Sandinista comandantes, men's exclusion of women from positions of responsibility and authority in postrevolutionary organizations of all kinds, appeared in Sandinista policy papers such as "El FSLN y la mujer en la Revolución Popular Sandinista" (in Gilbert and Block 1990; see also Olivera and Fernández 1991). Yet despite this distancing from an orthodox classist position on the part of the Frente and the incorporation of some elements of mainstream feminist discourses, the Frente resisted the identification of its policies toward women as feminist and leveled harsh criticism against those who worked to organize women outside of AMNLAE and its agenda:

The solution to the specific problems of women, i.e. the struggle against discriminatory political ideas and the development of socioeconomic conditions to assure women an effective equality of opportunity, are not issues having to do exclusively with women but with all of society . . . We reject tendencies that promote the emancipation of women as the outcome of a struggle against men, or as an activity exclusively of women, for this type of position is divisive and distracts the people from their fundamental tasks. It is the work of the FSLN and all revolutionaries, of all the advanced sectors of society, men and women together, to lead the ideological, political and socioeconomic battles that will result in the elimination of all forms of oppression and discrimination in Nicaragua, including those which women endure. (Dirección Nacional of the FSLN, in Gilbert and Block 1990: 260)

This positioning in Sandinista ideology should be measured against recent anthropological work emphasizing that nation-building projects both in Europe and the colonized world have always been gendered and genderizing. In other words, constructions of national identity rely upon the policing of specific gender roles in the daily lives of men and women, and at the same time aspects of national identity are themselves imbued with a gendered significance (see Verdery

1996; de la Cadena 1996; True 1996). Brackette Williams asks: "How have masculine and feminine, man and woman, come to 'embody' the logics of the 'national' in the shifting practices and ideas about the norms of domesticity? How have the subordinated 'subnationals' operating on the same terrains of various states confronted, contested, or assimilated these logics in diverse efforts to construct gendered selves . . . ?" (1996: 4). Carol Smith writes: "Women thus became the key icons around which a modern nation of culture would be built in cultural, biological, and material terms. And reproductive control over women—control over their sexuality—became the instrumental means by which economic, political, and cultural dominance of the elite in a new nation is assured" (1996: 55). Attention must thus be focused on how different kinds of women and their voices are suppressed, silenced, and channeled in national cultural identity discourse, and how these different women's sexualities and reproductive capacities are specifically controlled as a part of nation-building.

Interpreting early Sandinista positionings on "the woman question" within the context of the project at hand—artisans, culture, and nation-building during and since Sandinismo—in light of recent anthropological work concerning gendered national identities leads back to my ongoing critique of elite representations of *El Güegüence* as national parable. The only named female character in the play is the governor's daughter, Suche-Malinche. Traditionally, as Brinton (1883) pointed out, Suche-Malinche and her entourage of women were all played by men, which he considered a feature of indigenous drama. Suche-Malinche never speaks, and acts merely as a deus ex machina for first the conflict and later the problematic alliance between the socially, economically, and culturally disparate families of Güegüence and Governor Tastuanes. Her person and preferences receive no respect.

Güegüence: Well then, Governor Tastuanes, shall we not make a trade and a treaty between this prick without prickles [Don Forsico] and the lady Suche-Malinche?

Governor: Don't you already know, Güegüence?

Güegüence: No, I don't know, Governor Tastuanes.

Governor: Chief Captain Alguacil, my son, stop all work at the royal secretary's home so that he may obey our orders: to enter my royal presence with the lady Suche-Malinche.

(The Alguacil goes to speak with the Royal Secretary)

Alguacil: I pray God protect you, Sir Royal Secretary.

Secretary: I pray God that you prosper, Chief Captain Alguacil. Are you well?

Alguacil: I am here in front of you, Sir Secretary. You will enter the royal presence of Lord Governor Tastuanes in order to obey his orders, and the same with Lady Suche-Malinche.

Secretary: Well then, my son, Chief Captain Alguacil, we shall stop the music of "El Rujero" and all such things in the homes of all the important lords so that I may obey, and the same with the Lady Suche-Malinche.

Alguacil: At your service, Sir Royal Secretary.

(They play "El Rujero" and both dance)

Secretary: I pray God protect you, Lord Governor Tastuanes.

Governor: I pray God that you prosper, Sir Royal Secretary. Are you well?

Secretary: I am here before you ready to obey your orders, and the same with the Lady Suche-Malinche.

Governor: So, Señor Secretary, there is an agreement between this useless man, Güegüence, a rich man, and the Lady Suche-Malinche.

Secretary: Lord Governor Tastuanes, let the agreement stipulate that he dress her in a silk coat from China, a vest huipil, a feather huipil, silk stockings, shoes of gold, and beaver-skin hat, in order to be your son-in-law.

Governor: Ah, Güegüence, it irritates me that you have chosen so presumptuously.

Güegüence: Humpingly?

Governor: Presumptuously, Güegüence.

Güegüence: I have made neither a deal nor a contract with you. It's for my boy.

Governor: That I do not know, Güegüence.

Güegüence: Hey, boys! What deal or contract have you made with the Lord Governor Tastuanes?

Don Forsico: For me to get married, Daddy. (Lejarza 1993: 39–41)[1]

After an exchange of nasty insinuations between Güegüence, Don Forsico, and his other son, Don Ambrosio, concerning the women in Suche-Malinche's entourage, Don Forsico and Suche-Malinche are abruptly wed. But the marriage itself immediately becomes of secondary importance, as the governor takes the opportunity to demand that Güegüence provision the festivities with fine wine. When Don

Forsico obtains the wine, another exchange takes place, showing just how catholic Don Forsico's sexual experiences may be:

Don Forsico: Don't go, Dad, I have already found two bottles of wine.
Güegüence: Where did you get them?
Don Forsico: In the house of a "friend."
Güegüence: Who taught you to go around and make such "friends"?
Don Forsico: You did, Dad.
Güegüence: Shut up, boy! What will people say if they know that I taught you to make that kind of friend? (Lejarza 1993: 45)[2]

Once again, one is struck by the utter strangeness of interpreting *El Güegüence* as a parable of Nicaraguan national identity. For if the marriage of Don Forsico and Suche-Malinche is the kind of romance meant to seal the union between disparate social sectors in order to produce national citizens, as Sommer (1991) succinctly describes for national literatures elsewhere in Latin America, then this is a marriage that is neither consummated nor reproductive, at least during the course of the play. This is doubly ironic considering Suche-Malinche's name. In Mexico, La Malinche was the indigenous woman from the Gulf of Mexico whom Cortés used and then discarded after defeating the Aztec Empire; her role in history as well as in the mythos of the creation of the Mexican nation has been subjected to vitriol, as in the classic work by Octavio Paz (1959) and more recent feminist reinterpretations (see Cypess 1991; Anzaldua 1987) that rescue her reputation and revise the place of women in Mexican identity. If the Nicaraguan elite's reading of *El Güegüence* is taken at face value, the woman who should be the mother of the Nicaraguans is neither a woman nor a mother, and the father of the Nicaraguans has sex with men in exchange for wine. The possibility, as Brinton long ago asserted, that the mule Macho Ratón is Güegüence's alter ego stresses even more that reproduction is not the theme of this play.

Revising the meaning of Suche-Malinche is simultaneously a fraught and a novel proposition. Certainly, elite authors do not appear to have thought the silence of women problematic for narrating national identity; Sofía Montenegro's (1992) manifesto, about which I will have much to say at the end of this chapter, utilizes the story of the Mexican La Malinche to narrate a feminist vision for Nicaragua. Let us again depart from an essentialist reading of *El Güegüence*, spinning out new interpretations, thinking of the play more as a parable that instructs audiences or directs their attention in various ways. The words of the wife of an actor who has performed the play in Diriamba inspire such a revision. "How could a nation be born of such foolishness?" she admonished Flavio; "I really don't think so," she added. If women are excluded and silenced, men's alliances must become sterile and unproductive, a series of ruses and poorly executed schemes. Community—much less the nation—cannot be created without the involvement of women. Thus, if men mourn the passing of the familiar and the loss of their sons, as Güegüence does at the end of the play, they will belatedly realize that without women loss is permanent, and all endings simply end in death or farce. From this perspective, the play does not really end—it drifts off, awaiting new subversions of the absurd hierarchies of powerful authorities and the pretensions of wealth.

This chapter thus addresses women's voices in the artisan communities where Gia and I worked, for whom the silence of Suche-Malinche may be an invitation to speak. Not unexpectedly, the voices of these *artesanas* are complex: what they have to say concerns not only their consciousness of themselves as women; at the same time, what they do have to say about their experiences and thoughts as women has been subject to the conventions of silence in Nicaraguan society during and since Sandinismo. Previously (Field 1987) I struggled to analyze *artesanas'* condition of life: their instrumental role in the production of pottery, and thus in forming collective identity, yet their voices quite muffled in the case of San Juan and transmuted in the case of the *cerámica negra* women. In the end, that text included much of what the *artesanas* with whom we worked told us in life-history interviews, at the same time making clear that their voices, especially those of the San Juaneras, found little forum for expression in the existing discourses of Sandinista Nicaragua.

In the years since 1985 and particularly since the electoral defeat of the Frente in 1990, the influence and prestige of Nicaraguan feminist authors of prose and particularly of poetry have grown tremendously. Feminist critiques of the Sandinista era have been written, and new discourses concerned with women's rights to health care, control over their bodies and sexuality, and legal and social protection against rape and physical abuse have appeared and exercised a profound influence on the discourse of women's rights in the country. Although the role played by authors of prose and poetry within Nicaraguan feminism has given the feminist movement there an international profile, none of the San Juaneras we have known has become involved in any aspect of the feminist movement so far. Yet for all this, artisan women, like so many other subaltern social sectors, experienced a transformation during Sandinismo, which, as Montenegro (1992: 50) relates, permitted these sectors to "leave behind their victim role and to become protagonists in their own history." This is the process that I referred to in the introduction as the creation of local, organic, articulatory intellectuals. Such local articulations of identity are unlikely to be unidimensional; it may also be difficult for either insiders from the local environment or outsiders such as an anthropologist to detect what is shared among a group of local intellectuals who appear to belong to a single collectivity such as "women" (see Stephen 1991 for a resonant ethnographic case study).

In this chapter, I illustrate these observations with ethnographic descriptions from our work with two groups of *artesanas*. First, I recount the stories told by women who make or made *cerámica negra,* a craft dominated by women. Their stories about the origin of the craft, coming on the heels of a reconstructed history authored by officials in the Ministry of Culture without any input from the *artesanas,* is the only explicit discourse about women's history and creativity that I heard among Nicaraguan *artesanas.* Yet the stories were told in the context of these *artesanas'* involvement with the class discourse of the artisans' union. In my consideration of San Juaneras' narratives, and the gender-based conflicts and outcomes among Co-op *socios* over the past decade or so, different stories about women's conflicts with men and each other and their own individual and collective agendas emerge in several voices. The effect of the San Juan ethnographic material is thus less cohesive than the *cerámica negra* narrative, and what emerges are the disparate voices of individual women who in some ways were alone in attempting to break the silence of Suche-Malinche.

In the final section of the chapter, I review the feminist literature of the late Sandinista and post-Sandinista period, searching for analyses that illuminate, explain, or even relate to the *artesanas'* discourse and the larger issue of drawing together disparate women's voices with the broader project of reconstructing Nicaraguan identity(ies) in sight. I recognize that recuperating the ethnography of San Juanera and *cerámica negra artesanas* in light of the feminist discourse that has taken shape in recent years, even when that discourse has not explicitly impacted the lives of these *artesanas,* lends a certain constructed quality to this analysis, making this chapter a "fiction of feminist ethnography," in Visweswaran's (1994) terms. The ideas of Montenegro (1992) in the end connect most strongly to what I describe here about the *artesanas,* and it is through her work that the transection of *artesanas'* identities as women, as artisans, and as residents of localities comes back into focus once again, leading to the arguments made in the rest of the book.

The Stories of Doñas Silvia, Carmen, and Carmela, and the History of *Cerámica Negra*

Gia and I sat with María Dolores and Ramona in the house of their mother, Doña Silvia, on a cool and rainy February day. We had just finished preparing the clay by mixing a number of different dry powders into a wet mass on a rickety table outside the door in their small patio. Doña Silvia served us lukewarm sweetened coffee and *yoltamales,* tamales made from young green corn, and she said sternly, "Don't forget that *cerámica negra* has never been work for men!" Perhaps she admonished us in that fashion in part to respond to her daughter's praise of me, as I mixed the clay moments before. "It's beautiful," María Dolores had said, "when a man tries to learn what he doesn't know. In Nicaragua, the men don't like to do what we call 'woman's work.'"

We had already learned that the topic of relationships with men, whether in production or reproduction, was a treacherous one. On the one hand, Ramona and María Dolores spoke disparagingly about their brothers, all "conservative jerks" with the exception of their youngest brother, Jacinto, who sometimes helped them to haul powdered clay from the hills to their house. On the other hand, we were told in whispers that Doña Silvia had been "a real tyrant" who had kept them under tight rein and not informed them about anatomy, menstruation, or sexuality. This led her daughters to rebel, leave home, get pregnant, and take a very different approach bringing up their own daughters, Chepita (twelve, María Dolores's eldest) and Carlita (seven, Ramona's only child).

Ramona and María Dolores told us that as teenagers they had been intensely interested in the history of *cerámica negra,* and it was when they began to relate what they knew that Doña Silvia reminded us that men had never worked the craft. Clearly, Doña Silvia wanted to tell the story her way. She told us that Marta Pineda Gadeas, her grandmother's sister, was the first person to make *cerámica negra,* early in this century. Marta had been trying to fix a hole in the wall of her house, related Doña Silvia, which she filled with wet clay. After the clay dried, she polished it with a smooth stone, making the dried surface shiny and level with the wall. Her sisters, including Doña Silvia's grandmother, Teodora Gadeas de Pineda, liked the way the repaired wall looked, and decided to try to form clay jars using the same material and technique. Teodora experimented. Together, the women discovered a way to harden the clay by placing dried vessels in burning piles of sawdust. When they switched to burning the pots in pine needles, they found that the pots became uniformly black and glossy. Doña Silvia hypothesized that Marta and her sisters had learned something about ceramics from their mother, Guadalupe Pineda, whom Doña Silvia was sure had emigrated to Nicaragua from Spain.

Gia and I were curious to find out whether the Matagalpa branch of the family would tell a different story, especially after María Dolores said that she doubted the Matagalpa women knew anything about the origins of the craft. At this time, the Ministry of Culture officials were putting together *their* history of *cerámica negra,* and I showed María Dolores of Jinotega and María Esthela of Matagalpa these documents, one of which I cited in the last chapter. In another document, we read: "we [in Nicaragua] are lamentably not Indians, but neither are we Europeans; all of European culture, in its global form, is foreign to our continent, and we must take 'steps backwards' . . . it would be an error to try to change the designs of cerámica negra, introducing different forms when the most important thing is to maintain the forms based in our indigenous roots; the important thing is to improve the methods of work and to supply adequate tools for this improvement" (Ministry of Culture 1985a, document 4: 2). This, along with the draft document that connected *cerámica negra* to the pre-Columbian Castillo Esgrafiado culture and an article in *Barricada* that explicitly called *cerámica negra* an indigenous *artesanía* with pre-Columbian origins (Barricada 4/11/85) led María Dolores to say that "they [the Ministry people] disregard us because we are women." The articles and documents also helped to stimulate discussion of the craft's history in Doña Carmen's house, where, notwithstanding María Dolores's doubts, the women also maintained knowledge about the origins of *cerámica negra*.

According to Doña Carmen, Teodora Gadeas had nothing to do with inventing the craft. Carmen said that Teodora's husband's sister, Lorenza Pineda de Pineda, and her daughters, Josefa and Remejia, began the craft by making miniature figurines out of clay as well as large vessels for carrying and storing water.[3] These women, Doña Carmen claimed, had taught her mother's generation to make clay things, and her mother's generation had discovered the process of firing and blackening the pots. Doña Benita added that Carmen's mother had invented a clay filter for well water as well. However, much of the innovation in the craft had begun very recently, according to Doña Carmen. After the enormously destructive 1972 earthquake in Managua, the women learned to make more than miniature figurines and large jugs for water, and had experimented with their clay formula to arrive at the durable mixture they currently use.

The significant differences between the two narratives of *cerámica negra*'s origins notwithstanding, the dominant role of women in both led us to visit the last living individual from the older generation, Doña Carmela Pineda. She lived on a small farm in La Trinidad, just south of another large northern city, Estelí. María Esthela accompanied Gia and me to Doña Carmela's farm. We found a hale eighty-year-old woman, who told us that she had given up making ceramics some years ago, and who immediately agreed to relate the history of the craft. She did so, drawing attention to her support for the Revolution and the opportunity thus provided for such research. "We are living in the epoch of light," she said, "but we were in darkness, and because of that we cannot remember our history very well."

Nevertheless, she remembered enough to mediate the divergences between what we had heard from Doña Silvia and from Doña Carmen. Doña Carmela had grown up in Jinotega early in this century and had lived there for forty years, she said. Lorenza Pineda, Teodora Gadeas, and Lorenza's daughters had *all* taught her to make *cerámica negra*. She recalled that Lorenza had been the first to experiment with making pots and that she had also first discovered the art of blackening the pots in burning beds of sawdust or pine needles. Thus, Doña Carmela reckoned the blackening technique to be generation older than what Doña Carmen had said. She also credited Teodora with the discovery of the polishing technique, using smooth beach stones to create a vitreous gloss on the pots. Like both the Matagalpa and Jinotega women, Doña Carmela asserted that the first pieces of *cerámica negra* had been large. Lorenza had decided to make miniatures, Doña Carmela said, because their manufacture required less clay, they were easier to fire, and they found a readier market in Jinotega and environs in the 1910s and '20s.

Doña Carmela urged us to write down that many women had contributed to the process of discovering and improving *cerámica negra*, using different tools, clay mixtures, and methods of polishing, firing, and blackening the pots during the one hundred years she said the craft had existed. "For all this time," she said, "ceramics have made us the money we needed to survive; it has been our work all this time, but it has also been a pleasure, something for us [women] to enjoy." Although she mostly laughed as we related to her the differences between what we had heard about the craft's history in Matagalpa and Jinotega, one detail caused her to raise her voice, the only time she did so. She insisted that no one in her family had emigrated to Nicaragua from Spain, or from anywhere else for that matter. "We," she exclaimed, using the form *nosotras,* meaning "we" in the feminine plural, "we have always been Nicaraguans, pure Nicaraguan, to our fingernails, as we say!" By the same token, Doña Carmela's insistence did not mean she thought of her family as Indians; she shook her head sharply when I asked her about that.

The *artesanas* of Matagalpa and Jinotega perceived that their gender had led Ministry officials to embark on historical research about their craft without consulting them, as well as to disregard the women's ideas about improving production. María Dolores had concluded, "They [Ministry people] didn't respect us; we are women and they think we are uneducated and ignorant—they don't take our ideas seriously." Doña Carmen elaborated in another conversation: "They didn't put our ideas and problems into their plans, I think, because we are women . . . they don't know very much about our ceramics, our history, and I suppose if men made *cerámica negra* these people would try to find out more."

The absence of men from both family life and the production of *cerámica negra* in the lives and households of these *artesanas* did not elide the effects of patriarchal social relations, which emerged in their treatment by male-dominated government institutions. Yet, the *artesanas'* analysis of their situation as gender-based oppression had led them to participate in a class-based organization, the artisans' union UNADI, where they felt their experiences and understanding of them would be heard. Without necessarily stating it as such, by working with the union against the Ministry, the *cerámica negra* women believed that they battled against their gender oppression—not "as women," if by that term an unqualified or nonspecific category is referenced, but as *artesanas,* women artisans. This transection of two vectors of identity spoke to their life experiences and therefore composed the voice through which they broke the silence of Suche-Malinche. This circumstance, as I later discuss, bears upon and suggests a nascent critique of the construction of the social category "women" in Nicaraguan feminist discourse. Next, however, I contrast the fact that a gender-based oppression could be articulated with class analysis and class-based activism among the *cerámica negra* women with the lives of the *artesanas* in San Juan de Oriente during the Sandinista period.

Silence, Creativity, and Women's Lives at the San Juan Co-op: The 1980s

No one thinks about the special needs of women here. (Ester Bracamonte, *socia* of the Co-op in San Juan de Oriente)

Men almost always leave women. You should know someone for a while, I think, before marriage. My Mom married at thirteen or fourteen, but she's been married for twenty-six years. It all depends. If you behave well, I think men will [also] . . . I've seen my sister Ester, eighteen years old, have a kid, and now she has double the responsibility. Cleaning, cooking, ironing, and then she goes to work. That's double the responsibility. Maybe I'll meet a man who will be a help . . . I want it like this: if I'm going to work, he also will work double-time. (Catalina Bracamonte, *socia* of the Co-op in San Juan de Oriente)

In San Juan, as among the *cerámica negra* women, the making of ceramics had been historically carried out by individual women with the help of their daughters in their own homes. Before the founding of the Co-op in 1978, ceramics production formed a part of women's daily labor, blurring into their other domestic tasks, such as cooking, cleaning, and caring for children (Field 1987). In the Co-op during the 1980s, the division of labor between men and women clearly favored men over women, relegating women *socias* to the most repetitive and physically exhausting tasks, while marginalizing their access to the most creative and interesting jobs. Conflict over this inequality—in other words, over gender-based division of labor—burst into the open during 1984 and 1985, while I worked at the Co-op.

Like the *cerámica negra* women, San Juanera *artesanas* working at the Co-op have also perceived their problems as gender-based, at least in part. For the San Juaneras, however, the discourse of the artisans' union during the Sandinista years did not provide a means to analyze and address the role of gender and gender-based contradictions in their lives. San Juanera *artesanas'* consciousness of their oppression as women, as the two sisters' declarations above indicate, formed in response to the gender-based division of labor both within the spheres of production, that is, during the process of artisanal manufacture, and reproduction, that is, through the domestic labors within the family unit. Their understanding of their predicaments focused on the enforcement and significance of the division of labor in both production and reproduction within the context of a highly patriarchal sociocultural milieu. Since the late 1970s, many San Juaneras have faced men every day in both ceramics production and in the home, and because many of these women produce ceramics both in the Co-op and in their homes, the lines between male domination over production and reproduction processes have tended to become blurred.

The Co-op represented the brainchild of the old Banco Central, the product of its study of Nicaraguan artisan production, *La Situación de la Artesanía Nicaragüense* (Industrial Division 1976), which had recommended the technification of artisanal workshops as a route to both the survival of artisanal production and a means to enrich Nicaraguan society. But the brainchild bore other fruit in the arena of gender relations in San Juan. The foreign staff brought by the Banco Central and its successor, the Sandinista Ministry of Culture, trained both men and women as *socios;* this support and technical staff, composed of Spanish, German, Mexican, and other foreign men, inevitably brought their own sexist notions to bear upon the training of Co-op personnel, notions that resonated with or exacerbated the in situ gender contradictions. The genderized division of labor at the Co-op that Gia and I witnessed thus played out from a preexisting structure of discrimination against women built into the foundations of the "technical advance" of ceramics production in San Juan.

Given that women had been the only people producing ceramics in San Juan before the appearance of the Co-op, we were curious to investigate, if we could, what ceramics production had been like prior to 1978. In 1984, Agustín Amador and Bladimir Nororís at the Co-op directed us to the house of Joséfa Nicoya and her daughter where, they said, ceramics were produced "in a traditional manner." We walked a few blocks away from the Co-op to the conical straw roof and mud-walled house of the Nicoyas, one of the few such structures remaining in San Juan and another significant marker identifying them as "traditional" in the eyes of the Co-op *socios*. After several brief visits to their house over a two-week period, we felt comfortable asking Joséfa and her daughter, María Isabel, about their ceramics production. They told us that they brought crude clay from a deposit near San Juan and mixed it into the desired consistency with their bare feet on the floor of their bamboo and straw house. To fire their pots, they cut wood by themselves in forests located between San Juan and Diriá, the neighboring village to the south, and building piles of their pots interspersed with layers of firewood, set it all ablaze in the street in front of their house, burning the pots until all the wood was consumed.

The Nicoyas employed the coil technique to make large pots used for planting herbs or holding water and plates for cooking. They too called this the "traditional" technique, but were aware that the pots were brittle because of the low temperatures of the flames. During the rainy season, they said, they could not get a fire going in the street, so they did not produce ceramics. In any event, they depended on the patronage of particular clients from Managua, who did not always come to San Juan when the women most needed to sell. So they supplemented their precarious income by buying fruit from farms in San Juan and reselling the produce in the Masaya market. In this way, they often earned more than they could by making pottery, and could afford to pay someone to haul the clay from its source to their house rather than having to do it for themselves. María Isabel confided that she liked to experiment with her pottery, trying out new forms and affixing decorative relief to the pots. Thus, categorizing their production as "traditional," in the sense that the Nicoyas' pottery somehow represented an unchanging and unchanged relic of the way pottery used to be produced in San Juan, inaccurately portrayed what they did and how they thought about it. Perhaps the most traditional part of their production was that it remained in the hands of women, that it provided women's livelihood even in the complete absence of men, and that these women managed both the production and the marketing of their craft.

In analyzing the changes in gender relations in San Juan brought about by the Co-op and the Revolution, I have considered how these processes both resemble and depart markedly from ongoing transformations in gender relations among artisans elsewhere in Central America. Nash's (1993) analysis of such changes among the potters of Amatenango del Valle, Guatemala, describes a community where women have historically produced pottery, and where individual artisans' households have greatly intensified the production of ceramics. Nash argues that "there are conditions defining domestic relations of production in the context of community-controlled norms of production [that] are so linked to the gender ideology that any change in the levels of production and means of commercialization affects marital relations, reproduction rates, and norms of male/female interaction in ways that are not predictable in advance" (131). In Amatenango, men are increasingly involved in helping women to obtain and transport raw materials for pottery production, while the growth and intensification of production has shaped situations in which women are more and more responsible for marketing the finished products. Nash concludes: "Change in the division of labor within the household is affecting the position of women within and outside the domestic sphere, necessitating more powerful means of suppression exercised by men than in the past to preserve the patriarchal relations in the family" (148). At one time a production cooperative formed in Amatenango, but during the violent conflict in Guatemala its coordinator was killed and its *socios* disbanded. Notwithstanding the differences between the cases of San Juan and Amatenango, Nash's attention to changes in marriage, male-female interactions, and the patriarchal relations within families applies as much to the former case as the latter.

In speaking with Juanita Bracamonte, one of two women *socias* from the first training course, the only one organized by the Banco Central, we learned about how women were assigned particular tasks within the overall rotation of jobs at the Co-op during its earliest period. We asked: So the women who entered into the first course already knew how to make things by hand? "Yes; there were two women, there was Doña Enriqueta Gallegos and myself. And the men, they wanted us to learn to throw on the wheel." And the men didn't want to learn? "No, only the women. I don't know why, I saw only that the women stuck with it. Your legs hurt, your head and back hurt too. I don't think they [the men] liked that."

Juanita told us that she remembered being subtly but unmistakably encouraged at first from learning to use the kickwheel, and discouraged from learning to paint pre-Columbian designs. She reflected that women were not often given positive reinforcement to continue developing their skills. During the first training course and later on during the second course organized by the Ministry of Culture after the Sandinista triumph, the instructors simply assumed that women did not have the creative talent to design the individually painted and designed *vasos mayas*. "If you wanted to learn anything," she recalled, "you had to be very persistent."

Juanita left the Co-op "because of the situation with my kid." When she had a child, the Co-op made no provisions for child care, so she needed to stay home and care for him. She saw this as one of the unfortunate but expected consequences of womanhood for which men have little or no understanding, even though she responded to Gia's inquiry as follows: For you, how was it working with many men [in the Co-op]? "At first, they gave me a hard time, but then afterwards, we made friends, and we respected each other."

Then in 1982, Juanita's husband abandoned her, a circumstance historically familiar to San Juaneras,[4] but in the post-1979 period, one that did not necessarily lead to the same condition of extreme impoverishment it once had. The departure of her husband facilitated Juanita's decision to spend all of her savings to buy a kickwheel, the first woman in San Juan to do so. She did not, however, direct her energies toward pre-Columbian design, as the Co-op *socios* were doing at that time. The pottery she showed us was all utilitarian, although bearing the jaguar motif first used in the Co-op. In 1984, Juanita introduced a new product into the ceramics market when she and her children began making colored ceramic beads strung into necklaces. The necklaces sold in sizable quantities in Masaya and at the huge Huembes Market in Managua. Using her children's science fiction comic books, Juanita also made children's whistles and flutes, telling us that she enjoyed making different and unique things. Ediberto, the oldest of her four children, declared, "My mother is single, but independent—she makes things!" Notwithstanding their creativity and pride, Juanita's family have lived in a house made of bamboo and straw, equipped with electricity and a hose that is connected to the village's water system, but impoverished in comparison with other San Juan homes, according to Juanita herself. The house still looked like this in 1995. Her efforts, she told us, provided only enough cash to feed herself and her four sons, nothing more.

In 1985, Juanita told us that under the circumstances she had little reason to feel positive about revolutionary Nicaragua. Given that her training at the Co-op had been funded by the prerevolutionary Banco Central before the Sandinista victory, she did not believe the Sandinista government had anything to do with the successes of the Co-op, and especially not with the artistic and technical strides made by independent producers such as herself. We asked: What has been the most important change [since 1979]? "I believe that I haven't seen any changes, because everything was already here, from the work of the Banco Central, and since the Banco, nothing has been done." So for you, you don't think the government will help you? "I am not expecting that nor thinking about it because it's the government that needs *us* right now."

The government represented a threat to Juanita and her family, because the military draft of the mid-1980s prevented her from sending her older boys to school for fear they would be taken from her. This came out in the following exchange, with its sudden shift of topic and emphasis: And for you as a woman, how do you feel about politics now? Has the organization of women helped? "Yes, there is more respect for women, because before [the Revolution] only men could organize themselves, but now women are worth the same as men. [Long pause.] My son is seventeen years old. The army says he must enlist." "Because they are more interested in this war," she said, the government's promises to protect women meant little; the Sandinistas did nothing to enforce their own laws concerning the palimony due a wife after a husband's desertion of her and their family, she said. So Juanita believed that women had to protect one another, and she told us that she felt a special responsibility to encourage women still working in the Co-op to continue to study and improve their artistic and technical skills. Thus, although removed from gender inequalities at the Co-op, she still felt tied to the struggles of the women *socias*. She was acutely aware of the conditions constricting the options of independent women such as herself in Sandinista Nicaragua, which for her created a feeling of great distance from revolutionary discourse and process.

Seven women received their training during the second and third courses of instruction at the Co-op. They were integrated into the existing production processes at the Co-op and experienced similar problems on the trail blazed by Juanita. Several of these women told us that Juanita's career provided a model not only for women as Co-op *socias* but as independent, home-based producers. During the mid-1980s, women's roles at the Co-op were vital to the production of both kinds of ceramics churned out there. Women worked at the kickwheels making the versatile, utilitarian, and highly successful vessels, particularly mugs, which were fired at high temperatures with a lead-free vitreous glaze. They also were integrally involved in the production of the so-called pre-Columbian ceramics, a basically decorative earthenware that included bowls, plates, cups, and saucers, inscribed with a single pre-Columbian jaguar motif and fired in a low-temperature wood-burning kiln. Of all the pottery produced at the Co-op, women were least involved in the making of the purely decorative *vasos mayas* (Mayan vases), the large high-rimmed bowls, also fired in the wood-burning kiln but individually inscribed with unique, artistically brilliant adaptations of Mayan, Aztec, Mixtec, and other pre-Columbian motifs gleaned from a variety of published sources. Women never worked at the *vaso maya* production table until after 1986, until that time the only exclusively male preserve at the Co-op. The most menial tasks—sanding the dried mugs to be dipped into the transparent vitreous glaze, slip-coating both types of pre-Columbian pieces, and polishing these pieces with smooth stones—were shared by men and women. Hard labor, such as loading the kilns, feeding wood into the wood-burning kiln, and using the clay-mixing mill were also not considered off-limits to women. Using the mill, which required that a person break off large, heavy pieces of clay from a pile of unmixed clay, feed the chunks into the mill, and then remove the mixed clay, now in cylindrical rolls, was a particularly taxing labor. But in all these tasks, women more than carried their weight at the kickwheels. Ester held the record for the production of mugs: 120 in a single five-hour morning. She and her sister Catalina produced more mugs on a daily basis than any other *socio*.

The Co-op in fact depended on the physical strength and endurance of the *socias* during the mid-1980s, which some of the men *socios* recognized. Men's refusal to recognize women's creative capacities constituted the de facto inequality at the Co-op, a condition of work reproduced at the *socios'* general meetings by women's unwillingness to raise this topic for discussion and men's inability or unwillingness to acknowledge the existence of the inequality. In retrospect, many of the *socias*, some of whom still worked at the Co-op in 1995, blamed the two men who monopolized the painting of *vasos mayas*, Agustín and Bladimir. Yet in 1985, Agustín attempted to train one woman, Patricia, to paint pre-Columbian design. His attempt brought gender contradictions finally into the open, threatening to destroy the Co-op for a time and leading to a massive turnover in personnel in the years that followed. This conflict revealed much about power relations undermining women's creativity in the lives of five *socias*— Patricia, Catalina, Ester, Ena, and Digna, a group with multiple perspectives on the evolution and resolution of gender conflict at the Co-op and its relation to their lives and labors.

Patricia Bracamonte was eighteen in 1985, the youngest of nine children.[5] During the first six months of my fieldwork, I was unable to sustain a conversation of any length with Patricia. After Gia arrived and had spoken to Patricia on a number of occasions, I was shocked by the first question she posed for me. "I have heard many things about this subject," she said shyly one day, as I watched her throwing bowls on the wheel that were to be decorated with the Co-op's trademark pre-Columbian jaguar motif. Yes? I queried, alert to her opening line. "But I thought I ought to ask you directly," she continued. "Tell me, Les, what exactly does it mean that you are a Jew?"

Patricia told me that her mother had started her own ceramics business in their home when Patricia was a young child, which is why she said that "ceramics is an inheritance from my mother." Her mother used the coil technique to make large pots and planters, and she fired these pots in a wood blaze in the street in the manner familiar to us from spending time with the Nicoyas. Patricia learned these techniques, but became interested in the Co-op when she saw the beauty and skill of the pottery the *socios* produced in the early 1980s. So she enrolled in the second course at the end of 1981. Early in our conversations, Patricia claimed that she enjoyed all of the tasks at the Co-op equally, but preferred to paint. One of her jobs was painting the jaguar motif on the simple pre-Columbian pieces. Later, she admitted that what she had meant to say was that she really wanted to learn to paint *vasos mayas,* and that toward that end she was studying pre-Columbian art in her spare time, copying designs from Samuel Lothrop's *Pottery of Nicaragua and Costa Rica.*

Different styles for throwing pots, glazing them, and designing pre-Columbian motifs had been taught at the Co-op during each training course, shaped to a great extent by the varying philosophies of the foreign staff brought to the Co-op by the Banco Central and the Ministry of Culture. During the second course, when Patricia, Agustín, Bladimir, and others had been trained, a Spaniard named Arturo Lengán had imparted a highly creative and original approach to clay. Those who took the third course, including Catalina, Ester, and Ena, learned from Heinrich Heyne, a German, whose approach to ceramics was mostly technical, according to Agustín. Patricia's technique thus most closely resembled the work of the men who did the most creative tasks at the Co-op. That gave her the confidence, she said, to think that she could attempt to design *vasos mayas.* In early 1985 she made a prototype *vaso* that depicted priests making offerings to the gods, embedded in a delicate hatchwork pattern. Despite the technical and aesthetic success of her work, her self-esteem was very low. Patricia's father was an alcoholic who had abused her and her mother psychologically and had encouraged her brothers to do the same. Thus, instead of saving a portion of her salary earned at the Co-op to purchase her own kickwheel or books of pre-Columbian design, Patricia gave all of her earnings to her mother.

Patricia's skills and her potential as a painter of *vasos mayas* did not remain hidden once Agustín took an interest in helping her. His encouragement, she told me, provoked her to wonder why women had not been trained to design *vasos mayas* in the first place, and she decided to raise the issue with the Co-op's three-person directorate. Orlando described the directorate to us as always dominated by male personalities, if not always monopolized by men, just before a meeting during which job rotation was to be discussed. At this meeting, however, Patricia asked if she in particular could learn to paint *vasos mayas,* instead of raising the more general point of the exclusion of women from this labor. The directorate agreed to permit Patricia to be so trained. That decision ran afoul of Digna Gallegos, the only woman employed at the Co-op in 1985 who was older than twenty-two. Digna told me that she thought her son Silvio should be the next person to receive training as a *vaso maya* designer. Silvio had in fact been working on his own adaptation of designs from the Lothrop book since early 1984, and I, upon request, had also gifted him a book concerning the ceramics of pre-Columbian Mesoamerica. His illiteracy had hindered his progress, but he was determined and had become Bladimir's apprentice by late 1984. The Co-op's directorate had appointed Silvio and Angel to oversee job rotation, and I learned that in that capacity Silvio had informed Patricia that she would be expected to produce as much as Agustín and Bladimir immediately upon completing her training. She backed down under the pressure of this threat, and once again felt quite stymied.

Such experiences reinforced Patricia's overall negative attitudes toward men that she had learned in the domestic realm. In her home, she had learned that women in San Juan are expected to stay at home once they are married, to keep house and care for children. If she were to marry, she said, she fully expected to be forbidden to continue working at the Co-op, as well as prevented from spending time with women friends in San Juan and in other nearby villages and towns. Women who insisted on retaining such "liberties" (her term) could expect their husbands to desert them. As resigned as she was to the frustration of her creativity in her workplace, she refused to consider marriage, even though she longed to raise children. "When women fall in love with men, the men get them pregnant and then leave them," she concluded.

The other women whom Gia and I came to know intimately enough to talk about their lives did not necessarily go through the same processes and conflicts to reach the same conclusions; perhaps similar conclusions did not always leave them as personally disempowered as Patricia felt at that time. Ena Bracamonte, twenty years old in 1984 and cousin of Catalina and Ester, denied that she possessed creative talents such as those that made Patricia's life at the Co-op so difficult. She told us that she felt content doing the repetitive tasks she performed at the Co-op, that she did not prefer any one task over any other, and that she worked at the Co-op to earn a salary, nothing more. She did, however, enthusiastically undertake the responsibility of managing and expanding the Co-op's food and clothing commissary, a benefit the Co-op had established to help the *socios* cope with the accelerating hyperinflation of the mid-1980s. But if Ena chose to interact less with the male *socios* at the Co-op than any other woman working there, she expressed attitudes toward men perhaps even more fatalistic than Patricia's.

Ena's father had abandoned her mother when Ena was still very young, and her mother's second husband, she said, was no father to her. Healthy and happy marriages are rare and unlikely, Ena told us. But what she found particularly repulsive was the way San Juaneros of both genders excused men's behavior: "The men do those things. They have a wife here. Over there, another woman who is pregnant. Over there, a third woman with a child by that man. And the people say, 'Well, that's just the way they [men] are!'"

Ena's poor opinion of and consequent distancing from men was coupled with her belief that if a woman does get pregnant out of wedlock, "it is God's will, not ours." Thus Ena had come to terms with the male behavior she denounced. She planned to marry, actually, in the hopes that her future husband would not desert her. But if he did: "I will accept that too. My mother will help me, my friends will help me. I'll be okay with the help of God."

Ena's cousin, Catalina Bracamonte (twenty years old in 1985), did not accept this point of view: she had experienced childhood very differently. Both of her parents had been present, and both had constantly encouraged her to pursue a great variety of endeavors, such as cultivating their family's roughly five-acre plot, learning to ride horses, experimenting with clay, painting and designing ceramics. She observed that in her family, her father had learned to carve stone from a *maestro* in Masaya, and her mother had managed the cultivation of the family plot, becoming completely responsible for the plot after Catalina's father fell ill in 1984. As a result of both parents' admonitions about the necessity of being economically independent and versatile, Catalina had received more formal education than any other woman working at the Co-op in the 1980s. She had studied to be a secretary in Granada, learned to type in Masaya, and taken an accounting course offered to Co-op *socios* by the Banco Nacional in 1982. After two years of working at the Co-op, she used her savings to buy a kickwheel from Don Arturo, the second woman in San Juan to own one, after Juanita. "I like to study," she declared; "I like to take opportunities when I can. What if the Co-op were to close? I need to be prepared to find other kinds of work. I need alternatives."

Although Catalina confidently pursued studies of pre-Columbian design at home, and began producing her own line of ceramics in

1985, she expressed disinterest in challenging the division of labor at the Co-op. Were there limits, we asked, on what you learned at the Co-op—a policy about what they did or didn't teach you? "I mostly learned to throw [pots on the wheel], and not much about design." Why? "I don't know. They always said they would teach us women [design], but they preferred us to throw at the wheel. Maybe they had the idea that women wanted to throw, because of the success with Juanita Bracamonte, the first women to throw." So what did you think about that? "I was fine. Once they used to say that women couldn't throw, but it wasn't like that! We did learn to throw and we dedicated ourselves to it." When I asked her whether she would like to use a motif she had shown us based on her study of a book about Quetzalcoatl in her work at the Co-op, she laughed derisively and with heavy sarcasm said, "That's not allowed!" Her house was the place she felt free to express her creativity, experimenting with her sisters, talking with her father, and taking up other tasks in the home when she wanted to. I suggested that she did not want to risk making herself as vulnerable as Patricia by revealing her talents at the Co-op, but Catalina only laughed in reply.

Catalina's attitudes toward the Co-op as a workplace, and the household as the realm of creativity, were accompanied by her aversion to marriage and its division of labor. "It's good to be alone," she said. "I imagine that when you get married, you don't control your own life anymore." She would only be willing to marry if her husband agreed to take on the same load of responsibilities as she did, a relationship that she conceded was utterly unlikely in Nicaragua. I asked, Catalina, have you thought about having children? "Sure." How many? "Not many." Tell me why. "You have to think about lots of things, about work, obligations. Men almost always leave women. You should know someone a long time, I think, before marriage. My Mom married at thirteen or fourteen, but she's been married twenty-six years. It all depends. If you behave well, I think men will. But men have to understand, and well, sometimes, they have problems. That's what they learn from their fathers. I'm careful." Will it be different for you—you know, can it be equal with a man? "Maybe I'll meet a man who will really be a help." That's your hope? "That's what I would want to be understood. I want it like this: if I'm going to work [outside the home], he will also have to work double-time."

Catalina criticized her sister Ester's relationship precisely because

Ester had ended up with twice the workload of her husband, Roberto, managing both the home and working at the Co-op. Ester (only seventeen in 1984) was consistently the most productive Co-op *socia* in 1984–85, and she worked almost to the last day of her pregnancy. After her daughter was born, Ester became sick from exhaustion and kidney infections and could not work for some months. Nevertheless, Ester took on the responsibility for maintaining their home after her and Catalina's father became sick. While their mother managed the farm, Ester resumed work at the Co-op, giving over her entire salary; Catalina, said Ester, "had become like the father in their home." While Roberto traveled a good deal because he had become a delegate to the artisans' union UNADI, Ester remained with her natal family: "We women relate better with each other, we trust each other more. I don't know how I would live without my sisters. Anyway, with our father sick, look at my mother doing the [farm] work. We have good examples." Ester did not believe that she would ever be able to express her creativity in her job at the Co-op, but she told us that she wished the Co-op provided young *socias* with information about birth control. I asked her whether she had considered raising that issue at a Co-op meeting, but she did not reply.

Digna, in her mid-forties, did not include herself, nor was she included in the circle of support and trust that included the younger women so far discussed. She herself expressed a distaste for the younger women and for their friendship with one another that went beyond the threat she perceived they might pose to her son Silvio's ambitions if the younger women were to demand a place at the *vaso maya* table. As such she demanded that her daughter Maritza and Silvio's wife, Myriam, both *socias,* keep their contacts with the other young women to a minimum. In 1984, Digna freely admitted to me, as I helped her attach handles to mugs, that at the root of her anger lay dissatisfaction with her own life. Before becoming a Co-op *socia,* she had worked as a maid in Managua, as an agricultural day laborer in the north picking coffee and in Chinandega picking cotton, and had also visited Costa Rica twice before the Sandinista triumph in 1979. Digna had given birth to eight children and told me that "the wealth of the poor in Nicaragua is their children." Yet between her job at the Co-op and her domestic labors, she often felt too exhausted to pursue production of ceramics at home with which to supplement her family's income, given that her husband had left her long ago. Gia and I concluded that this situation lay at the heart of her resentment of the younger *socias,* who were not as burdened with responsibility and therefore could find the time to produce ceramics at home and study pre-Columbian design. Thus, Digna's perception of inequality centered on the differences between herself and younger women; men hardly entered into that equation. Emblematic of her malaise, Digna reacted acrimoniously to a picture of herself that appeared on a map of the folkloric attractions of Nicaragua that the Ministry of Culture published in 1985: "Why didn't they choose a picture of a younger person for that map instead of me? I'm old, and will be dead soon enough. Then what will that picture mean? Nothing. I'm old and bored with this work. I want to travel, but I must still work."

The conflict between Digna and her family on one side, and the younger *socias* on the other simmered through early and mid-1985. When it became apparent that Agustín was helping Patricia, Digna accused him of pilfering paints from the Co-op and demanded that he resign. Agustín preferred to leave at that point, but Bladimir admonished him not to because without him, he said, the quality of the *vasos mayas* would diminish. Moreover, Patricia, Ester, Catalina, Ena, and others all threatened to resign if Agustín left. Ultimately the dispute was mediated by a state-run organization that promoted and helped cooperatives, and the conflict subsided. The following year, Agustín, Bladimir, Ester, Ena, Digna, Maritza, and Myriam all left the Co-op. Patricia continued to work there into the 1990s, and as of 1995, Catalina now works there two days a week. Currently, both Patricia and Silvio paint *vasos mayas.*

Back in 1985, I talked with Orlando about the conflict that had nearly torn the Co-op asunder. He told me that he had witnessed such divisions since he had first taken the job of coordinator. Digna had already succeeded in getting one *socia* to resign in 1983, and ugly incidents between Digna and other women had continued. As a result of this pattern, Orlando continued, the *socios,* both men and women, had voted to exclude women applicants when they discussed training a new cohort to work at the Co-op during 1985. "The *socios* decided," Orlando told me, "that too many women make for problems." It turned out that Orlando had been analyzing the gender contradiction at the Co-op and in the whole country for some time, although he was at first somewhat hesitant to talk despite my questions. He relented, and began by saying that "women are the oppressed gender of Nicaragua . . . Look, in this situation it is safer for a woman to get angry toward another woman than toward men. It's men who have the real power, and if women decide to go ahead and complain about men they might really get into trouble." According to Orlando, other women have little or no power to inflict real damage, so women end up expressing their frustration with and resentment of men through their fights with other women. Yet Digna's ambitions for her son had led her to disregard caution and attack Agustín, a man. Patricia observed that even though the *socios,* both male and female, blamed the women in the Co-op for causing trouble, everyone also valued the quality of women's work. When the new cohort of students, all male, began producing mugs and other ware, the craftsmanship was shoddy. Though dismayed, none of the *socios* expressed any real surprise. When we left Nicaragua at the end of June 1985, I thought that the frustration of the younger *socias* would continue as a sideshow while the men would maintain their control over both the administration and the creative work at the Co-op. Although I did not perceive that among the *artesanas* at the Co-op a single "women's experience" or "women's critique" of work and family life existed, it had become apparent that the organizational structure at the Co-op, contextualized by the deepening economic crisis and the strident politics of a nation at war, created a set of parameters under which all the *artesanas* operated.

Outcomes and Assessments for San Juanera *Artesanas* in the Post-Sandinista Era

Eight years passed. I returned to Nicaragua alone in May of 1993. During that month and another visit two years later, I learned how the women we had known had managed their work and home lives during those years, arriving at different living arrangements and intellectual understandings of and accommodations within the constrained social, economic, and cultural possibilities available to them as *artesanas.*

In 1993, I discovered that the Co-op no longer produced the clear-glazed mugs, plates, cups, and saucers that had paid the bills during the mid-1980s. Production now focused on a simplified pre-Columbian design inscribed on small vases, large bowls, and other pots, which does not display the creative virtuosity of earlier days. No new women had been trained as *socias,* but Catalina, Patricia, and Ena continued to work, at least part-time. In general, the Co-op appeared somewhat "run down," as Agustín put it; to my eyes, it looked more like the facilities' capacity for production was being only partially utilized. All of the remaining *socias* also produced ceramics in their homes, and what they produced looked very similar to what the Co-op *socios* turn out; if anything, the former appeared of better quality than the latter. In the ensuing years, the home-based production of ceramics has in general exploded—but domestic production of ceramics no longer takes the form of what we had witnessed at the Nicoya home. Rather, domestic production of ceramics has been clearly influenced by techniques and technologies first pioneered by the Co-op *socios,* and disseminated to the entire community mostly through former and current *socios* working at home. It is no exaggeration to state that *socias,* Juanita and Catalina in particular, pioneered this new kind of domestic production.

Ester and her husband, Roberto, organized the new Cooperativa Quetzalcoatl, a retail cooperative, after the defeat of the Sandinistas in 1990. The new cooperative's *socios,* mostly women, produce ceramics in their homes, under an agreement with the co-op that it will buy a certain number of pots of consistent artistic and technical character every month at a given price. When I visited San Juan in 1993, the artisans of both the new and old co-ops as well as those producing independently at home were still reeling: the old base of customers for San Juanero ceramics—the constant flow of North American and Western European *internacionalistas* coming to see the Revolution—had dried up after Doña Violeta took power. The return of many of the old bourgeois Nicaraguans from Miami had done very little to take up the slack in the market for Nicaraguan *artesanías.* By 1995, both the old Co-op and the new, as well as virtuoso independent producers such as Agustín, had come to rely on large orders that they received mostly but not always from foreign buyers. Throughout San Juan, I heard much the same story. As I walked around San Juan's first public ceramics exhibition, held in front of San Juan's primary school in May 1995, I saw that all of the fifteen or twenty sellers' booths were staffed by women. In informal conversations with these women, they told me that although both they and their husbands participated in domestic production of ceramics, the men were also involved in cultivating whatever small parcels of land each family owned,[6] and in picking up income in any other possible way. If women do not monopolize ceramics production as they once did before the advent of the Co-op in the late 1970s, in the post-Sandinista era they again seem to predominate and are not now excluded from any aspect of its production.

After Agustín and Bladimir left the Co-op in 1987, Patricia became a designer and painter of *vasos mayas*. Even after the Co-op stopped producing them, she continued to make them at home. Yet her home life did not nourish her any more than it had before. She had not married, but had given birth to a daughter, eight years old in 1993. Her situation had increased the psychological abuse her father and brothers heaped upon her, and Patricia had internalized their extremely negative appraisal of her. She was afraid that Gia and I would think less of her, that we would no longer want her friendship, and that we would judge her negatively, as she thought the rest of the community had. Although out-of-wedlock children are and have been as common as ceramic pots in San Juan, a fact of life exploited by many men and met with resignation by many women (which Ena had so fervently denounced in 1985), Patricia believed that everyone had judged her and despised her. I assured her that mutual friends had told me about her child and that no one had expressed anything but support and empathy. But it was no use. Increased creativity in her production pottery gave her no relief from guilt and fear. When I returned to San Juan in 1995, Patricia had very recently married a man from the neighboring village of Masatepe who owned and operated a gas station north of Jinotega. Patricia was away visiting him constantly, and most of our mutual friends in San Juan had concluded that this marriage was at least in part Patricia's ticket out of the torment she had endured in her hometown.

Ena's life seemed the least changed among the women we knew. We reminisced over her own prediction that she would inevitably marry. I asked her why she had not: Actually, Ena, you look happier than you did years ago. Why is that? "I *am* happy. I can take care of my parents, I am making ceramics on my own, whatever I want." A husband? "It didn't happen, at least not yet. I am content to stay at home, producing what I like." She showed me her pots, small and well made on her own kickwheel, engraved with a variety of small designs from Lothrop's book. Ena also managed her parents' small store, the kind of corner grocery that had sprung up all over the Masaya region in the wake of the Sandinista defeat. She still had young siblings to look after. Ena had a life she was proud of.

Ester's life had also improved during the ensuing eight years, even though in founding and administering the new co-op, she and Roberto had increased their workload enormously. By 1995, they had four children; given that Roberto was staying at home much of the time to make pots, Ester frequently had his help in caring for their children, help she had not counted on years ago. In the open-air workshop behind their house, they attended to several tasks in the production of pottery: throwing pots, applying clay slip, polishing dried pots, applying glaze, loading and unloading the kiln. Their children played, were fed, took naps, were scolded amid the pots. Although when I have visited them since 1990, they have always been in the midst of filling large orders, Ester said: "You can't count on this [pointing to the large number of pots]. Maybe we won't get another order for a while. The situation is worse, but at least we work together." He's a good man, isn't he [nodding toward Roberto]? "He's all right. It's good he's at home."

Juanita's life had improved in a similar fashion after her husband returned in the late 1980s. "He left his 'other' family," Juanita told me, referring to the other woman he had lived with and the children they had together after leaving Juanita. Juanita's husband contributed some income to the household now, and helped to care for their younger children. Fortunately, Juanita had secured a relatively stable market for exporting her pottery through the agency of a North American man who bought her products on a regular monthly basis. Her main preoccupation originated in what had been her greatest fear during the 1980s: her second son, Juan, who had been only thirteen in 1984, had ended up serving in the military in 1987 and 1988. He had been stationed on an army base located in a densely wooded, moist area on the eastern slopes of the northern mountains. He had suffered a severe injury to his head, but Juanita was not sure what had actually happened to him. All she knew was that he still experienced occasional blackouts, severe headaches, and loss of peripheral vision. Juan had been the boy who made the most humorous and innovative figurines out of clay ten years earlier, and although Juanita's life had improved overall in that time, nothing could ameliorate the pain of his injury for her.

Among all the women whom we had befriended, the developments in Catalina's life took me most by surprise. Catalina had in the end and against her own estimation of life's possibilities married a man who was willing to share her life and labors relatively equally. With her husband, José Dolores, she had three children. We talked at length in 1995: What is it like in your marriage? "For example, when I am working at the Co-op, if there is anything that the children need, if there are things that should be done in the house, like give them food, help them with schoolwork, dress them, well, he does it—well, everything except washing clothes." Why is he like that? It's very different from the ways of the other Nicaraguan men we both know. "He likes to share, and if I don't get a chance to eat or to rest he understands that this is not fair; he is conscious of the need to share our tasks. So if it happens like that, I come home and take care of myself first. I don't have to take the kids right away if he's been with them." Catalina, excuse me, but I'm still amazed. You were never going to get married compared to your cousins who were. What happened? "Look, since I was young, I did the same things as the guys, whatever the work. Out on the farm too. My parents were special, I suppose. I liked to do every kind of work, everything that needed to be done. So I went with my Dad everywhere. My older sister dedicated herself to getting an excellent education. Ester was a little more choosy than me; she stayed in the house making pottery. But I always liked riding horses! So I went with my parents wherever they went, and I learned to do all the tasks that each one of them knew how to do."

With respect to the changes of the last few years at the Co-op, Catalina reiterated points we had gone over in past conversations, but she summed up her views in a clearer and more forceful fashion. What happened, I asked, to change the way work is divided at the Co-op? "Before, we women were not taught to do many things. It was this way because of the egotism of the men. They told us: these are the labors of men, these the labors of women. Then certain men left the Co-op . . . you know who they are. It was necessity, really, that gave us women the opportunity to design and paint. And now, the majority of women know how to paint." And how is it, for women in general, let's say, since the defeat of the Sandinistas? "In reality, life is quite limited, as far as economics goes both for men and women, because neither the husband nor the wife can find work in this country anymore. But much more serious is that there are very many men who do not share domestic work with their wives. Worse still are the men who do not agree with their wives on limiting the number of children [they produce]. And it is always the woman who must confront this problem in the end . . . and now, you know, in the terrible [economic] situation, children are getting sick so frequently."

Catalina has found satisfaction and fulfillment in her life, to an extent she had considered only implausible years ago. If the remarkable degree to which she has achieved an acceptable situation in both her home and work lives is exceptional, I think it is also true that none of the five women (Juanita, Catalina, Patricia, Ena, and Ester) with whom I have been talking since the defeat of the Sandinistas has experienced a reassertion or strengthening of patriarchal family relations or male control over ceramics production.

In sum, the common perception among these San Juaneras of gender-based oppression and their struggles with the genderization of their labors at home and in the workplace during the 1980s conditioned a set of demands and desires among them. *Artesanas,* like other women in Nicaragua, as the next section relates, demanded the end of violence and abuse in the home after the triumph of the Sandinistas and since their defeat as well. In loathing the conventional norms of masculine behavior, some of these *artesanas* dared to imagine a different sort of man with the capacity to share the labors of the home. *Artesanas* also demanded the right to express their creativity in *artesanía.* The two sets of demands were intricately intertwined during the early years of the Co-op; without a realignment of the division of labor in the home, women were usually unable to work in artisanal production outside the home in the old Co-op, where access to technical and aesthetic innovations was available. This did not mean that women who produced ceramics domestically were incapable of innovation, as examples from the Nicoya women and Juanita Bracamonte show. Nevertheless, the existence of the Co-op has been the main venue by which innovation has been introduced among San Juaneros as a whole and for women in particular. Changes in home-based production and reproduction in San Juan have had everything to do with women's participation in the Co-op, and the rippling out of information and techniques to other women in the community has started with current and former women *socias.* Thus, the presence of the Co-op offered the *artesanas* of San Juan both the opportunities to learn advanced production techniques and technologies and the possibility of economic empowerment within their families through the wages they earned. The changes fostered by the presence of the Co-op created the space where women could but certainly did not always confront the power of men to limit their economic options and especially their creativity. The processes of learning and struggling in the workplace, especially as the ceramics production workplace has re-extended into the home during the past ten years, thus shaped the ways these women have navigated and conceptualized the contradictions and limitations of domestic life. Have the discourses of Nicaraguan feminism since the mid-1980s addressed or illuminated *artesanas'* experiences and struggles? Given their distance from the ostensible realms of feminist politics, what can be concluded about these women's conscious subjectivity of their own lives *as women* which I have explored here?

Artesanas as Political Subjects: Conceptualizing "Voice" in the Context of Nicaraguan Feminist Discourses

My review of Nicaraguan feminist discourses is necessarily not innocent of contemporary currents in North American feminism. The deconstruction of the category of "universal woman" by Rapp (1992), of a unified feminism by Fox-Genovese (1993), E. Martin's (1996) recent historical summary of both processes, Stephen's (1993b) specific critique of the essentialized "Latin American woman," and Babb's (1997) cross-cultural comparisons of women's participation in urban informal economies together force me to reconceptualize what is meant in using the term "voice" in reference to empowerment of what are in fact many different sorts of women in Nicaragua. With respect to *artesanas,* "voice" has not necessarily manifested itself through conventional forms of discourse, such as words written or spoken, but on and through pieces of pottery, a fact I have taken a long time to realize. Then, too, the deconstruction of a universalizing concept of "woman" in Nicaraguan feminist discourse must necessarily occur in ways distinct from that process in the United States. In Nicaragua, as in the United States, this process has realigned the vectors that define identity and the relationships among these vectors, particularly class, ethnicity, and gender, in the post-Sandinista period.

Although I seek to illuminate the struggles of San Juanera and *cerámica negra artesanas* using Nicaraguan feminist discourse, it is important to remember that none of these women has ever belonged to AMNLAE or to any of the myriad organizations that form a part of the larger women's movement in contemporary Nicaragua. They did not and continue not to utilize the organizational and ideological apparatus of Nicaraguan feminism to articulate themselves as political subjects called *women*. Nevertheless, I conclude that the existence of active and vocal feminists in Nicaragua during and since the Sandinista period has made it difficult for San Juanero men to reassert the traditional patriarchal family relations in response to women's increased incomes and technical/aesthetic skill, as men did in Amatenango del Valle according to Nash (1993). Thus, without direct involvement in the feminist movement, the San Juaneras with whom we worked have benefited from it. This would be difficult to prove conclusively, and there is more than enough evidence to show that Nicaragua remains an extremely patriarchal society. Yet, as Montenegro (1992) declared, under Sandinismo women, like other subaltern groups, seized the opportunity to become political subjects. Randall (1994) writes:

The Sandinista Revolution brought young women, with their Spanish Catholic heritage of chastity and submission, out into the arena of public struggle. A decade of revolutionary government promoted women's rights in health, education, labor, leadership, and more egalitarian legislation— some of it successful, some not . . . throughout the Sandinista administration the FSLN retained control over AMNLAE and the women of AMNLAE proved incapable of cutting the cord that prevented autonomy. Still, it would be incorrect to underestimate the liberating effect that Sandinism has had upon generations of women. (34)

The words of Doña Carmela, the oldest woman in the *cerámica negra* families, underscores how the "coming of the light" after the revolutionary triumph also meant the coming to light of opinions and perspectives the Sandinistas may not necessarily have expected or wanted to hear. Such unintended consequences resulting from the mass organizing of the Sandinista period are a theme of the women's movement and of feminist discourse since the mid-1980s.

By the mid-1980s, many women among AMNLAE's leadership and rank and file emerged as advocates specifically for women's rights, especially such legal rights as child support from biological fathers, recourse from physical abuse, and equal access to land inheritance.

This rights agenda was elaborated by the same group of influential women within the Sandinista bureaucracy and from the literary intelligentsia discussed previously, and it is likely that their broaching of such themes as reproductive rights and issues of sexual identity in the Nicaraguan context stemmed from their interchanges with the international, especially the U.S., feminist community (see Randall 1981, 1994; Molyneux 1986; Angel and Macintosh 1987; and Stephens 1988). The introduction of discourses specifically focused on women's rights laid the groundwork for pointed critiques of AMNLAE and its relationship with the Frente. For example, notwithstanding AMNLAE's defense of poor women, researchers Olivera and Fernández (1991) found that the organization's political positions did not effectively reach out to or organize this constituency during the era of Sandinismo.

By the late 1980s, many of the feminists who had occupied important positions of power in the Sandinista government had grown profoundly disenchanted with AMNLAE, which they viewed, according to Michele Najlis, as "nothing more than an appendage of the [Sandinista] Party . . . run by male members of the national directorate who frequently made terrible comments about women and women's issues" (in Randall 1994: 57). These women began meeting in independent study and discussion groups, such as the PIE (Partido de la Izquierda Erótica, or Party of the Erotic Left), which addressed both the nature of women's disempowerment within the Sandinista Front as well as other feminist issues, such as abortion and lesbian and gay rights, that the Sandinistas had refused to address. Gioconda Belli, Milú Vargas, Sofía Montenegro, and the other women in the PIE who held positions within the Frente and the Nicaraguan cultural elite, used their privileged access to media, governmental forums, and educational institutions to disseminate feminist points of view. Moreover, as Montenegro confessed (in Randall 1994), their agitation bore fruit outside the centers of power, as university-trained women organized and carried out sophisticated investigative research projects concerned with conditions of life among campesina women. Initially, some of this research was sponsored by research institutions connected with the Frente, such as CIERA; by the end of the 1980s, entirely independent research was being carried out by women in CIAM (Centro de Investigación y Acción para los Derechos de la Mujer, or Center for Investigation and Social Action in Favor of Women's Rights), Cezontle (a women's resource center based in Managua), and the Centros de Mujeres health centers in Matagalpa and Masaya, among others. These investigations, many concerned with women's participation in land reform and agricultural cooperatives, focused on the gender-based division of labor in the home and the workplace and the status of women's reproductive and domestic labor. Even with this growing corpus of work, women working from both within and outside of the Frente were still unable to exercise decisive influence over the modus operandi during the last years of Sandinista rule. Doubtless this resulted from the overall economic collapse and the draconian scaling back of all state activities. Nevertheless, the outrageously sexist nature of the Sandinistas' electoral campaign of 1990, which alienated many women, cannot be entirely blamed upon either of these factors.

Women's organizations entirely independent of the Sandinista Front and committed to a broader, feminist-socialist understanding of the tasks of revolutionary transformation have greatly expanded since 1990. Such organizations have been locally focused—the Ixchen Women's Health Centers in Masaya and Matagalpa, for example—or have set out to investigate and document conditions of life for the vast majority of impoverished Nicaraguan women following the work of this kind pioneered by women working within Sandinista public policy research groups during the 1980s. In *La Mujer en las Cooperativas Agropecuarias en Nicaragua* (Women in agricultural cooperatives in Nicaragua) (1984a), the researchers of CIERA-MIDINRA outlined economic and ideological factors that either favored or impeded the participation of campesinas in the mass cooperativization of agriculture the Sandinista Front sponsored during the revolutionary period. The authors cited four case study cooperatives in the provinces of León, Chinandega, and Rivas and in the Nueva Guinea region to describe the lives of agricultural women and their roles in production, management, and reproduction in order to formulate policy recommendations specifically in favor of improving campesinas' lives across a broad spectrum of conditions. Research of this kind continued as researchers from Cezontle (see Olivera et al. 1992; Olivera and Fernández 1991) and Paola Pérez Alemán carried out a series of documentation and analysis projects. Pérez Alemán worked with the government's Instituto Nicaragüense de la Mujer (Nicaraguan Institute of the Woman) and produced *Industria, genero y mujer en Nicaragua* (Industry, gender and woman in Nicaragua) (1989) concerned with women workers in the textile industry. As an independent researcher with the nongovernmental CIAM, she published *Organización, identidad y cambio* (Organization, identity, change) (1990), which again focused on campesinas in agricultural cooperatives. These works emphasized the economic, political, and ideological analysis of women's labor in both the home and the workplace that shaped my discussions of *artesanas'* life experiences elaborated above.

Underlying the work of Pérez Alemán and the Cenzontle researchers is a socialist-feminist perspective,[7] as distinct from an orthodox Marxist or class analysis. This position is predicated on an understanding of Nicaragua's "inheritance of a dependent capitalist society, in which profit, the growth of wage labor, and private ownership of resources generates class differentiation between the owners and non-owners of the means of production, accompanied by unequal distribution of wealth and power. In this exploitative system of production, associated with capitalist development, women take the roles of agricultural day-laborer, campesina, market vendor, artisan, industrial worker, [or] maid" (Pérez Alemán, Martínez, and Widmaier 1989: 22). But a socialist-feminist position also describes women's oppression through analysis of the "system of gender, which is created and reproduced, as much in the domestic sphere as in the realm of production, [as well as in] hierarchical relations of unequal power between men and women, expressed in male-female roles, in the sexual division of labor, in 'the masculine' and 'the feminine,' which are nourished by the socialization [of individuals] at various levels, generating and maintaining these asymmetries" (21).

Cezontle's Mercedes Olivera and her research team have used the socialist-feminist analysis to address the historical origins of both patriarchal ideology and women's economic domination in the domestic and public spheres. In *Nicaragua: El poder de las mujeres* (Nicaragua: The power of women) (1992) Olivera used the work of historian German Vargas Romero to identify the eighteenth century as the period during which Nicaraguan patriarchy and machismo coalesced. The demographic crash of indigenous civilizations, the predominance of males among the Spanish colonists, and the economic imperatives of empire determined a "model of domination":

[Male] sexual license created a cultural form, a model of socially acceptable conduct that greatly subordinated women. This was fundamentally due to the utilization of women as reproducers of the [greatly diminished] workforce, with the consequent devalorization of female sexuality . . . [Thus] the model of domination conjugated subordination of women, class exploitation, and ethnic discrimination . . . The "double day" [of women] also was part of the model. Women were obligated to give service as part of colonial tribute. Their free domestic labor, sometimes for government officials, or plantation owners, or church authorities, was frequently accompanied by sexual relations, always disadvantageous for women . . . [therefore] the "double day" originated under colonial domination . . . [and] we can affirm that the roots of the model of marital relations also originated during colonialism. (Olivera et al. 1992: 66–68)

In the previously mentioned *Organización, identitidad y cambio* (1990), Pérez Alemán used socialist-feminist insights to examine the role of UNAG (Unión Nacional de Agricultores y Ganaderos, National Union of Farmers and Ranchers), the Sandinista campesinos' organization, in responding to the main problems confronting the peasants as a class. She found that UNAG had also addressed problems of key concern to peasant women, such as food supplies, commodity prices, and public health, which because of the division of labor in the countryside became the responsibility of women. UNAG's leadership, according to Pérez Alemán, had not remained bound to a purely class-based analysis, and had worked actively to recruit women into the agricultural cooperative movement and to provide resources to them for their survival and the survival of their families. They did so without challenging to any significant extent the way that gender structures the division of labor and the inequalities women suffer as a consequence. This was particularly problematic because by becoming involved in agricultural cooperatives under the current regime of the domestic division of labor, campesinas doubled their workload:

There is no explicitly conscious analysis that reflects a more challenging approach to the subordination that women endure. Alongside the attention to women's survival, there is no attention to their subordination, which stems from problems of abuse, the double shift, lack of control over reproductive capacity, male irresponsibility, etc. For example, the fact that domestic reproduction is female work has not been questioned on a collective level. There is scarcely any attention paid to getting men involved in community work, which is considered exclusively women's responsibility.

So, while UNAG has departed from a strictly class-oriented approach, its attention to the private domestic sphere comes from a purely traditional perspective. (Pérez Alemán 1990: 136)

Pérez Alemán saw no alternative except a direct attack upon the patriarchal ideology ensconced among the Nicaraguan campesinos. She advocated a radical educational project based in the agricultural cooperatives, the purpose of which would be explicitly to generate new, nonsexist social values and relations. This project would also demand a consciousness-raising campaign among UNAG's local and national leadership, who would in turn work toward a gender-egalitarian society in the countryside. In such a society, women would cease to be the objects of oppression in the workplace and the home and become instead fully empowered political subjects.

I think that Pérez Alemán would likely be the first to admit that these proposals are highly optimistic, perhaps even utopian: Nicaragua's persistent and ever-increasing impoverishment, the defeat of the Sandinistas and the advent of a nonrevolutionary Nicaraguan state under UNO's weak leadership that made no commitment to challenging patriarchal culture (in fact, much to the contrary), have simply exacerbated the overall crisis confronting Nicaraguan campesinos in the form of resource decline, decreasing productivity, and competition from imports. Nevertheless, the socialist-feminist perspective and the programmatics of Pérez Alemán and others advanced a specifically Nicaraguan feminist discourse in two vital ways. First, the independent researchers empirically established the complex relationships between women's roles in and the genderized inequality of domestic reproduction and commodity production. Second, these researchers created a basis from which to begin combining feminist analysis with other analyses of social inequality, out of which a multidimensional picture of daily lived identities can emerge. The campesina, in other words, must be understood and heard both as a woman and as a farmer, a member of an agricultural cooperative, and a rural person.

The extent to which this literature, which focuses so overwhelmingly on peasant women, is relevant to the experiences, choices, and ideas of *artesanas* is still questionable. One example of research conducted among *artesanas* is a chapter in a volume of women's life histories, *La vida cotidiana de la mujer campesina* (Daily life for the woman peasant), published by CIERA in 1989. In this volume, the experiences of a San Juanera named María Dolores as told in her own words is shown to differ very little from the life histories of the seven agricultural women whose stories constitute the rest of the book. María Dolores learns to make ceramics from her mother, and from the first enjoys this work with a tremendous gusto that enables her to support herself through the production and sale of pottery. Unfortunately, she and her children also undergo a cycle of physical abuse from her alcoholic husband, abuse that her mother suffered at the hands of María Dolores's alcoholic father and which in the context of the other life histories in this volume comes to typify the lives of campesinas. Forced by her husband's perennial irresponsibility to support her children through ceramics production, her body is wracked by illness and exhaustion caused by the double load of labors she bears. The editors of this volume represent the patriarchal brutality of the home as the source of rural women's oppression. The information we gathered from among San Juaneras with whom we worked does not necessarily depart greatly from this description. It is not so much that male alcoholism, irresponsibility, and abuse do not play as large a role in the lives of the San Juaneras I know as they did in the life of María Dolores. The difference, I would argue, is the role played by the Co-op in the lives of the women we came to know. Working at the Co-op shaped a complex understanding of themselves, their creativity, and the range of choices available to them in the home and at work, once again underscoring the need for an analysis of these *artesanas* that combines the vector of gender with other identity factors.

Montenegro's work offers parameters to frame such analyses. In her article "Nuestra madre: La Malinche" (Our mother: La Malinche) (1992), Montenegro reviewed the way the story of La Malinche—a young woman from a people conquered by the Aztec Empire, who was sold into slavery and ended up in the hands of the Spaniards, who became trilingual and highly knowledgeable about the political complexities of central Mexico—has been perverted by the patriarchal mythology of the Mexican Revolution. In Octavio Paz's (1959) highly influential reading of that mythology, La Malinche is considered the mother of the mestizo Mexican nation, but at the same time is despised and blamed as a defiled, fallen, raped woman: a whore. Like Cypess (1991) and Kaminsky (1994), Montenegro uncovered the ideological roots of women's victimization in Latin America's mestizo societies in the patriarchal interpretation of La Malinche, and then called for a revisionist view of La Malinche that celebrates instead of denigrates her role in the creation of the mestizos. In a more profoundly realized, unpublished manifesto entitled "Identidad y colonialismo: El retorno de La Malinche" (Identity and colonialism: The return of La Malinche) (n.d.), Montenegro linked her revision of La Malinche to feminist scholarship concerned with the origins of patriarchal social relations and religion. In this text, she outlined a feminist theory of race and ethnicity with at least two goals in mind. First, she fused the analysis of gender inequality to the analysis of ethnic and racial hierarchies and oppression in Mexico and Central America. Second, Montenegro proposed a "re-Indianization" of the mestizo peoples of this region that would begin with a reconstruction of gender relations. Her utopian vision, inspired by the hypothetical society Eisler (1987) called "gilania," creates a paradox: Montenegro's call for a re-ethnicization and a re-genderization of Central America seems to be a nonnationalist emancipatory project that would take place within the framework of the existing nations of the area. This particular anchoring of gender relations to ethnic and race relations poses new questions for the analysis of the artisans of Nicaragua, of national cultural identity, and of the significance of *El Güegüence* to these histories, as the next chapter investigates.

When I received the following letter from María Esthela Rodríguez de Pineda, I realized that, in a way that seems to resonate with Montenegro's declarations, the *cerámica negra* women were linking their own analysis of gender to another vector of identity: ethnicity. The "re-Indianization" of their craft, a decade after they had rejected the Ministry of Culture's attempts to do so in favor of hitching themselves to UNADI's class project, stems from a more widespread realignment of views about ethnic and national history in the north of Nicaragua bound up with the indigenous rights movement of the 1990s, as we shall see. I was nonetheless initially quite surprised by the manifestation of this realignment in María Esthela's letter.

Dear Les:

I hope that this finds you well, together with your family, and greetings to Gia.

I am very sorry that I was so late in writing what follows, but we have had many problems and I could not get to it before.

Cerámica Negra of Nicaragua: A History

Cerámica negra has been dated by archaeologists to the formative period (1500 B.C.–A.D. 400).

Careful study of indigenous art attributes to the Chorotegas the Bright Polychrome Ceramics exemplified by the zoomorphic and anthropomorphic spherical vessels from the great pre-Columbian culture of Nicoya.

Cerámica negra, with its smooth polished surface, is the unknown treasure of the northern mountains of this country, above all from Matagalpa and Jinotega. Jinotega is where cerámica negra originated. This form of ceramics is characterized by a velvety jet-black finish, with delicate floral engraving achieved with indigenous techniques from the pre-colonial era.

At present, only nine women from the family are working in cerámica negra, who are afraid that within an appointed time the craft could die out, for there are no longer any people in the family interested in maintaining this art-form.

Cerámica negra is distinctly a hand-made craft, and there is no use of any kind of mold in making a piece. After the piece has dried out to the extent deemed necessary by the women, they proceed to level all the rough edges of each piece, leaving it wholly even, after which they go on to give it its first polish. After a determined time, they proceed to give it a second polish and after more time they go ahead and give it a third polish with sea-stones. After they have brought out the necessary gloss on the piece, they go on to give it the jet-black color characteristic of cerámica negra. The color of cerámica negra is natural; no type of oxide is used in our ceramics. The tools used in making this ceramics are crafted by the women that make it.

In the past, they made cerámica negra pieces which were utilitarian, for example jugs or pitchers. This pot was used to cool water in the days when refrigeration did not exist. Pots were also used to cook soups or other foods, such as coffee pots for making coffee as well.

At present, we have formed a collective in which we are organized to make cerámica negra and to sell it ourselves, without any intermediaries but instead directly from producer to customer.

We have carried out many experiments in order to improve the quality of cerámica negra and to increase our production. While we have achieved improvements, increasing production is very difficult, I dare say impossible. For if we make large quantities of pieces we could lose them because all our work is by hand and we do not have the capacity to finish more than ten pieces weekly. If the pieces are big, we can only finish off two. When all is said and done, the women who make cerámica negra do so because we enjoy it and because it is our source of work. We have experimented with it from love of this art which is a gift that God has given us and placed in our hands. If it were not this way, I do not believe we would be making ceramics.

There is much variety in cerámica negra, since each woman has specialized in her line of work; some make miniatures, others medium-sized pieces, others pieces a bit larger, and others even larger, each according to her style of work.

The techniques for making cerámica negra do not differ much from other types of ceramics; what constitutes the unknown technical aspect is the technique for blackening the pieces.

The technique consists of placing the piece in a bed of wood shavings and coffee-bean shells when it reaches a very high temperature. When the piece is in contact with the heat this produces a natural chemical reaction, catching on fire around the piece which acquires almost immediately the black color which is characteristic.

From the task of going to the mountains to bring the raw materials, to the process of making and finishing the pieces, this is the work of women. Within the craft of cerámica negra, there are men, but none of them have taken this art-form as their profession.

Fear grows stronger among the women every time they fire pots they have made because more and more frequently they are losing more pots than are coming out well. For this reason, cerámica negra is costly, for it is after firing all the pots that they record whether a few or many pieces broke, and such is their disenchantment. But they continue making it as before, for they carry this art in the blood.

Well, Les, I believe I have contributed a few ideas for your book. I would like to have some news from you all, and know whether these ideas arrived in time for your editing because I forgot in what month you were going to send it to be printed.

Regards to Gia and all the children, and also to you.

Your sister,
María Esthela Rodríguez, Coordinator of Cerámica Negra

In light of Montenegro's work and the turn toward reexamining the ethnic history of western Nicaragua which I discuss next, it occurs to me that there is a more pointed way to read the silence of Suche-Malinche as an anti-essentialist parable. Whereas the Mexican

Malinche was an Indian who was sold to the Spaniards and subsequently birthed the first mestizos, the Nicaraguan Malinche was the daughter of the Spanish governor who does not appear again with her ostensible mate. I wonder why the author(s) of *El Güegüence* inscribed such a key reversal of the position and thus symbolism of La Malinche vis-à-vis the Mexican narrative, where her name and symbolic history originated; pondering that reversal fuels my retelling of her silence as parable. In Nicaragua, Malinche was a European and thus imbued with that power: in the play she is costumed and adorned with the symbols of Castillian wealth. If her silence renders her power just implicit, we may ask nevertheless where, if she chooses to consummate her marriage with the son of the subaltern Güegüence, the power in that marriage will reside. Who is to say what the identities of their children may be? As silent figure in this parable, Suche-Malinche draws the attention of readers and spectators to the power La Malinche holds merely by keeping quiet amid so much absurdity. The men, the powerful and the disempowered alike, are either buffoons or taken in by buffoonery, and thus we are left to conclude that it will be she who decides the future identity of community after the end of the play. This parable resonates with Montenegro's utopian notion that feminism will provide the basis for reconstructing ethnic identity in Nicaragua, but leaves hanging the question of the identities of the ethnic groups implicated.

Chapter 4

The Time of the Blue Thread

Knowledge and Truth about Ethnicity in

Western Nicaragua

Interpreting the Blue Thread

The most essentialized nationalist interpretations of *El Güegüence,*
such as those presided over by Pablo Antonio Cuadra and Francisco
Pérez Estrada, celebrated the last moments of the play in particular.
When Güegüence proclaims "Ah, in my time, when I was a boy, in
the time of the blue thread [*el hilo azul*], when you could see in the
fields of the Diriomos, lifting up those packs of guavas [*fardos de
guayabas*], isn't that right, boys?" (Lejarza 1993: 49), these authors
understood this as an admission of the final defeat of the indigenous
peoples of western Nicaragua and their submission to the domination of a new mestizo people: the Nicaraguan people. In his ever-
popular volume of essays, *El Nicaragüense* (The Nicaraguan) (1981),
Cuadra almost gushes: "The lands of the Pacific [in Nicaragua] are
the region of the easy life. Their great fertility, healthfulness, and the
ease with which communication can be maintained over its terrains
have attracted since prehistory the densest populations and initiated
the development of the principal indigenous cultures from which our
mestizo Nicaraguan culture was created" (209).

The time of the blue thread was the good old days, as Arellano explained, and the nostalgia Güegüence evokes underscores just how
distant those days already had become by the end of the play and how
irretrievable they would forever be. This trope is the backbone for
the characteristic assumption among twentieth-century elite Nicaraguan intellectuals: "the commonsense notion that Nicaragua is an
ethnically homogeneous society," which Gould calls the "myth of
Nicaragua mestiza" (1993: 428).

The myth of Nicaragua mestiza, in both Somocista and Sandinista forms, narrates the transformation of communities of indigenous peoples into lower-class individuals whose formerly collective ethnic identity was replaced by allegiance to a nonethnic, Nicaraguan national identity. For elite intellectuals such as Cuadra and other *El Güegüence* commentators, this narrative occasionally recognized that the supposedly extinct indigenous societies had in some way "contributed" to the richness of Nicaraguan national culture. The Sandinista Front's explicit rejection of the social injustices of the long history of elite domination that had culminated in the tyranny of Somocismo and the economic prostration of Nicaragua was not accompanied by a decisive departure from the myth of Nicaragua mestiza, as Wheelock's *Las raices Indígenas de la lucha anti-colonialista en Nicaragua* (1981) showed. Throughout the twentieth century, the myth thus produced bodies of knowledge that confirmed its initial assumptions, becoming an integral part of the elite construction of Nicaraguan national identity.

Focusing on the indigenous communities of Sutiava (1990b), Matagalpa (1993), and the central plateau province of Chontales (1995), Gould punctured the Foucauldian regime of truth established by the myth of Nicaragua mestiza, even showing how peasants without readily identifiable indigenous history utilized a discourse of indigenous ethnicity to defend their lands (see 1990a). At cross purposes with the myth of Nicaragua mestiza, western Nicaraguan communities that self-identify as indigenous and are locally and nationally recognized as ethnically indigenous continued to exist into this century. The entrance of Gould's counternarrative of indigenous history coincided with the appearance of an indigenous movement among these communities in western Nicaragua during the postrevolutionary 1990s. Like Gould's work the history of western Nicaragua, according to the indigenous movement's leaders, documents the extent to which indigenous peoples survived into the twentieth century. By demonstrating the failure of the myth of Nicaragua mestiza, movement leaders foreground contemporary struggles by indigenous communities to regain land and cultural rights. These counterhistories recall Alejandro Dávila Bolaños's interpretation of *El Güegüence,* which construed the play as an anticolonial guerrilla theater that proclaimed Nicaraguan identity in opposition to the domination of Spanish culture, the Catholic religion, and white skin.

My contact with and understanding of the contemporary indigenous movement in western Nicaragua derive primarily from my
friendship with Flavio Gamboa, which began in 1993. Flavio's particular counterhistory of Nicaragua and Nicaraguan indigenous peoples is not a full-fledged counterparable that simply reverses the
nationalist parable narrated by Cuadra and the others. For Flavio,
the blue thread *is* a symbol of indigenous survival rather than of defeat, a manifestation of the historical thread of continuity; however,
Flavio does *not* assert that the blue thread in this guise is a trope for
a very different Nicaraguan national character based on indigenous
identity. In a resonant manner, the indigenous movement is struggling for the indigenous minority in western Nicaragua, rather than
for a full-scale reconstruction of Nicaraguan national identity. But
Flavio's (and the movement's) counterhistory may not be the only
way to reconstruct the meaning of the blue thread.

As in the previous chapter, I choose to understand Güegüence's
elusive reference to the time of the blue thread as an anti-essentialist
parable. In this chapter, I will illustrate this understanding by means
of two thematic contrasts. First, the contrast between the reactions
of different artisan communities to the appearance of the indigenous
movement since the electoral defeat of the Frente exemplifies the contrast between the blue thread as counterhistory, on the one hand, and
as anti-essentialist parable on the other. The *cerámica negra* women
have embraced an indigenous origin for their craft, as María Esthela's
letter at the end of the previous chapter indicated, and aligned their
families with the indigenous movement of the Matagalpa region and
its narrative of indigenous survival in western Nicaragua. The artisans of San Juan de Oriente have not become involved with the indigenous movement, even though one of its central arenas is located
in nearby Monimbó, where Flavio lives. Instead, San Juaneros and
ceramic production in San Juan have entered a new period of highly
individualized production and marketing of their wares, described
at the end of the previous two chapters. My attempts to draw San
Juanero friends and acquaintances into a discourse about identity—
mestizo, indigenous, or any combination thereof—have been met by
a consistent response drawing my attention back to their work, back
to their daily lives as potters.

"What do *you* mean by indigenous identity, Les?" Agustín Amador asked me at his house. He was not necessarily tired of the topic,

which we had been discussing for two weeks already, but he seemed to enjoy turning the questions back on me in front of Flavio. Flavio was showing Agustín a ceramic pre-Columbian ocarina he had found near Monimbó, and listening intently to this exchange.

"Language, beliefs, dress, that sort of thing," I responded, immediately surprised by my instinctually trait-driven responses.

"There is none of that here," Agustín replied dryly. "Here, we are potters, the old families that have always lived here, and the newer families as well. Pottery is being Indian. But pottery is what we do, and being Indian is not really our concern."

In another conversation some days later, Catalina Bracamonte remarked, "I guess being a Bracamonte, in my family, that means you are a potter. And if you are a potter here, you are an Indian. Although some people don't like to be called Indian, Les, I'll tell you that, well, this is what we are."

In a third conversation, Juanita Bracamonte laughed at the subject when I brought it up. "You know that already," she observed. "Here in San Juan, we make pottery. That's enough said about our identity."

These remarks, laconic, friendly, and tolerant, draw my attention back to Güegüence's precise words in his famous declamation. He did not wax nostalgically for a declining indigenous language or religion or other specifically ethnic traits, but recalled two aspects of daily life: homespun, hand-dyed thread and agricultural labors. His words are those of a native of Masaya-Carazo, whose memories reference the products of artisan-craft and local agriculture. His nostalgia is thus for the life of this region, which he gave up to become a con artist and parasite of the rich, and it points back to the bedrock of that daily life: cloth, its characteristic color, the fruit from the hills of Masaya-Carazo, the rhythm of work. As a parable told from the vantage of Masaya-Carazo, Güegüence's words suggest that if continuity and community are to be found they will be found in the practices of daily work and the materials out of which life is made, rather than through either the pretensions of the wealthy or the illusions of the foolish. Such a parable reinforces a sense of identity that is not specifically ethnic but is local and communal, and underscores the meaningfulness artisans find in their daily lives.

This rereading also outlines the second and more profound thematic contrast in this chapter: between my own interpretations and the interpretations of my colleague, informant, and friend, Flavio

Gamboa. The sections that follow contrast our different perspectives concerning the decline of indigenous ethnic markers, especially indigenous languages. In many ways, we disagree about the nature of continued indigenous identity, notwithstanding the decline of indigenous ethnic markers, about the nature of mestizo identity, and the significance of the contemporary indigenous movement, especially vis-à-vis the artisans. The contrast between our views is complicated by both the collaboration between us, over which in this text I continuously exercise the authorial power to have the last word, and by the larger framework of transforming relationships between local organic and metropolitan intellectuals at the close of this century (see Field 1996). Ethnic and racial identities as elaborated by organic intellectuals are almost always discourses concerned with traits that define who is and is not included in groups; meanwhile, contemporary anthropologists and other social scientists are engaged in analyses that inevitably attempt to deconstruct identity discourses by laying bare their historical construction. It is well to recall Friedman's (1994) warning, even if, as I have previously stated, one disagrees with his near-dialectical opposition between the work of metropolitan and indigenous intellectuals:

If one is engaged in "negotiating culture," that is, involved in the construal and interpretation of ethnographic or historical realities, then one is bound on a collision course with others for whom such realities are definitive. Culture is supremely negotiable for professional culture experts, but for those whose identity depends upon a particular configuration this is not the case. Identity is not negotiable. Otherwise it has no existence . . . The constitution of identity is an elaborate and deadly serious game of mirrors. It is a complex temporal interaction of multiple practices of identification external and internal to a subject or population. In order to understand the constitutive process it is, thus, necessary to be able to situate the mirrors in space and their movement in time. (140–41)

The contrasts between Flavio's and my selective historical reconstructions present a test case for whether or not social science can offer nonessentializing analysis of identity discourses, and whether this can be carried out in the context of relationships with the intellectuals elaborating those discourses. Both Flavio and I realize that our historical projects have not been as comprehensive as academic historians would prefer, nor have our projects maintained a discrete boundary separating them from each other; but we have agreed to follow topics of mutual interest toward different ends. I cannot deny, however, that this text inscribes his projects within mine, even when we disagree.

The juxtaposition of our different analyses in this book also constitutes an attempt on my part to evaluate the changes in a nationalist regime of truth—the myth of Nicaragua mestiza—and the possible implications for an overall reconstruction of Nicaraguan national identity. Such an attempt has been carried out in light of the shortcomings, or better said, the difficulties encountered in operationalizing Foucauldian theories of power and knowledge and the Gramscian hegemony/counterhegemony dynamic which I discussed in the introduction. It would actually be quite foolhardy to argue that an absolute decline of the myth of Nicaragua mestiza is taking place, given the election of successively more conservative, conventional, and elitist governments since the Sandinista defeat.[1] Yet Sandinista cultural policy helped to underwrite the current proliferation of identity discourses in western Nicaragua, and in the aftermath of the Sandinista electoral defeat identity politics, even among the artisan communities, have not assumed a single or coherent form. In the current situation, competing sorts of knowledge about local and national identity form part of the social, political, and economic struggles of non-elite sectors whose intellectual voices were unleashed by the revolutionary process of Sandinismo. This is a cat neither the Sandinistas nor the elites can put back in its bag.

The ongoing transformations of local and national identities in Nicaragua are haunted by the grimace of Macho Ratón, Güegüence's potential alter ego. At the very end of the drama, Güegüence once again nostalgically declaims: "Let me recall my old times, that I may console myself with that. Say, boys, are we going forward or backward?" (Lejarza 1993: 49).[2] This question is now more appropriate than ever and more worthy of a grimace. In the elite parable of national identity, Macho Ratón's expression signified ironic and pained self-deprecation in the face of the putative extinction of indigenous peoples in western Nicaragua. At the end of the twentieth century, Macho Ratón's grimace could express disgust at the multiple indeterminacies of indigenous and mestizo identity situated within the disastrous neoliberal economics of a revived elitist state.

Histories of the Indigenous Peoples:
Converging and Diverging Analytic Strands

Flavio and I have fueled one another's respective fascination with the decline of markers of indigenous identity, especially language, in relation to the historical transformation of indigenous peoples in western Nicaragua following the Spanish Conquest. Such a focus originates in multiple ways for each of us. My interest in part reflects the conventional Boasian linkage between language and cultural identity, as well as the cultural survivalist preoccupation with the fate of minority and endangered languages. Beyond such stereotypical anthropological concerns, linguistic anthropologists such as Hill and Hill (1985) and Urban (1991) have suggested that the speaking of indigenous languages may not necessarily map onto discrete indigenous ethnic identities. But the central focus of my inquiry is necessarily the place of artisan communities in the history of Nicaraguan identity politics, during which these artisan communities have on the whole maintained an anomalous, even capricious position. My perspective relies on a social constructionist analysis of the presence and absence of indigenous languages and other markers vis-à-vis the construction of identity.

This metropolitan view is frequently tangential to Flavio's motivations for tracing and analyzing the decline of indigenous languages in western Nicaragua. He is concerned, first of all, to demonstrate the relationship between that decline and the oppressive nature of colonial and postcolonial states in Nicaragua, such that it became necessary for indigenous peoples to cease speaking their languages in order to survive that brutality. His other major concern is to create sentiment within the contemporary indigenous movement in favor of resuscitating at least one indigenous language, Nahuatl, as a way of epitomizing the survival and revival of indigenous peoples in the region; this is not immediately evident in the following essay, but he has told me so. Much more apparently, Flavio's essay constitutes an attempt to contribute new information to the interpretive discourse about *El Güegüence,* which valorizes the specific ethnic Mangue essence of the play, and emphatically validates local history and identity in the Masaya region, an agenda that is both explicitly political and academic in nature. In general, he is not as concerned about artisans as I am.

THE MANKEMES AND THEIR LANGUAGE
BY FLAVIO GAMBOA

The territory of the Mankesa, a broad band of land on the Pacific coast of Central America, stretches from the [shores] of Lake Xolotlan to the Gulf of Nicoya [Costa Rica].[3] Its inhabitants were known as Mankemes and their language Mangue, and it was composed of twenty-eight chiefdoms or states. The capital was "the City of the Peaks," Diria. Each chiefdom had its own social structure, and the twenty-eight local governments met every seven lunar *soles,* that is every seven years, to elect between them the Diriankeme that would govern them from his power as "Prince and Lord of the Twenty-Eight Chiefdoms for Seven Years." The Nahuatl speakers named this person the Calachuni. The Mankeme were the only ethnic group in Cemanahuac (the Americas) that, having settled and established their social structure, traveled northward occupying other lands, such as Quirigua, Copan, Palenque, and the eastern Aztec coasts (Chiapas).[4]

This territory was split by a migration of Nahuatl speakers who came from Mexico and was led by Xutecucali in the years between A.D. 1000 and 1100, taking possession of a small territory from the Ochomogo River (Nicaragua) to the Sapoa River (Costa Rica).[5] From this territory six chiefdoms moved north in the modern territory of Nicaragua and others moved southward into what is now Costa Rica. Of the fifteen remaining chiefdoms that stayed in the original territory, a few survive even to this day. Every time disagreements occurred among the chiefdoms, they sent an ambassador with food as a declaration of war. Before entering into the combat of war, the bravest warriors moved forward and forming an entrenchment on either side, the adversaries made a series of gestures towards each other in order to display their bravery, capacity to intimidate and thereby obtain a final victory through these sorts of mimicries which today are known as theater.[6]

On the twelfth of October 1492 began the total destruction of Cemanahuac, exterminated and brutalized by the Spanish system which initiated the colonial effort with the scourge of Spanish prisons. Antonio de Mendoza, in 1550 made the first viceroy of New Spain (Mexico), experienced problems understanding the subjugated populations that still spoke innumerable languages. For this reason, it was necessary to establish a single language for which he sought the help of the king to find a solution. After a long time, Antonio de Mendoza passed away and Luis de Velasco took his place as the second viceroy. By order of the king, he named the alcaldes de vara,[7] a nominal position without any authority that likely served as a spy for the viceroy against his own people.

The royal order abolishing languages arrived and was enforced without delay. All legations, warrants and official requests had to be in Nahuatl and written as the Spanish authorities mandated. This law extended over the confines of the entire New World, and in this way played a role in the definitive and mortal blow to the Native peoples of Cemanahuac which was the expropriation of the Mother Earth from them. Without the right to use their own languages and to worship their own deities, this was total genocide.

The Mankemes spoke their own language until the middle of the seventeenth century, at which point the Nahuatl language was introduced and the Castillianization of Native personal names began. However, historians, researchers, and writers agree that the writing of *El Güegüence* dates from the sixteenth century and the first performances of it occurred in the streets of Masaya, due to the discontent of the Native peoples against the sub-deputy of the governor and the other Spanish authorities who committed all sorts of abuses. These authorities lived in the town which is now the city of Granada, which has been attacked constantly by buccaneers and pirates.[8]

In his memoirs, Agustín de Gamboa [Flavio's great-grandfather] tells us that in 1810 the performances of *Güegüence* were suspended for a number of years by the higher authorities under the pretext of the immoral phrases uttered in the play, such as "natikupunah" (son of the great whore), "nasamame" (sickly person), "kuylón" (hermaphrodite), "guatepok" (prostitute), "naha pendíh" (cuckold). Such phrases provided motivation for mutilating various speeches in the play. In this year (1810) the play was performed by old men, who confessed that they were no longer good for much else, that if they were imprisoned or killed for performing, they had nothing to lose. By contrast, the young people were persecuted for their participation by the judges from Milpa with forced labor without payment and peonage to landlords who might sell them into slavery to work in the silver mines of Bolivia. Thus the play *El Güegüence* is known as the dance of the old men.

Anonymous works do not enjoy much prestige, and much less those of indigenous origin. The famous Nicaraguan Rubén Darío categorized this work as frivolous, "the moan of a jungle Indian," and other authors who preceded Rubén said much the same. The only author who had the courage to affirm that which is indigenous and born of Mankesa was Alejandro

Dávila Bolaños.[9] His version of *El Güegüence* is the best translation of all those that exist. In his book, this writer accepted two words as Mangue: "ñonguan" and "cumbataci." By contrast, Carlos Mántica accepted only one, "ñonguan," and two as origin unknown: "escataci" and "incumbataci." These and the other translators view the word "mo" as Nahuatl and they attribute to it diverse uses as an honorific, used not to indicate authority but courage. Walter Lehmann did not find an explanation for this phrase and the others, although his version is the one used in Diriamba during the performances of the patronal celebrations there. Most Mangue words have many meanings, and are not used in a singular mode or expressed with only one set of tones, but instead are used in agreement with the subject under discussion. Wherefore, this idiom is more expressive than the Spanish language, and for this reason the translations that do not address variations in tone, form and meaning have stayed static and mordant.

For example, "Ñonguan" is not a man named Juan, nor is "Don Juan" more accurate. The word becomes a reference to power, nobility, and wealth if it is used to initiate a conversation; it can also be used in conjunctions if it comes after a subject or in the middle of a declamation, or if it is pronounced as a smooth proclamation: "Ñonnguann." The correct interpretation would be "Ñor" as in "señor."

"Escataci" refers to God the Father of the white people, as seen in line 113 in the *El Güegüence* of Alejandro Dávila Bolaños.

"Incumbataci" is an entreaty to the son of God of the white people who lives in the clouds or high places.

"Mo" is a Mangue word which can be said with various tones—weak, strong, and harmonious—which lends meaning of variable significance depending upon the position of the subject. In any of the translations of line 238, we can find the word "mo" used to apply to two persons, one of authority and high lineage, the other without commission or office but with lineage. The first usage is a strong expression directed at the alguacil mayor as a man of authority, but in a petitioning tone of voice.

The second usage is an expression with a smooth harmonious tone, directed at a lady of high lineage such as Lady Suche-Malinche. If the lady does not possess any such rank, "mo" would have a weak tone without harmony.

However, in line 8, the alguacil gives two different phonetic tones to the word "mo." The first use represents authority and is directed toward the governor, who requires this.

The second was used with someone who once held but no longer holds power, and the tone in this case is calm.

The variety of forms and tones is similar to the case of "hó" in Chinese, which features guttural tones and must be understood in its various forms in accordance with the subject of the sentence, or in the case of the letter "N" in other languages, including among the Mayas for whom the symbol or glyph "N" was the symbol of the snake at the same time that the word for this reptile was written with that symbol as the letter "N" (also the case for the Sanskrit "naga," the Thai "nahh," or the Hebrew "nahash").[10]

The tonal diversity in many of the words of the Mangue language made this a rich idiom and difficult to compare to other languages.

Flavio's essay represents not only his historical recounting of Spanish colonialism and its repression of Indian identity, but an attempt to reclaim the Mangue language from the obscurity of extinction, and thus to reinsert its significance in a literary and world linguistic context. This is the reason, I believe, his essay becomes steadily oriented more toward linguistics and less toward history as it develops, serving to assert an essentialized notion of identity based on language. While embracing Dávila Bolaños's interpretation of *El Güegüence,* Flavio emphasizes the local over the national: he tells an anticolonial story about the Mangue of Masaya-Carazo, not about the entire country. His essentialism is also both anticolonial and antiquarian — because Mangue is irretrievably lost and the Mankesa homeland has not been included in any atlas for hundreds of years. This is an essentialism that is not readily accessible or composed of common knowledge materials; it has been elaborated and made real by someone willing to expend time and resources carrying out extended research by himself and with scholars who can access more sources than he can alone. Undoubtedly, this explains a great deal about Flavio's collaboration with metropolitan academics, including myself.[11]

My historical reconstruction of the decline and transformation of indigenous ethnic markers in western Nicaragua relies on several sources, some of which remain unavailable to Flavio because they have not been translated into Spanish. Ultimately, however, I am not sure how different our presuppositions are. Never mind my nonessentialist intentions: the sources for my narrative are mostly bound up with the essentialist schema of anthropological convention. For example, to discuss the linguistically diverse waves of emigration from central, western, and southern Mexico that prior to the arrival of the Spaniards in the 1520s settled the Pacific littoral of what is now western Nicaragua, anthropologists have used ethniclike labels for regions and groups, notwithstanding our usually very partial understanding of their languages and despite our almost total ignorance about how these peoples understood and named their political and cultural identities and boundaries. Mason (1973) described two large linguistic populations: first, the speakers of Mangue and other Chorotega languages, which form a part of the Oto-Manguean language family and whose settlements reached from the Gulf of Fonseca to just south of the colonial city of Granada by the tenth century; and second, the speakers of Nicarao, a Nahuatl dialect, who had concentrated on the Isthmus of Rivas by about A.D. 1200. A smaller group, the speakers of the Maribio language, of an uncertain linguistic affiliation called Tlapaneca-Yopi, lived in the region where the colonial city of León was later built. Demographer Linda Newson (1987), whose work is widely cited and respected, archaeologists such as Lange and Bishop (1988), as well as Nicaraguan scholars such as Julian C. Guerrero and Lola Soriano de Guerrero (1982) and Jaime Wheelock (1981), whom Flavio has also read, have characterized the political organization of all three linguistic groups as socially stratified, materially wealthy chiefdoms, or *cacicazgos*. In the highlands zone, Newson has described the societies populated by speakers of the Matagalpa language as less stratified and more dispersed; their language, likely related to modern Sumu and other macro-Chibcha idioms spoken in eastern Nicaragua, was probably highly dialect-variant, according to Mason (1973).

The first factor in the transformation of indigenous peoples that I take into account is the demographic collapse of pre-Conquest populations estimated by Newson (1987) at between 600,000 and 1.4 million, or what should be considered one of the most densely populated zones in what became the "New World." Some twenty years following the arrival of the Spaniards, the population in the western region had dropped to between 12,000 and 30,000 (Newson 1987), stemming from epidemics, the slave trade, and the brutal imposition of Spanish colonial rule, all linked to the founding of León and Granada. These two rival colonial cities obstructed the political and economic unification of western Nicaragua for four hundred years. Between these two elite centers, colonial Masaya was built adjacent to the indigenous center of Monimbó, which the earliest reports (see Incer 1990) describe as the center of artisanal production in western Nicaragua. By Incer's and Romero Vargas's (1988) reckoning, Masaya lived off the marketing of Monimboseños' labors. By 1600, the major colonial cities had emerged alongside major pre-Hispanic indigenous population nuclei: Jalteva, the Indian town next to Granada,[12] the Maribio speakers of Sutiava adjacent to León, and Monimbó, the Mankeme companion of colonial Masaya. Other important Indian populations reemerged in the highlands, where Matagalpa speakers continued to live in village-centered societies sprinkled over the sparsely populated region adjacent to the initially very small colonial town of Matagalpa. In Romero Vargas's (1988) history, the variation in indigenous population centers emerging from the colonial period—from Indian towns bordering on colonial urban centers to isolated rural villages—shaped later national efforts to control and appropriate indigenous resources as part of the Nicaraguan nation-building project.

Wheelock (1981) makes clear that the transformation of indigenous lands into resources for the national political economy intertwined with both the metamorphosis of indigenous cultural markers (language, presentation of self through clothing, ornamentation, etc.), about which he was not terribly interested, and continuous resistance by indigenous communities to elite authority, which captured most of his attention. Continuing a historical pattern set in the late seventeenth and throughout the eighteenth centuries, the major indigenous communities (Sutiava, Jalteva, Monimbó, and villages in the Matagalpa region) continued to carry out insurrections against the elites of León and Granada during the conflictive years of early Nicaraguan independence, as both Wheelock (1981) and Romero Vargas (1988) have described. Romero Vargas suggests that these rebellions were led by the "traditional" leadership of indigenous communities, but this leadership was itself derived from the new conditions of colonial rule. The significance of these institutions and their histories differs depending on one's point of view.

The Conquest clearly demolished the political structure of the old *cacicazgos,* and by the eighteenth century indigenous leadership was encapsulated in two institutions. The council of elders (*consejo de ancianos*) was very likely a pre-Hispanic institution but one that the Spanish colonial regime transformed in important ways, particularly with respect to gender. Mercedes Olivera et al. (1992), as noted in the previous chapter, argued that the Spaniards eliminated women from positions of public power; early observers such as Oviedo (1976) stressed that women's role in politics had been considerable before the arrival of the Spaniards among the Mangue-speaking peoples, a view still accepted by Newson. Recently Nicaraguan sociologist Membraño Idiaquez (1992) and Spanish ethnographer García Bresó (1992) have shown that the colonial regime also enabled particular families to maintain control over the council and to accumulate resources for their own benefit in indigenous communities that co-operated with the Spaniards. This was especially true for the families among whom the colonial authorities appointed the *alcalde de vara* ("mayor of the cane"), the leader of the council authorized by the silver-headed wooden cane received from the Spanish king. The latter institution continued to exist into the independence period in both Monimbó and Sutiava, whereas the council persists only in Monimbó (Membraño Idiaquez 1992). Flavio is well acquainted with this history. Although I see the history of the *consejo de ancianos* and the *alcalde de vara* as demonstrating the nonessentialized nature of indigenous identity in Monimbó, he sees them as evidence for the persistence of traditional leadership.

The history of the artisans enters these transformations obliquely; in other words, I have mostly deduced what happened to artisan communities. For example, Vilas (1986) and Dunkerly (1988) argue that during the nineteenth century inexpensive artisanal manufactures functioned as a subsidy for capitalist accumulation by keeping low the costs of reproducing the labor force. Because artisanal production dominated Monimbó and was at least important in Sutiava during this period, I conclude that the economic expansion under Zelaya at the end of the nineteenth century would have stimulated artisanal production of basic personal and household commodities, practically ensuring the survival of part of the economic base of urban Indian communities. However, the incorporation of the artisan sector into the national political economy must have stimulated economic differentiation within these indigenous communities that undermined communal solidarity. Community solidarity was also undercut by the rapacious seizure of the communal land base by elites in León and Masaya, lands that had provided space for agriculture and the gathering of wild plant and animal foods for the people Sutiava and Monimbó, respectively (see Gould 1990b; Membraño Idiaquez 1992). When Zelaya left power in 1909 under heavy U.S. pressure, indigenous communities became cannon fodder for new interelite confrontations, which ended up further eroding their remaining land base. Flavio's great-grandfather's memoirs record this taking place in Monimbó.

Zelaya's regime remains doubly important in understanding the transformation of indigenous peoples in western Nicaragua, because his attempt to create a unified strong state was also a nation-building project. In effect, the historical moment in which the Nicaraguan *state* began to emerge out of internecine chaos was also the moment in which the myth of Nicaragua mestiza was deployed to construct the Nicaraguan *nation,* which is why after Zelaya intellectuals took for granted the truth that Nicaragua was becoming or had already become an ethnically homogeneous society. One paradigmatic element of this assumption was, of course, the transformation of *El Güegüence* into the symbol of *mestizaje.* Stigmatization of all people readily identifiable as Indian accompanied the mestizoization of the Nicaraguan state and nation. García Bresó (1992) asserts that this stigma was the stimulus behind the fading of identity markers in Monimbó; but let me argue that this was a more multidimensional process. On the one hand, the fading of clear markers of indigenous identity likely encouraged elites to appropriate indigenous communities' resources under the pretext that these communities were no longer Indian and did not enjoy any special relationship to land and locality. As far as elite history and literature were concerned, their inhabitants did not look, act, or sound like Indians. On the other hand, an increasing number of individuals in Monimbó and Sutiava learned to read and write Spanish, and such educated individuals constituted a new core of local intellectuals distinct from the traditional leadership. These new local intellectuals were consequently unlikely to initiate a discourse of Indianness and more likely to articulate a version of the elite national discourse of progress.

It is difficult for anthropologists to analyze this outcome without reference to the profoundly conventional disciplinary concepts of assimilation and acculturation, which are epitomized in Adams's 1957 work. Much like the myth of Nicaragua mestiza, assimilation narratives elide indigenous identities when they do not conform to anthropologists' etic parameters, greatly simplifying complex cultural transformations (see Field 1994a). Historians too can gloss these linguistic transitions far too lightly. In reference to the extinction of both the Mangue and Maribio languages, Burns (1991: 126), for instance, asserts that "the Indians of the Pacific coast found it necessary, desirable and useful to abandon their languages and speak Spanish." These superficial assessments are perhaps easier to pass off in western Nicaragua than elsewhere because indigenous languages faded out so long ago. Nineteenth-century ethnographers Squier and Brinton found only a few isolated speakers of Mangue, Nahuatl, and Maribio (see Brinton 1883); Berendt (1874) elicited very limited Mangue vocabularies in Masaya. Maribio persisted in Sutiava until the early twentieth century among a very few old people (Lehmann 1910 in Gould 1990b); and although the disappearance of the Matagalpa dialects is still muddled, Nahuatl faded in the seventeenth and eighteenth centuries as it merged with Spanish. During the past two decades, Flavio is the only person I have met in Monimbó and all of Masaya-Carazo in whose family even the memory of having spoken an indigenous language is preserved.

Gould (1995) understands western Nicaraguan language extinctions as the aggregate effects of several generations of indigenous individuals who internalized the stigma against Indianness. García Bresó's (1992) ethnography of Monimbó provides evidence for such a conclusion as well. In this vein, however, we should remember that Friedlander (1975) has shown that although stigma denatured Indian culture in Hueyapan (central Mexico), Nahuatl survived as a spoken language that both stigmatized and perversely empowered people to carry out their lives in secret from the mestizos. Such a dynamic is by no means uncommon in the history of the Americas; and as Hill and Hill (1986) showed in Mexico, and Urban (1991) in Paraguay, the speaking of "Indian" languages is not necessarily the marker of indigenous identity. In her work near Cuzco, Marisol de la Cadena (1995) finds that "while the social indicators of ethnicity (the everyday masks of Indianness of non-Indianness) might change, the ideology of ethnic hierarchy may endure at the micro or macro level . . . material appearance (the disappearance of Indian homespuns, the spread of Spanish and urban cultural forms to rural parts) might on the surface indicate that "Indians are disappearing," [but] the discursive practices of everyday life on the edges of Cuzco or in the countryside continue to differentiate Indians from mestizos and even to deepen the stigma of Indian for some sectors" (30).

The stigma against Indianness remains audible in this region in the denigration of Indians in common expressions celebrated by folklorist Enrique Peña Hernandez (1986) cited in chapter 1. The effects of stigma were also demonstrated in the artisans' rejection of Ernesto Cardenal's *indigenismo* during the Sandinista period. But if stigma helped to erode ethnic markers in western Nicaragua, that factor alone cannot explain why all indigenous languages had completely disappeared by the mid-twentieth century in this region: language retention does not always correlate to indigenous identity. Perhaps one option—and an attractive one in a nonessentializing analysis coming from a metropolitan intellectual—is to disentangle indigenous identities from language survival altogether. If this is done, the survival of each individual community—Monimbó, other communities in Masaya-Carazo, Sutiava, and the communities of the northern highlands—must be explained with reference to divergent and locally specific factors. The Indians of each of these areas are in this light different *kinds* of Indians, and by "kind" I do not mean in an explicitly ethnic sense as discernible through ethnic markers or essences. Masaya-Carazo Indians are Indians because they are artisans, and artisans because they are Indians. Even so, indigenous Monimboseño identity diverges from indigenous San Juanero identity over their respective relationships with the state, a relationship that also forms a key part of defining specific Indian communities, both historically and currently. The close relationship between Indianness and resistance to the state counterbalanced the stigma against Indianness, facilitating the reproduction of Indian identity from one generation to the next in particular cases.

The emergence of the Somocista state in the early and mid-twentieth century, which was the "solution" to renewed internecine warfare arranged by the United States and its new military proxy, the Nicaraguan National Guard, following the fall of Zelaya, activated political resistance to the state in Sutiava and Monimbó. Resistance to the state then became a key marker of indigenous ethnicity in these two communities, a statement about which Flavio and I agree both historically and analytically. In Sutiava, the successful expansion and modernization of cotton and beef production under the first Somoza (Somoza García 1936–56), which forced thousands of farmers off their lands in the Chinandega-León region (see R. G. Williams 1986), became the specific stimulus to resistance. Gould (1990b: 110) writes that most Indians in that community "came to understand that at the heart of their ethnicity is found an ideology of resistance rather than a series of endogamous relations of kinship." The *consejo de ancianos,* which remained in control of cultural resources, such as the community library, became the organizational center for planning increasingly violent attacks on the National Guard and local plantation owners (see Gould 1990b). García Bresó (1992) has shown that Monimbó's oppositional history and the stigmatization of Monimboseños by non-Indians in Masaya were the decisive factors congealing Indian identity there. Monimbó, which continued to elect its *alcalde de vara,* gained a reputation as a dangerous place, where Guardsmen and police were attacked by drunken Indians and where the population continued to favor their own artisanal manufactures over the flood of cheap imports that was the product of Somocista trade policy. At the same time, the municipal Somocista government in Masaya expropriated the last bits of communal land in Monimbó, according to Membraño Idiaquez (1992). As impoverished artisans and proletarians came to dominate the population of Monimbó and Sutiava, people in these communities continued to consider themselves Indians. The existence and character of twentieth-century indigenous communities thus directly challenged the elite regime of truth about *mestizaje* in Somocista Nicaragua, and these communities were consequently under continuous attack by the Somocista state economically, militarily, and ideologically.

The Somocista state characteristically used both co-optation and repression to build its corporatist state (see Walter 1993). With respect to the Indians, one form of this co-optation meant wooing intellectuals from active interest in Indian persistence in order to substantiate the elite truth that Indians had disappeared from western Nicaragua. Nicaraguan sociologist Mario Rizo Zeledón (1992: 61) comments: "If one looks for a body of national literature specifically concerning indigenous communities of the [western] region, we are met with thematics that absolutely ignore their existence." Another form this co-optation took, at least to drive a wedge between intellectuals and Indians, was a weak romantic *indigenismo* about the "Indian soul" of the Nicaraguan people compatible with a literary conception of the inexorable decline and disappearance of Indian cultures in western Nicaragua. That conception, epitomized by Cuadra, was also orchestrated in the 1950s journal *Nicaragua Indígena,* mentioned in chapter 1. This journal officially lamented the muting of indigenous cultural markers and the disappearance of indigenous languages, but in effect legitimized the annexation of cultural performances such as of *El Güegüence* to the truth of *mestizaje*. By documenting the muting of clear symbolic and behavioral markers distinguishing Indian from mestizo, and because the resistance by indigenous communities to Somocismo was not within the realm of the discussible, readers of *Nicaragua Indígena* could rest assured that Indians really had disappeared.[13]

In the northern highlands, the region of the *cerámica negra* women, the history of indigenous identity and artisanal production clearly diverged. Resistance to the nation-building state provides a common theme, however, between indigenous communities in the highlands and those elsewhere. Zelaya's nation-state project impacted the indigenous communities in the northern highlands because his aggressive pursuit of economic modernization depended on Nicaragua's first truly successful entrance into the world economy: the introduction of dependent capitalist development based on large-scale cultivation of coffee by European immigrants in Nicaragua's northern highlands beginning in the 1870s, as detailed by Robert Williams (1986). Agro-export production of coffee in Nicaragua required the dispossession of the communal lands of Matagalpa Indians that composed a large percentage of the landowners in the highlands during this period. These intrusions met with persistent insurrections against the elite-dominated state by the rural Indians. Their struggles were rendered politically salient for nation-building by Wheelock (1981) and romantically heroic by local historians Julián Guerrero and Lola Soriano de Guerrero (1982). Gould (1993) has described how elite intellectuals and coffee plantation owners characterized the Matagalpa Indians as savage, primitive, marginal, seminaked brutes, whose communal control over land constituted an impediment to nation-building and economic progress. The defeat of the Matagalpa Indians' armed attack on elite power in the 1881 War of the Communards thus entrenched the idea of victory over "the primitive Indian" in the nation-building project in Nicaragua under Zelaya.

Rose Spalding's (1994) portrait of the weakness of Nicaraguan elites for the first half-century of independence suggests that Nicaraguan elites may have felt especially compelled to confront, defeat, and disgrace any force they perceived as impeding the progress of the nation's political economy and identity. When the majority of Matagalpa Indians lost their land, they not only joined the ranks of semiproletarians working for the benefit of the elite's agro-export coffee capitalism; they also became the subjects of a new politics of stigma, as the lavishly documented and illustrated CIERA-MIDINRA (1984b) study of the Segovia region of the northern highlands also substantiates. As in Masaya-Carazo, cultural differences assigned to the category "Indian" became the signs that marked individuals and communities as outside the nation and part of the lowest social category; in the highlands, Indian status occupied a category below the subaltern status of mestizo agricultural workers. Under such circumstances, most Matagalpa Indians abandoned their clothing and other visible markers of Indian identity; at the same time, the issues of land ownership, community control over land, and resistance to the domination of export crops became the skeleton upon which the body of indigenous identity hung and still hangs. Thus, in the highlands, resistance to the state combined not with artisanal production but with specific relationships to land and farming, even if those relationships persisted mostly in memory, to define the kind of Indian that survived.

Perhaps one major exception to this argument is an indigenous community in the highlands in which identity did persist in association with artisanal production, or at least in tandem with the memory of communal land and a nascent struggle to regain it. In El Chile, an isolated village located in rugged terrain east of the city of Matagalpa, the artisanal production of cloth persisted, woven from locally grown cotton varieties. A woman's craft, until recently El Chile cloth was brilliantly tinted by vegetable dyes and by weaving together threads from varieties of cotton that grow in color. Several older women continued to clandestinely weave cotton cloth even when the Somocista state outlawed small-scale cultivation and processing of cotton, surely one of the most bizarre and irrational facets of that state's paranoid pursuit of power, as Angel and Macintosh (1987) documented. In the 1990s, these same women and their children speak with a distinctive accent and pepper their conversation with words from either Nahuatl or the Matagalpa language. The oldest people may still have spoken their language into the 1950s, although the stigmatization of indigenous identity in this region as throughout western Nicaragua meant that at the very least Indians ceased to speak it anywhere they might be heard by non-Indians. Concerning El Chile's Indianness, metaphorized more neatly by the blue thread of *El Güegüence* than perhaps anywhere else in western Nicaragua, Christina Hernández, one of the elderly women who continued to weave under Somocismo, related: "In the time of the grandmothers, [then] they still used the plant dyes, and also they could speak [the old language]. [We still use] the old kinds of cotton, make this pottery, cook that way [with a *comal*] over there."

The benefit of considering El Chile's Indianness as a combination of the northern highlands Indians' relationship to land with the Masaya-Carazo Indians' relationship to artisanal production (and their common resistance to the state) is that this helps to explain the realignment of the *cerámica negra* women of the city of Matagalpa toward indigenous identity in the 1990s. It was the *cerámica negra* women who facilitated the link between the Ministry of Culture and El Chile, where Ernesto Cardenal sponsored one of his last projects of "rescuing" a craft through a production cooperative ("Rescate" 1987; "Contra" 1987). María Esthela accompanied Ministry officials to the village during much of 1984 and '85, and later clinched the affiliation of the El Chile weavers with the artisans' union, UNADI. This affiliation turned around the other way when, in the 1990s, the involvement of the El Chile villagers with the indigenous movement over issues of land rights led their friends among the *cerámica negra* women to affirm indigenous history and identity in the Matagalpa region.

But I am jumping ahead of myself. In this section, I have argued that the history of the decline of indigenous ethnic markers led to the creation of different kinds of (nonessentialized) Indians in various regions of western Nicaragua. In the next section, I deal with the other side of the coin of transformation: the creation of the mestizo majority, who came to outnumber the Indians, of whatever kind, and who became thematically enshrined in the elite construction of the Nicaraguan nation. In the final section, the previous analyses of Indians and mestizos in western Nicaragua shapes a discussion of the Indians who are and are not participating in the indigenous movement of the 1990s.

In a Mestizo Country: Discourses and Narratives

Inquiring about the majority population, the nationality called "Nicaraguans," who are mestizos according to elite interpretations, indexes an established and currently burgeoning discourse within social science, literary criticism, literature, and political and social movements concerning mestizos and the process of becoming and being mestizo, or *mestizaje*. Although many meanings are attributed to *mestizaje* in this discourse, here I will refer to and contest *mestizaje* in three ways: as a process of biological miscegenation; as a process of nation-building that requires that mestizos, as individuals and collectivities, undergo "de-Indianization," both culturally-linguistically and in order to accommodate national identity in ways that Indians, who are positioned in opposition to the nation-building state, cannot; and as a process that necessarily creates a panoply of divergent mixed and mixing identity positions. The tensions coursing through this discussion are first, between critical use and citation of academic sources to build my own position, on the one hand, and Flavio's position, on the other, and second, between the divergences in Flavio's own positioning, which this textualization brings into high relief.

The extreme demographic tumble indigenous peoples experienced in the region that became Nicaragua, distinct from other demographic processes in the wake of Spanish colonialism in Mexico, Guatemala, or the Andes, surely affected the sudden emergence of mixed populations in this region. In León, Granada, Masaya, Managua, and the other colonial cities, peninsular and *criollo* (American-born) Spaniards ruled, while the majority of the population was composed of groups of people who were not Indians, not Spaniards, not *criollos* (see Stanislawski 1983). Most of this population had parents, grandparents, and other more distant ancestors from the indigenous civilizations of the area, as well as from Spain, and in many cases from regions of Africa as well. They spoke Spanish, usually mixed with words from indigenous languages, were at least nominally Catholic, dressed in a European style, and from early on were known as mestizos, the mixed people. It is undeniable that these new populations in colonial western Nicaragua figured importantly early on (Newson 1987), weighing heavily upon the construction of elite notions of Nicaraguan national identity as featured in the literature about *El Güegüence*. Essentialist ideas of race construe such biological miscegenation as the materials for mestizo nation-building and mestizo national identities.

The likelihood of incurring such essentialism is, however, no less a hazard for the social scientist than for the nationalist. Carol Smith (1996) has discussed the profound implantation of the symbolics of blood in Western consciousness, with its associated concepts of purity of descent and the degradation of mixture. The symbolics of blood, she argues, are the key components in the conflation of race, class, and culture in social science as well as in nationalist ideologies. Indeed, Friedman (1994) has broadsided key concepts and processes in the anthropological imaginary on this basis:

Creolization is an inevitable consequence of the use of the [essentialist] notion of culture that we have criticized above . . . this mingling of cultures, the fusion that leads to supposedly new products, is a metaphor that can only succeed in terms of a previous metaphor, that of culture as matter, in this case, apparently as fluid . . . the use of the concept creole in colonial contexts was a stable mechanism of identification based on an essentialized view of culture . . . Cultures don't flow together or mix with each other. Rather, certain actors, often strategically placed actors, identify the world in such terms as a part of their own self-identification. (208–10)

The difficulties involved in deploying conventional anthropological analytic idioms such as "culture" and the historical conflation in this discipline between culture and race are recurrent. In Esteva-Fabrigat's (1995) analysis, static, predefined, and ahistorical concepts of race simply reassert Eurocentric assumptions about racial groups as a priori categories. Nevertheless, his emphasis on racial categories and demography is moderated by deeper realizations, inconceivable to ignore since Ronald Stutzman's (1981) analysis of Ecuadorian *mestizaje:* "Thus, mestizos, or Indians, and even blacks, have not always been categorized by either color or genealogy. There are many cases where they were conferred a Hispanic status just by living on the Spanish way or by being economically strong. Indians become mestizos, and mestizos become whites, when they adopted the Hispanic cultural form . . . racial mobility is culturally conditioned. As a result, many mestizos would be Indians or Spanish depending upon their cultural status" (Esteva-Fabrigat 1995: 56).

For nationalists, the fact of biological miscegenation is clearly insufficient to build national identities, and social categories are manipulated to do so. In Nicaragua, the conceptualization of the non-Indian majority changed during the period of Somocista nation-building following the elite internecine struggle that recurred after Zelaya's fall. Gould (1993) writes: "Before the 1930s, all sectors of [Nicaraguan] society employed the term 'ladino' to refer to non-

Indians or to 'whites.' During the same period the term 'mestizo' meant the offspring of unions between Indians and whites (broadly defined). By 1950, however, 'mestizo' not only had supplanted 'ladino' but had become a self-description for the whole of society. This linguistic transformation symbolized the triumph of the myth of Nicaragua mestiza" (397). By the same token, the recognition among many social scientists and historians that racial categories are sociocultural constructions at least as much as biological constants has not necessarily meant the abandonment of rigidly bounded definitions of mestizo and Indian identities. The work of Bonfil Batalla (1992a) represents a particularly sophisticated version of this kind of definition of ethnic identity, grounded in a relational discussion of Indians and mestizos in the specific historical contexts of Spanish colonialism. On the one hand:

the definition of the Indian cannot be based in the analysis of particularities of each group; the societies and the cultures called indigenous present a spectrum of variation and contrast so wide that no single definition stemming from internal characteristics can incorporate the sum total of them all without the risk of losing all heuristic value. The category of Indian, in effect, is a superethnic category that does not denote any specific content for the groups to which it applies, but rather a particular relationship between them and other sectors of the global social system of which the Indians form a part. The category of Indian denotes the condition of being colonized, and necessarily makes reference to the colonial relationship. The Indian was born when Colón took possession of the island of Hispaniola in the name of the Catholic Monarchs. (30)

On the other hand:

the mestizo is, simultaneously, a segment of colonial society and a product of biological mixing between the colonizers and the colonized, but with the understanding that in addition to those socially categorized as mestizos, there were fruits of the large-scale miscegenation who continued to belong to the indigenous population, and surely as well, to the criolla . . . The Ibero-American colonial regime demanded a social layer capable of carrying out a series of tasks (administrative, service-oriented, of measurement and of intervention) that the distinctly colonizing population—which is to say the peninsular Spaniards and the criollos—were insufficient to accomplish . . . The mestizos, as a social category, as a sector distinct from the indigenous population, were the suitable means which the colonial system seized to satisfy this lack . . . the mestizos can see themselves as a sector of colonized origin that the colonial apparatus coopted in order it incorporate it into the colonizing sector, assigning to it a subordinate position. (33)

The colonial mestizos, Bonfil Batalla shows in another essay (1992b), functioned as the useful servants of the regime, carrying out the orders of the *peninsulares* and the *criollos* in the overall domination of Indians and slaves. Stemming from their functions within colonial regimes, Latin American independence struggles enshrined *mestizaje* as an essential element of state-led nation-building projects, and people called mestizos came to predominate everywhere. In the many versions of *mestizaje*'s marriage to nation-building, he argues, the Indian does and can only represent the past, a vanquished element that went into the making of the nation. In the contemporary world, then, people still called Indians can only be seen as throwbacks, anachronisms, static, retrograde, resistant to change. Bonfil Batalla stressed that although there had been considerable mixing of cultural elements among groups, *mestizaje* had not constituted "a new culture." Although nationalist ideologies eulogized the mestizo as the harmonious fusion of European and Indian, often expressed as the mind of the European with the emotions of the Indian, Bonfil Batalla (1992b: 44) viewed the formation of the mestizo as a "de-Indianization," or the compulsory loss of the original ethnic identity, and its substitution "not [by] a new hybrid or mestizo culture which marries the best of two different civilizations, [but] plainly and simply [substitution] by a western model," a modified version of Spanish worldviews and life-ways developed by the *criollos* in their new circumstances.

The pejorative view of *mestizaje* displayed by Bonfil Batalla characterizes much of the post–World War II literature among both North American and Latin American social scientists. Among North American anthropologists, a near total neglect of mestizos in countries with large indigenous populations (Guatemala, Bolivia, Peru, Ecuador) made clear which population was most interesting, complex, indeed "cultural" for ethnographers. Guatemalan scholar Guzmán-Bockler (1975) used the term *ningunidad* (nobody-ness) to describe mestizos, in that having been stripped of Indian somebody-ness, mestizos remain empty and undefined. Thus, although nationalists and social scientists might share either cultural or biological assumptions or both, they do not agree on the outcome of *mestizaje*. This simultaneous convergence and divergence between these two discourses is also present in the worldview of an outspoken indigenous intellectual, Flavio. If, for him, to be Indian is to maintain traditions of leadership and community organization, to be both rebellious and stigmatized, and alternatively, to work as an artisan, or own and farm land communally, mestizo identity is distinguished by the absence of such behaviors and traditions. I learned about his perspective in 1993, during a fieldtrip with Flavio which he called:

A Trip to Mestizo Country When I crossed the *solar*, the broad front yard to get to Flavio's house, he was waiting to expound to me once more his theory that several large villages had been located adjacent to modern Monimbó on the bluffs overlooking the eastern shore of Laguna Masaya before the arrival of the Spaniards. His grandfather had told him that this area had been one of the heartlands of the Manqueza, a population center like the area where the former Mangue-speaking villages of Diria, Diriomo, San Juan de Oriente, Catarina, and Niquinohomo are now located—except that the lakeside region is now almost completely depopulated. Once, during the early years of the Sandinista period, Flavio had spoken to archaeologists at the Museo Nacional in Managua about conducting an archaeological survey in that area, but they had dismissed his ideas. Because this was the fourth or fifth time we had discussed these ideas, we finally decided to wander the farmland around the lake to see what we could find.

Both of us had also heard from a woman who owned a general store (*pulpería*) on the main street in Monimbó that a clandestine excavation was going on near the lake. Her store featured the usual heterogeneous panoply of goods found in *pulperías*—fresh baked rolls, rolls of toilet paper, cans of tuna, cans of dried milk, cigarettes, vinegar, laundry soap, meat from the market covered with flies—but if anything an even more varied selection. I had bought bread and fruit in her store before but she also sold papier-mâché masks used in some of Monimbó's street dances. She had a mask of Macho Ratón, and also Arellano's 1991 edition of *El Güegüence,* the publication of which doña Violeta's Ministry of Education had funded. I bought the book and then, broadly smiling, she brought out a small funerary pot the *huaqueros* (grave robbers) had sold to her from the site, which she obviously wanted to show off to Flavio. She didn't really know where the *huaqueros* were digging, but she said that they had found *collares de jade* (jade necklaces), an intriguing detail that I did not believe.

One Saturday morning we set off for the lake from Flavio's house with six-year-old Elwin, one of Flavio's countless grandchildren. After ascending a long and very dusty hill, we entered a shallow basin which Flavio said had been a pond during the 1940s, before *despale descontrolado* (indiscriminate deforestation) had dried it up. Along the way we passed a small fruit and soda stand underneath a tiny awning at the bottom of the path that led to Don Italo's house, an acquaintance of Flavio's. We sat under the awning for some minutes and drank Cokes with the campesinos running the stand, and Don Italo walked over to talk with us. After a few minutes, an unpleasant controversy between the men about the New Testament had swallowed up the pleasantries of introductions. Don Italo, a Baptist, argued with the campesinos, who were *Pentacostalistas,* about the predictions in the Book of Revelations. Flavio tried to inject a note of tolerance and mutual respect, which the campesinos misread as an assertion of superiority. Don Italo turned to me and asked what religion I was. When I responded *"Soy judío"* (I am Jewish), Don Italo's face twisted in disgust. "So you're the ones who own all the banks in *Norteamerica,* and also all the newspapers!" I asked him where he had learned these things, and he retorted that the pastor of his church had told the congregation all about the *judíos.*

I stood up and started walking; Flavio was soon beside me. He wanted to reassure me that those people were ignorant, that this kind of ignorance was spreading, and then he said: "Well, they are only poor mestizos." We proceeded, after a half hour turning off the dusty road toward a house made of broad planks. The path was lined with very large mango trees laden with fruit, and Elwin and I picked up mangos that were not bruised. We washed them in the water that filled an old steel barrel next to the house, from which puffs of smoke and the smell of cooking beans wafted in equal measure. I never did catch the last name of Don Hernando, the campesino who lived there, or the names of all the young men, some of them his sons who worked for him clearing the fields and planting beans, tomatoes, and the green squash called *pepián.*

Don Hernando didn't know anything about any ongoing excavations around the lake, but he had found much of *la cerámica,* many pots, in his own time, selling them to foreigners and rich folk from

Managua. The land on this side of the lake had belonged to one family for a very long time, he said. He'd worked for them, and they had never been rich, he said. They didn't grow much, they just owned many *manzanas* of this land and used it to pasture their cattle. Then the Revolution came and took most of their land away because the Sandinistas in Masaya said the father was a Somocista. Anyway, he said, it didn't matter that the Sandinistas gave the land to a campesino cooperative, because all the young guys had to go to the *servicio militar* (military duty). After the war, Doña Violeta had broken up all the cooperatives, so the campesinos were now cultivating the whole area. He pointed out that they rented a John Deere plow in Masaya just the same as if they were still a cooperative.

"I don't go digging for *la cerámica* anymore," he said. "It's too much work in the hot sun. I don't see the value in it, unless you can get a foreigner to buy it." Flavio looked down uncomfortably, so I asked Don Hernando if he knew any stories, old stories about this place. I was wondering optimistically if perhaps something might be remembered about the old villages Flavio had described on this lake shore. Instead, Don Hernando told me this:

"Up there by the road in that meadow there, did you see, where the horses are now? In my great-grandmothers' time, that was a *laguna* [lake]. A small *laguna*, and not very deep, all around the edges it was very shallow. Except that in the middle it was deep. I don't know how deep it was. My great-grandma, her dad wanted to drain off that *laguna*, to farm it, but he could never accomplish that. And why? My great-grandma told me why. Because a very large snake lived in that *laguna*, in the deep part. Did you ever hear what an anaconda is? Where is it that they live? It is an enormous snake. Except this one was bigger than that. Until one summer, it was so dry, it never rained. For weeks there was no rain, and only the deep part of the lake was left. Then they found that snake and they killed it. The next day the lake was completely dried up and gone. That's what she told me."

After we heard the story, I asked Don Hernando if he had ever found any gold during his excavations. He told us about one of the graves he had found, that in this one grave the skeleton had been enormous, taller than me. They had found an arrow point in the man's chest, and gold beads scattered around him. "It was Italians, I think," said Don Hernando, "that bought that one, before the Sandinistas won, anyway."

Flavio said it was time to go. Outside the house, he whispered that he was embarrassed about what the man had told us, about selling off the ceramics and other remains. Flavio, Elwin, and I walked out into the fields leading away from Don Hernando's house toward the bluffs overlooking the lake. These fields formed part of the terrain that the campesinos were newly cultivating, land that had only grazed cattle since the Spaniards arrived, Flavio remarked. We were looking for bits of old pottery. We didn't have long to wait. Strewn over the land and, as we soon saw, over the several hectares all around us were thousands of broken pots, smashed to fragments by the tractors the campesinos had rented to prepare the land for planting. The more we walked, the more we found. "There's enough here to fill four museums," Flavio said mournfully. Elwin and I busied ourselves collecting fragments painted with intricate white, black, and red designs. The tractors had done heavy-duty work, because among the bits of pots we noted large *metates* and grinding stones carved from heavy basalt rock, also pulverized by the agricultural machinery.

As we walked stooped over the ground, I saw that the campesinos had plowed these fields literally to within centimeters of the rim of bluffs that descended precipitously hundreds of meters to the lake's surface.

"Don Flavio," I said, "these people must notice that all the soil is being washed down these cliffs when the rains come. Why don't they leave a few trees, or just some plants here at the rim to protect their soil?"

We had just found a tripod pot broken into about eight pieces, the first specimen we'd encountered for which there was any hope of piecing it back together. Flavio put the pieces into my backpack and peeled one of the oranges I had carried for Elwin.

"This is the work of the mestizo," he said finally. "Our campesinos don't value our past, don't value this land anymore. They are just thinking about today, about their *guarito* [rum]. The government of Doña Violeta says there is no money to save this history. But they have money for other things. That's what *mestizaje* did to this people."

This terrible view of *mestizaje* contrasts with other encounters I have had with Flavio, when it was possible to discover a less rigid boundary between Indian and mestizo, in effect calling into question his own assumptions and those of others. One direction to take in addressing these essentialisms is to show the extent to which the conceptualization and lived behaviors of being mestizo and Indian are in perpetual flux. In one conversation with Flavio regarding his own standards for defining Indian identity in western Nicaragua, he spoke about the importance of knowing family history and showed me passages from Romero Vargas's *Las Estructuras Sociales de Nicaragua en el Siglo XVIII* (1988). I read the following:

In order to climb the social hierarchy, the mestizos could refer back to laws that placed them at the same level as the Spaniards. On February 15, 1729, the Audencia received a request from Captain Antonio Gamboa, citizen of León, calling for recognition of his status. He was the son of Don Antonio Gamboa, a Spaniard, and a noble Indian from Subtiava [sic]. He recalled the Royal Cedula of March 16, 1697, because it conceded special rights to the descendants of caciques. The ecclesiastic council of León, after examining the proof offered by Gamboa, declared him "a legitimate mestizo, clean of all bad race, descendent of the caciques of the town of Subtiava." The Audencia pronounced itself in favor of Gamboa, who was accorded all the "honors, privileges, and exemptions," stipulated by law. (351)

Flavio then flipped to the rear of the book to show me the original document from which Romero Vargas had made this observation. I read from a text taken from the Archivo General de Centroamérica, Guatemala City, the following excerpt:

The Mestizo Antonio de Gamboa Solicits Recognition of his Status Captain Don Antonio de Gamboa, citizen of León, in the province of Nicaragua, by letter of the law, appears before your Highness, and declares that I am the descendant of the first caciques of the town of Subtiava [sic], enjoying the special privileges of my ancestors in possession of which I have lived all of my life which is justifiable through the information that dutifully and under the necessary oaths before you that which I request to be in my possession the Royal Cedula that your Majesty was moved to dispatch to generally favor all the caciques and [which] my ancestors inherited from one to the next [generation] that documents the purity of our blood as an expression of our heritage (without . . . that likewise I present) and I ask that the original [documents] be returned to me. (490)

This documentation, as far as I can see, establishes the rights of mestizos whose indigenous ancestry legitimizes their claim to nobility among colonial authorities; by contrast, Flavio used these passages to show me just how indigenous his family has been for centuries. Thus, a relationship to authority that marked mestizo identity in the seventeenth and eighteenth centuries has come to substantiate Indian identity in the twentieth.

Such plasticity has long been evident in the Andes, where the bowler hats, woolen shawls, and old-fashioned dresses of colonial times have centuries later become the embodiments of Indian identity. Aníbal Quijano (1980) described the intermediary stage between rural Indian and urban mestizo identities in Peru occupied by *cholos*, people currently in the process of de-Indianization, having migrated to urban areas. *Cholos* differ both from the Indians, who are by definition outside of national society, and from mainstream urban citizens by their distinctive but changing dress and linguistic and occupational traits that mark them as an ethno-class apart—Indians who are almost but not quite not Indian anymore. De la Cadena (1996) has drawn out this argument much further, finding that in contemporary Cuzco

drawing analytic boundaries (no matter how fluid) between present day "Indians" and "mestizos" is inaccurate and dismissive of subordinate definitions of both identities as relative social conditions. Among indigenous Cuzqueños calling someone mestizo/a (or Indian) is fixing momentarily (but only so) a point of reference inherently and fluidly related to Indian (or mestizo/a) . . . In Cuzco, de-Indianization is the process of empowering indigenous identities through economic and educational achievements, *and* displaying this identity in regional events of popular culture that take place ubiquitously in urban and rural stages. (138)

In Nicaragua, the radical nationalism of Augusto C. Sandino, whose forces controlled much of the northern highlands in the late 1920s and early 1930s, went partway down the road to developing alternative versions of Nicaraguan identity that transgress the Indian/mestizo boundary. Sandino's nationalism had been influenced by his exposure to the *indigenismo* of the Mexican Revolution during a sojourn in Tampico. He referred to the people of Nicaragua and all Central America as "Indo-Latins" or "Indo-Hispanics" or "Indo-Americans." He thus paid tribute to two heritages:

I am a Nicaraguan, and I feel proud because in my veins circulates, more than anything else, Indian blood . . . My highest honor is to have arisen from the bosom of the oppressed, who are the soul and nerve of the Race. (In Ramírez 1984: 117–19)

I used to look with resentment on the colonizing work of Spain, but today I have profound admiration for it . . . Spain gave us its language, its civilization and its blood, We consider ourselves the Spanish Indians of America. (In Hodges 1986: 108)

Sandino elaborated a nationalism of perfect harmony between Indian and Spaniard, suggesting that de-Indianization need not occur, but rather a process of adding Hispanic traits to existing Indian cultural traditions. This is indeed the fusion that Bonfil Batalla argued never occurred and that, it might be argued, Cardenal's *indigenismo* also aimed to fulfill. Because Sandino lost, we cannot know what his marriage between *mestizaje* and nation-building would have meant for the indigenous communities of the early twentieth century. However, Sandino's transgression of the mestizo-Indian border in western Nicaragua is resonant with both recent academic work and areas of Flavio's discourse. Jorge Klor de Alva (1995), for example, emphasizes that "different forms of colonialism . . . are likely to create different forms of mestizaje," writing: "The chameleon-like nature of mestizaje—Western in the presence of Europeans, indigenous in native villages, and Indian-like in contemporary United States barrios —is its crucial characteristic. It is the result of the ambiguous ethnic spaces that appeared in the wake of the demographic decimation of the indigenes, the introduction of enslaved Africans, and the extensive immigration of Europeans" (253). "Chameleon-like" suggests a certain opportunistic will behind the transformative nature of mestizo identity, which does not describe how the choices of individuals and groups in places such as Nicaragua change through time. A better description may be found in the following narrative taken from the pages of Flavio Gamboa's family notebooks. In the narrative, his great-great-grandfather attends a large gathering of people from indigenous communities located in Masaya-Carazo and in the Rivas region as well. The telling weaves together many people's memories; memories of one generation also become the memories of those that follow. Yet, the realm of individual taste and preference assumes at least as important a role as that played by "tradition." Clear lines are not drawn around "Indian" or "mestizo" in Flavio's notebooks; but in the image of the marimba, a musical instrument of African origin but firmly identified with indigenous cultures from Mexico to Nicaragua, ubiquitous at Indian festivals but disliked by Flavio's Indian ancestor, a multidimensional metaphor for the intertwining of Indian and mestizo in western Nicaragua emerges.

My great-grandfather, Agustín de Gamboa, says in his memoirs that his father, Antonio Luis, made a trip in a [bullock] cart in 1829 when he was 18 years old in the company of his father, Luis Antonio de Gamboa, to the town of Popoyuapa, to fulfill a vow. Two carts from Monimbó, three from Masaya, two from Nandayure, one from Bombonaxi, and nine from Tenderí. These travelers in carts, arriving at the plaza of Oxomogo, from all the Indian towns of Masaya, Granada and Carazo, added up to 46 carts. When night came, they formed a large circle in which they started to party; there were 5 marimbas playing [and] those who were playing the marimba the best were Salomé Mercado Potoy and Malaguias Lopez Pavón, both from Monimbó.

I [Flavio's great-grandfather] want to be honorable and honest, for although I am the descendant of the rose of Monimbó, I do not like the marimba, and for this reason I moved over to where the Granadinos were playing some beautiful Spanish melodies strumming on violins, mandolins and guitars . . . from the writings of my grandfather, [I know that] on these journeys they brought with them the music and performance of the marimba, the soft and rhythmically sweet dances of Monimbó, [as well as] exquisite and appetizing local foods, not to mention the intoxicating alcoholic beverages made at home, and the delicious orange jams unique in all Nicaragua. On this journey, it was indispensable to show appreciation, generosity, and affection to the family that lent their courtyard as lodgings for the itinerant hotel in which the travelers roamed, and especially so for those from Monimbó, who went looking for the best gifts to please the families they were visiting in Popoyuapa, from freshly woven reed mats, to delicate hand-embroidered tablecloths, to the unequaled finery of [Monimboseño] hammocks.

[*Here Flavio has interjected the following:* One of the noble families visited by my ancestors since the eighteenth century was the family with the last name Fuertes, who lived in a large mansion of many verandas in back of the Cathedral of Popoyuapa, a family that I had the pleasure of knowing there in the year 1948; from here I will go on with my great-grandfather's description of his father's journey.]

All of us travelers from Monimbó and Masaya took care not to arrive in Popoyuapa during the light of day, so that no one could see us all grimy from our journey, and also to avoid bothering anyone or making anyone do extra work for us because of our arrival. For all these reasons, we tried to arrive late in the night, so that they would find us already settled in the courtyard of our hosts. [The next day] my father had ordered that they shoot off 12 firecrackers and 12 skyrockets, and that they play a serenade with marimbas. When I heard the sound of fireworks I woke up, and it was 5:00 in the morning on Ash Wednesday in the month of March, 1829, and I was a bit scared. I went into the center of the courtyard, where I found a big surprise, for there were more than a thousand people who formed a huge circle, there in the courtyard of the Fuertes family, as I avidly watched each step of the graceful and beautiful dance performed by the men and women of Monimbó, one of the musical pieces that received the most applause from the assembled. It was the young women who played two marimbas together, and others played the guardiolita and the fiddle and "avocado" [drums]. Another thing which filled me with surprise was that my father brought in a wagon three barrels of a home-made liquor called "cususa." I believed that my father would sell that liquor in Popo-yuapa, for he was quite a merchant. He ordered [us] to put a barrel on the north side [of the courtyard] and another on the south side. And [in this way] he distributed the liquor for free among those who were there, and I considered this amazing as I watched each man taking out their bags, gourds, little clay containers so that they could put in some of this liquor. On this day I came to understand that my father enjoyed a tremendous esteem in the village of Popoyuapa, and that the indigenous dances of Mo-nimbó were the finest among all the peoples of Nicaragua, but from that day on I decided to let it be known that I did not like the marimba.

Both trait-driven schema and rigid ethnic boundaries are inade-quate to the specific histories in the making of identities in western Nicaragua, as Flavio's ancestor's narrative underscores for a metro-politan reader. If the mestizos are mestizos, the Indians are also mes-tizos. If artisanal production, "traditional" government, particular dances and musical instruments, the performance of popular drama, and community solidarity in resistance to the state emerge as a work-ing list of "traits" describing Indian communities in western Nicara-gua, "we" [14] are suddenly comfortable also knowing that not all of these traits apply to all Indian communities. Sutiava is not a center of artisanal production, and San Juan de Oriente has not been a focus of resistance to the state. Moreover, many of these traits apply to non-Indian communities: all of Masaya, and not just Monimbó, rose against Somoza repeatedly, as did all of León, and not just Sutiava.

Non-Indians make pottery and other *artesanías* elsewhere in western Nicaragua, and the marimba is played and popular drama performed outside of indigenous communities.

The understanding that *mestizaje* is fluid, and that Indian and mestizo identities overlap in a manner that shapes the historically dynamic emergence of both different kinds of Indians and different kinds of mestizos is thus already present in Flavio's discourse, despite his focus on indigenous cultural survival. The resemblance between such an understanding and contemporary work by Chicana intellectuals (see Anzaldúa 1987; Alarcón 1990; Sandoval 1991) that explores and celebrates the multiplicity of mestiza identities in the political/cultural/sexual borderlands between Mexico and the United States only briefly creates a comfort zone for the social constructionism of metropolitan intellectuals such as myself. Notwithstanding the fluidity between mestizo and Indian, the mélange of characteristics, and the varied individualities among them, the key difference between the two in Nicaragua, as throughout Latin America, has derived from the valorization of the mestizo in the construction of national identity. Elite constructions of national identity, rather than anything essential about mestizoness or Indianness, include and exclude, value and devalue, centralize and peripheralize. Consequently, there *is* a difference between exploring tensions and fluidity in Flavio's discourse—thereby weaving, if you will, an all-inclusive, multicultural cloth with blue thread—and his actual leadership[15] and the leadership of other local intellectuals in the indigenous movement of the 1990s. In that capacity, Flavio's discourse remains a counternarrative to the elite's myth of Nicaragua mestiza: the counterhistory of a blue thread which traces and substantiates only indigenous identity in resistance to the state. But there are prices to pay for such strategies, both in terms of the kinds of Indians who are willing to join such a movement, and the implications for how far such a movement can go in its struggles with the Nicaraguan state.

The Indigenous Movement of the 1990s:
The Limitations of Counterallegory

It was not necessarily a foregone conclusion that an ethnic identity movement would emerge in western Nicaragua after 1990. The fact that in the wake of a dozen years of catastrophic warfare, economic collapse, and ideological exhaustion on the part of most Nicaraguans in what had been to begin with a very poor country, the UNO state was the weakest Nicaraguan state since the U.S. interventions early in this century is insufficient to explain why an indigenous movement developed. In this final section, I argue that the post-1990 indigenous movement and its themes have been largely shaped by two intertwined factors. First, the Sandinista Front's mass organization of subaltern groups all over western Nicaragua and the simultaneous inability of the Frente to comprehend the nature of indigenous participation in the revolutionary process exercised a very important role in the emergence of the indigenous movement. Second, the Frente's incomprehension of indigenous identity on the Atlantic Coast and its decade-long struggle with the Miskitu, which the Miskitu basically won, conditioned the entrance into Nicaragua of particular ideas and strategies from the hemispheric indigenous movement which supported the Miskitu struggle. Because the Miskitu in effect defeated the Frente, their movement's ideas and strategies were validated over others, creating an ideological framework for the indigenous movement in western Nicaragua.

Chapter 2 showed that the extensive participation of indigenous communities in the uprisings that defeated Somocismo had posed conceptual challenges to Sandinista historiography, which had attempted to negotiate a marriage between Sandinista class analysis and the utopian *indigenismo* of Ernesto Cardenal. The internalization of central themes from the myth of Nicaragua mestiza in Sandinista analysis may have been related to the class origins of the Frente's leaders, which both Vilas (1992) and Stone (1990) have described as predominantly upper class and intertwined with the same Leonese and Granadino elite lineages that have dominated Nicaragua since before independence. By the same token, when the Frente Sandinista joined forces with such Indian communities to bring down the Somocista state, even the partial acknowledgment of the existence of indigenous communities necessarily unraveled one facet of the myth of Nicaragua mestiza. Sandinista guerrilla leader and revolutionary comandante Omar Cabezas detailed his experiences organizing in Sutiava during the 1960s in his book, *Fire from the Mountain* (1985): "Our work in Subtiava [*sic*] took off like wildfire . . . [a]nd we started presenting the image of Sandino . . . The Indians had a leader, an historical figure, who more than any other was representative of their people: Adiac. We presented Sandino as an incarnation of Adiac, then Adiac as an incarnation of Sandino, but Sandino in light of *The Communist Manifesto*, see? So from shack to shack, from Indian to Indian, ideas were circulating: Adiac . . . Sandino . . . class struggle . . . vanguard FSLN. Gradually a whole movement was born in Subtiava" (36–37). Cabezas's reference to Adiac, the last cacique of Sutiava, has not been forgotten by contemporary intellectuals from this community, such as Enrique de la Concepción Fonseca, who told me that "the fact that the Frente could respect our history kept our relationship with the Frente very close for a long time."

Indigenous communities' involvement with the Sandinistas in effect facilitated the emergence of local intellectuals who could articulate identity beyond the local level. The Sandinista transformation of Nicaraguan society spawned a proliferation of unions and other mass organizations that represented poor, middle-income, and rich farmers, students, teachers, and other sectors. The mass organizations, at least at first, enabled many local intellectuals among the Nicaraguan poor to explore their political voices through Sandinismo. As Maria Josefina Jarquin Moreno, an Indian leader from Matagalpa stated: "During the [Sandinista] decade we have just experienced, we learned, in one form or another, to participate in political processes." Jarquin Moreno, de la Concepción Fonseca, and others had worked with unions and later joined the ATC (Asociación del Trabajadores del Campo, Association of Rural Workers), the organization of the poorest, often landless people of the Nicaraguan countryside. The experience of local organizing in the ATC, both to attract scarce state resources and to oppose state policies deemed inappropriate or misguided, had profoundly affected many communities, including indigenous communities, and spawned new generations of local leaders/intellectuals during the 1980s, some of whom became leaders of the indigenous movement in the 1990s.

Yet the Sandinistas never did truly understand that the Sutiava, Monimboseño, and rural indigenous communities had participated in the revolution as whole communities, not as unified social classes. The alliance between Sandinista ideology and Cardenal's *indigenismo* could not address that analytic failure because it romanticized Indianness without addressing the stigma of being an Indian; the Monimboseños did not need validation for their Indian identity and rejected it, and the San Juaneros found *indigenista* discourse patronizing and not particularly useful for their needs. Notwithstanding the gap between the indigenous communities of western Nicaragua and the Frente, the Sandinista leadership's internalization of the myth of Nicaragua mestiza posed the biggest headaches for them on the Atlantic Coast. The myth obstructed the Frente's analysis of the Coast. Its colonial and postindependence character, shaped by its historic incorporation into the British Caribbean and later the U.S. sphere of economic domination, had suited not only the North American corporations that managed the extractive economy and their Somocista partners, but also, in many ways, the ethnically diverse inhabitants. As Hale (1994) observes, given their historical understanding of the fate of indigenous peoples in western Nicaragua, the Frente expected the Miskitu to behave as and have the consciousness of an oppressed class that would seek its liberation in the national revolutionary transformation. The Frente was wrong not only about the Miskitu, but about the indigenous communities of the western region as well.

The success of the Atlantic Coast indigenous peoples in legitimizing their identities and agendas during the last years of Sandinismo had been deeply impacted by the influence of pan-Indianist movements from North America. The relationship between the Miskitu insurrections and a number of North American Indian organizations, such as the American Indian Movement (AIM) and Akwesasne Notes, has been well established. The success of the Miskitu, a relatively small indigenous minority, in establishing their right to negotiate over land and community, even regional, autonomy established a tremendous precedent for the indigenous communities of the western region. Nevertheless, the Miskitu were also taken aback by early organizing by the western communities after 1990. Flavio described several scenes in the early 1990s, during which delegations of indigenous leaders from Monimbó, Sutiava, and the northern highlands had greatly surprised the Miskitu leaders by showing up for meetings with pan-Indianist leaders trying to organize for the quincentennial of the Columbus voyage. "It is for certain," Flavio told me in 1993,

that they [the Miskitu] didn't believe we existed anymore—just like the mestizos here [in the western region] didn't believe it . . . it was we, here in the western part, who did the work to organize for the quincentennial, and we also forced the UNO to include a Parlamento Indígena of our leaders in the Casa del Gobierno. It's true that the Revolution did not help indigenous communities develop. This is very ironic, because the participation of the indigenous communities of the Pacific was decisive in the Sandinista triumph. The Frente only recognized the rights of Indians on the Atlantic Coast; the *costeños* were against the Revolution, but they got autonomy. The Indians of the Pacific were always in favor of the Revolution, but they got nothing. Now [after the defeat of the Sandinistas] it is up to us in the indigenous communities [in the western region] to investigate our situation. Where are the titles to our lands? Why did our languages disappear?

Panindigenous organizations from Latin America exercised a direct influence on the movement in western Nicaragua through their sponsorship of a Nicaraguan section of the Parlamento Indígena de América (Indigenous Parliament of America), a panhemispheric organization to commemorate the quincentennial of Columbus's arrival in the Caribbean. The presence of panhemispheric organizations, and the high tide of their influence on the western Nicaraguan movement, culminated when the Third Continental Meeting of Black, Indigenous, and Popular Resistance was held in Managua from October 6 to 12, 1992.

The success of the Miskitu stamped an indelible pattern upon the thinking of the indigenous leaders from the western zone such as Flavio. The issues of control over land, community autonomy, and resistance to the state are the hallmarks of that pattern. Although these issues constitute the substance of many if not all indigenous movements elsewhere in Latin America, there are several movements—the indigenous Confederación de Nacionalidades Indígenas del Ecuador (CONAIE) (see 1989) in Ecuador, the sprawling Mayan movement in Guatemala (see Warren 1992, 1996), the Ejercito Zapatista de Liberación Nacional (EZLN) in Mexico (see Ouwenweel 1996; Gossen 1996)—which situate such issues within an overall demand for reconfiguring the nation and national identity. This would reconfigure national identities not only for Indian minorities, but for mestizo majorities as well. One might argue that the condition of being a minority dictates that the indigenous movement in Nicaragua must be a minority movement struggling for minority rights, but the example of the indigenous movement in Colombia (see Rappaport and Dover 1996) suggests that the option of larger goals for movements based among indigenous minorities exists. In western Nicaragua, the indigenous movement has its sights set on land rights for the small number of extant indigenous communities, which is the result not only of the mold set by the Miskitu, but also the origins of western Nicaragua's indigenous leadership in the mass movements of the Sandinista period, and this leadership's specific counternarrative of Nicaraguan history.

The public discourse of indigenous intellectuals such as Flavio, de la Concepción Fonseca of Sutiava, Jorge Hernández of Sebaco, and others is dominated by the struggle for land, particularly land in a communal form, and for community development through government support of infrastructure and education. The indigenous movement in the western region thus responds specifically to the exigencies facing indigenous communities in the northern highlands and north Pacific Coast. These communities, mainly small villages of farming folk as well as the large urban barrio of Sutiava, are located in zones of historically heavy agro-export production and massive concentration of land ownership in very few hands at the expense of the communal lands of indigenous communities. Notwithstanding important differentiating factors among these communities, I found that the focus on the search for original titles to lands and on ongoing battles with municipal authorities refusing to recognize either the legitimacy of indigenous land claims or the rights of the indigenous community to participate in municipal government stand out as their common themes (see also Rizo Zeledón 1992).

These concerns were highlighted during a 1993 meeting called by a national environmentalist group called PAANIC (Programa de Acción Ambiental de Nicaragua, or Environmental Action Program of Nicaragua) in connection with the World Bank's certification of the environmental credentials of the UNO government's economic development plans. Ecological concerns may have been the theme of the meeting, but the delegates from western Nicaraguan indigenous communities sounded the theme of land reform by reiterating demands for reconstituting indigenous communities' communal lands and for ecologically sound agriculture to replace pesticide-intensive agro-export production. De la Concepción Fonseca and other Sutiava representatives linked agro-export, environmental collapse, and disenfranchisement of indigenous communities because of their long experience with cotton in the León region, the most pesticide-intensive crop grown in Nicaragua. Although the Sandinistas had reduced the use of pesticides, the Sutiavas claimed this occurred more because of their expense than out of commitment to appropriate or clean technologies, which Biondi-Morra's (1993) study substantiated. The Sutiava people envisaged organic cultivation of cotton and other crops on reclaimed communal lands that had been lost to the large cotton firms decades earlier.

A tour around northern and central Nicaragua with Flavio hammered home the focal themes of the indigenous movement. In El Chile, where my interests focused on the weaving tradition, the linguistic evidence for Matagalpa words surviving in villagers' everyday speech, and the role of the *consejo de ancianos* in community affairs, Flavio went to meet with community president Hipolito Lopez concerning the recovery of communal lands—not about cultural issues. In Sebaco, Flavio met with Hernández, who like most people in the indigenous community raised cattle, about regaining title to pasture lands that had belonged to the community before the 1940s. Indigenous leaders in the tiny village of Samulalí, where people raised beans on their tiny plots and worked for minuscule wages on coffee plantations repossessed by their old owners after 1990, talked with Flavio about land. Gustavo Adolfo Gonzalez Cano, president of the local indigenous communities in the Jinotega region, reviewed land titles with Flavio and me. After this series of meetings I realized that although Flavio has published articles that analyze dance and ritual (Gamboa 1989) and dreams of Nahuatl language instruction in Monimbó, these remain rather private topics in comparison to the movement's goals of regaining land.

With respect to the experiences, problems, and aspirations of artisans in the indigenous communities of Masaya-Carazo, the relevance of the contemporary indigenous movement in western Nicaragua is far less clear. Monimbó's involvement with the indigenous movement does reflect a desire within that community to regain long lost outlying lands in the hilly countryside south of the barrio. But I would contend, and Flavio has agreed, that Monimbó's involvement may derive just as much from this community's historical opposition to a succession of Nicaraguan state-building efforts, opposition that the indigenous movement offers in the 1990s. Because San Juaneros are not engaged in a struggle over land, nor is their particular indigenous identity defined by historical opposition to the state, the contemporary indigenous movement does not offer very much of interest. The San Juaneros I have known have not joined the discourse on indigenous identity. In my discussions with Agustín, Roberto, Catalina, Juanita, and many others, I found that as the artisanal economy contracts and changes, the idea of ethnic identity makes little practical sense to them, even as people continue to make pots and perform the *chilillo* at the Fiesta of San Juan that reenacts and subverts the Spanish Conquest, much like *El Güegüence* in nearby Monimbó. By contrast, in Matagalpa, the women who make *cerámica negra,* formerly vociferous critics of the *indigenismo* of Cardenal's Ministry of Culture, who proudly defended the mestizo origins of their craft, have positioned themselves differently in the UNO era. The *cerámica negra* women in Matagalpa and Jinotega can potentially gain from a relationship with the indigenous movement because of the movement's high profile in the north. This helps to explain the latest version of the history of their craft in their cooperative's pamphlet, which reiterates what María Esthela had written to Gia and me: "Cerámica negra has been dated by archaeologists to the Formative Period (1500 BC–400 AD) . . . Cerámica negra has experienced the phenomenon of cultural persistence, maintaining in virtually the same form the technical and esthetic roots [derived from] aboriginal culture" (Sociedad Colectiva de Cerámica Negra 1990).

In 1995, María Esthela showed me the schedule of events from a newsletter of one of the several indigenous associations operating in the Matagalpa region. She was listed as a speaker for one event, called "Problems of Indigenous Artisan Women," along with one of the El Chile women. I asked her about the event and its implications, and she responded by reminding me how few artisans of any kind lived in and around Matagalpa, and that it was very important for her family to find other artisans with whom to pursue common goals. In the sociocultural milieu of the post-Sandinista state, which she emphasized does nothing to encourage artisans and artisanal production, the women see the indigenous organizations of the Matagalpa region as the best venue for their opposition to this state. The *cerámica negra* women have thus sealed their common cause with the indigenous organizations of Matagalpa by constructing an indigenous history for their craft. By making artisanal production a sign of indigenous ethnic identity, their connection to the indigenous organizations works through the El Chile people, who, like the other indigenous people in Matagalpa, are mainly engaged in a struggle to recover communal lands.

The San Juaneros' disinterest in the indigenous movement does not discredit the movement, but it does underscore that the movement's themes are irrelevant to some of the kinds of Indians who survived into the twentieth century. The counternarrative to the myth of Nicaragua mestiza promoted by the indigenous movement challenges the telos of the myth but also acknowledges one of its common-knowledge assumptions: the boundary between Indian and mestizo. Thus, the blue thread is again only about being Indian, but narrates survival rather than disappearance. Unfortunately, this counternarrative of the blue thread seems to stimulate knowledge and truth-making mechanisms that reify the assumptions of the myth of Nicaragua mestiza rather than undermining the myth as a regime of truth. "Say, boys, are we going forward or backward?" Güegüence wonders. The post-Sandinista literature written by Nicaraguan academics concerned with the persistence of indigenous identity understands that persistence through fairly conventional analyses of essential cultural traits and ethnic markers. Membraño Idiaquez (1992), for example, concludes that the persistence of ritual, traditional community organizations such as the *consejo de ancianos* and the *alcalde de vara,* artisanal production, and the institution of communal land are among those objectively observable traits responsible for maintaining indigenous identity in Monimbó and Sutiava. But at the heart of such persistence, he argues that "what has made possible the creation and recreation of a historical and sociocultural continuity between the present and the pre-Columbian past of the Sutiava and Monimbo communities is the persistence of systems of clan and lineage-based kinship" (141).

In the same volume in which Membraño's Idiaquez's article appeared, Alessandra Castegnaro de Foletti (1992), an Italian anthropologist who has worked in Nicaragua, has essentialized the pottery making of La Paz Centro as an indigenous "Chorotega" tradition in a manner akin to the same *indigenismo* promoted by Cardenal's Ministry of Culture that was resoundingly rejected by the San Juanero artisans in the 1980s. In a later volume, *La estructura de las comunidades étnicas* (The structure of indigenous communities) (1994), Membraño Idiaquez elaborated his theory of the clan and lineage basis for indigenous identity, particularly in Sutiava and Monimbó, in terms of structural Marxist theory. The temptation to legitimize indigenous persistence in western Nicaragua through the identification of cultural essences emphasizes the profound entrenchment of the "knowl-edge assumptions" upon which regimes of truth such as the myth of Nicaragua mestiza are built. Even Gould's work, which has turned the myth on its head, still relies on a boundary line between Indian and mestizo that sets Indians outside the nation and mestizos within.

To ultimately undermine the myth of Nicaragua mestiza means to abandon the ethnic boundary and redefine Nicaraguan national iden-tity for all of the peoples within its borders. This is not the purpose of the contemporary indigenous movement in the western region, as I have shown, notwithstanding the places within Flavio's discourse that appear conducive to such an endeavor. Treating the time of the blue thread as a parable of daily work and life in Masaya-Carazo does not offer a ready-made solution to this challenge, but it does point away from ethnic identity discourses. Discourses about revo-lutionary class identities and universal gender categories have also proved inadequate. If a parable makes a point, the point seems to be that entirely new narratives must be told about the Nicaraguan peoples to reconstruct the truth(s) about the nation and reconfigure the knowledge-producing mechanisms of the state.

Chapter 5

Whither the Grimace?

Reimagining Nation, State, and Culture

Unfolding a Parable for Change

In the previous three chapters, I have explored why several forms of collective identity have posed different kinds of predicaments for the western Nicaraguan artisans with whom I have been working. As I have shown, artisan communities were not able to pursue their collective goals as a revolutionary class except very temporarily, and only some artisan communities have found the contemporary indigenous movement a viable option for them. At the same time, the feminist movement has not addressed the interests of *artesanas,* which are indeed distinct from and at times opposed to those of male artisans. The framework for these discussions has been the elite demarcation of Nicaraguan identity epitomized in the literature about the ancient play *El Güegüence* or, in more general terms, the state-led construction of the Nicaraguan nation.

Elite appropriations of *El Güegüence* construed the play as a parable of mestizo national identity, in which *mestizaje* is defined as the victory of a national majority of ethnically bounded non-Indian individuals in active collaboration with the state. By contrast, I interpret this play as a parable of cultural history that is not necessarily a declaration of cultural identity. As an anti-essentialist parable, the play is a scatological reflection upon power and the state, at the same time evoking collective loss and humor broadly associated with the national experience of disempowered social groups. As I describe in this chapter, for those most intimately involved in the performance of the play, *El Güegüence* tells a story about the passing of time, the absurdity of authority, and the contradictions of coping with the inheritances of the past. Ultimately, I suggest that interpreting *El Güegüence* as a parable of the passage of time and power provides the necessary critical and humorous skepticism toward all state and national projects wherein to quarry a vein of hope: the possibility that diverse groups of Nicaraguans might reimagine their nation. If the artisans' experiences of the past two decades at all prefigure this reimagining, then it will be shaped by both utopian and quotidian needs and desires. So it is appropriate to invoke Güegüence, imploring Governor Tastuanes to "[p]ermit me to offer up this morning star, that shines to the other side of the sea, and this vial of gold with which to heal the Royal Court of Lord Governor Tastuanes" (Lejarza 1991: 63). In response, the raucous laughter of the Monimboseño audiences whom Flavio recalled seemed to liberate them from the fantasies of both the powerful and the powerless, and then remind that audience, with a grimace, of the necessities at hand.

This chapter, then, is about general preconditions for reimagining the Nicaraguan nation, illustrated by ethnographic accounts among the artisan communities in the Masaya-Carazo region where I have been working. If I have shown the inadequacy, incompleteness, even exhaustion of using class, gender, and ethnicity to name and organize identity in western Nicaragua under the terms spelled out by elite and revolutionary discourses of culture and nation, it is necessary to re-interrogate anthropology's role in this conceptual straitjacket. The same concepts that have been and remain the most limiting upon the imaginaries of nationalism (B. Williams 1989, 1991) are in many ways replicated in anthropological discourses (see Diskin 1991; Field 1994a, 1994b; Hale 1994). Anthropologists should examine and then divorce themselves from the complicity of their discourses, especially of identity and culture, with the assumptions of nation-building and nationalism, a complicity that limits the range of thinking about the possibilities of change. Nandy (1987) has prescribed three skepticisms for social scientists which would facilitate such a divorce: skepticism toward the nation, toward the notion of scientific progress, and toward teleologies of history. Nandy views these positions as a means to advance the accountability of academic work toward the subaltern and the disempowered. Based on the paradoxes I have encountered in working with artisans in western Nicaragua, I would add another skepticism: toward discourses of identity.

In anthropology, calls for disavowing bounded conceptions of identity have been sounded for some years now (e.g., see B. Williams 1989; Alonso 1994; Field 1994b; Trouillot 1991). Dominguez (1989), moreover, has shown how the anthropological understanding of culture as trait-defined and bounded, a thing that is malleable, can be destroyed unwittingly or controlled willfully, acts complicitly with state-led projects to preserve, modify, or erase aspects of culture considered vital or dangerous to a state-defined "national heritage." These scholars have outlined alternative analyses of identity distanced from the logic of nation-building projects, often in solidarity with the politics of diverse social groups engaged in what have been called "new social movements," which I discuss in detail later in the chapter. Several kinds of new positions are possible for anthropologists: directly contributing to analytic discourses within new social movements; using the positioning of new movements as frames of reference for academic work; attempting to bridge academic and political discourses; constructing analyses that are overtly opposed to nation-building projects that utilize concepts of race and ethnicity to reify the oppression of subaltern groups; and doubtless others. Smith's (1990) analysis of Indian identity in Guatemala, for example, addresses an anthropological literature characterized by representations of localized and bounded ethnic identities marked by language, dress, and behavior. Taking up debates within indigenous opposition movements concerning the relationship between class and ethnicity, Smith addresses Indians' historical resistance to the ladino nation-state and its structures as a source of identity. As a heterogeneous collection of ethnic groups that compose a political bloc in opposition to the Guatemalan nation and state, Indians are currently engaged in local resistance struggles through the cultural community created by municipality, indigenous languages, presentations of self, and rituals. The scope of Smith's analysis thus encompasses both local and national but, like the Indian movement, is opposed to the nation-building project of the Guatemalan state, and can be seen as helping to build the intellectual buttresses of that movement.

Within the North American academy, but also writing for those outside of it, there are also intellectuals working from subaltern perspectives. Writers such as Anzaldúa (1987), Moraga (Moraga and Anzaldúa 1981), Sandoval (1991), and Menchaca (1993) are exploring oppositional positionings in alliance with subaltern groups in order to bridge the chasm between new social movements and descriptions of identity appearing in the academy. Anzaldúa (1987), as mentioned in chapter 3, has worked to redefine mestiza identity.

Her feminist perspective explicitly attacks the dualist thinking about mestizo-Indian identity typical of both Latin American nationalism and social science analysis, although she maintains a boundary between mestizos and Indians that differs from the historical slipperiness I found in Flavio's discourse:

numerous possibilities leave la mestiza floundering in uncharted seas . . . the new mestiza copes by developing a tolerance for contradictions, a tolerance for ambiguity. She learns to be an Indian in Mexican culture, to be Mexican from an Anglo point of view. She learns to juggle cultures. She has a plural personality, she operates in a pluralistic mode . . . not only does she sustain contradictions, she turns the ambivalence into something else . . . en unas pocas centurias, the future will belong to the mestiza. Because the future depends on the breaking down of paradigms, it depends on the straddling of two or more cultures. By creating a new mythos—that is, a change in the way we perceive reality, the way we perceive ourselves, and the ways we behave—la mestiza creates a new consciousness . . . the answer to the problem between the white race and the colored, between males and females, lies in healing the split that originates in the very foundation of our lives, our culture, our languages, our thoughts. A massive uprooting of dualistic thinking in the individual and collective consciousness is the beginning of a long struggle . . . (79–80)

The difference between intellectuals operating within versus those observing from outside the struggles of social movements tended to blur to a certain extent during the Sandinista period in Nicaragua. This has allowed me, a white North American male, the privilege of folding my collaborations with artisans and *artesanas,* Indians and mestizos into this text, in an effort to struggle against the conceptual frameworks that constrict the future of these subaltern Nicaraguans.

In this chapter, I critique three assumptions that in effect stymie the original thinking that is necessary for the Nicaraguan future: the assumption that the state can act as a patron for the production of culture; the assumption that the state is an appropriate site for changing the nation; and the assumption that the nation-state is a viable entity for political transformation. To pursue the first critique, I explore contradictions in cultural policy engendered by the Sandinista state's attempt to straddle the model of socialist accumulation (Verdery 1996) and its need to mobilize the population through revolutionary organizing, both of which transpired in the context of the global implosion of socialist and revolutionary states since 1989. To pursue the second critique, I discuss the artisans' movements of the past two decades as a distinctive form of "new social movement," the explosion of which across Latin America underscores the crisis of state-led nation-building in the region. Finally, I question the nation-state as a viable platform for pursuing the politics of liberation, using both the suggestive terminologies Appadurai (1996) has introduced and the imaginative work of Bolt (1990), a Nicaraguan author who has reintroduced parable as a means to pursue critique and possibility in Nicaraguan history. Ethnographic narratives are used to illuminate these theoretical discussions, which are not proposed as utopian blueprints but as a set of preliminary tactics.

Critique of the State as Cultural Patron: A Postsocialist Frame

In the previous chapter, I argued that proliferation of revolutionary mass organizations during the 1980s facilitated the emergence of a wide range of social movements, particularly the new intellectual voices in the feminist and indigenous movements. Whereas I consider these phenomena largely unforeseen consequences of Sandinismo, others, such as Martin (1994), assume that these effects of the Sandinista revolutionary process were part and parcel of the liberating effects of socialist transformation. Whether intentional or accidental, the stimulation of local intellectual discourses under Sandinismo took place in the context of the battle over cultural policy which the "democratizers," led by Ernesto Cardenal, lost. As chapter 2 and authors such as Beverley and Zimmerman (1990), Dawes (1993), and Martin (1994) chronicle, Cardenal and his followers in the Ministry who favored rural, campesino, and nonprofessional groups of poets, painters, and performers lost out to Rosario Murillo and the Association of Sandinista Cultural Workers (ASTC), who wanted to fund primarily urban, professional artists. While the battle raged, the artisans' union UNADI emerged, and after Murillo won the Ministry of Culture closed and state support for artisans dwindled. Behind the struggle over funds, the two groups were promoting variant ideological visions of the sort of culture the revolution was all about.

It would be futile at this point in history to engage in labeling the Sandinista revolution according to rigid definitions of socialist, national-popular, national liberation, or other categorizations of revolutions derived from Marxism-Leninism. Vilas's (1986) analysis, which fruitfully distinguished the role played by class analysis in Sandinista ideology and practice, underlined the limits of such categorizations. But it is relatively unproblematic to acknowledge the very important influence of several strands of Marxist theory—Leninist, Gramscian, social democratic—on the Sandinista leadership, as well as the very significant political and economic relationships between the Sandinista state and the socialist states, especially Cuba, East Germany, and Bulgaria. These influences, at least in terms of cultural policy, always combined with and perhaps were overwhelmed by the experience of another Latin American revolution, the Mexican, which was itself shaped by several currents of socialist and anarchist thought earlier in this century. Granted these realities, the revolutionary process under the Sandinistas was heavily imbued by socialist theory and practice.

The logic behind both Murillo's and the ASTC's campaign to monopolize state funds for cultural policy and confine funds to small groups of professional culture producers and thus the conflict between the Murillo and Cardenal factions to secure state patronage stemmed, I argue, from a model of socialism that Verdery (1991) has elucidated, based on her work in Romania. Verdery explains that the overall strategy of socialist states was to accumulate means of production, including cultural means of production. In Romania, where the state had far more access to funds than was ever true in Nicaragua (whatever the cost to the Romanian citizenry), the Communist Party trained intellectuals to produce cultural knowledge, through which the rule of the Party was legitimated: "the [Communist] apparatus sees cultural production as a minor category of ideological activism and the function of art as indoctrination, providing clear answers to social questions" (1991: 88). Unfortunately for state elites, intellectuals' training made it possible for them to reject this function. By controlling the means of cultural production, including research funds, access to publishing, and especially the language of intellectual discourse, and always seeking as with all else to accumulate more of those means, the state had the capacity to recruit those intellectuals whose work best served to legitimate the Party. Verdery argues that socialist states were actually extremely weak, lacking any but the most fragile legitimacy in the minds of their citizens and therefore, "no socialist regime can countenance the production of ideological effects contrary to its purposes, effects that would reveal its nakedness" (90-91). The state's patronage became the essential factor in the success of intellectuals' cultural production, causing infighting within the ranks of intellectuals over the relationship to the state:

Because cultural and knowledge claims are intellectuals' only justification . . . the currency of competition [between them] will be a defense of culture, of "authentic" values, of standards of professionalism and knowledge . . . Often these will be wrapped around definitions of national identity and national values. The stakes are who gets to write the school manuals that present a particular version of reality, or to produce an official history, or to define the literary "canon," or to render the lineage of philosophical knowledge; whose books will be published, and in what press runs; whose projects will receive investments that will facilitate still other investments later; whose work will receive prizes—valuable not because they increase sales and, therefore, incomes, as in the capitalist world, but because the mere receipt of the prize enhances one's claims to future allocations and promotes the values on which one has staked one's work . . . Authors under socialism need mass publics to buy their works less than they need the attention of bureaucrats who will fund their projects . . .

Claims and counterclaims directed at the bureaucracy for allocations that will sustain culture's producers are what animate the abstract tendency . . . for the center to acquire "allocative capacity" even over the symbolic constitution of society. (94, 97)

I think such effects were produced by the state patronage system in Nicaragua, although more subtly than overtly and more or less in an embryonic form.[1] The Murillo supporters in the ASTC clearly wanted a more monopolistic control over cultural production and a steady accumulation of the means to produce culture. But both her faction and Cardenal's attempted to lay claim to state patronage by using ideological appeals to the central leadership and its control over the revolutionary nation-building project, rather than by demonstrating the greater efficacy of one policy over another through recourse to the logic of the market or other data. Artisans, as seen in chapter 2, rejected affiliation with any of the factions fighting over cultural policy and thus avoided being pigeonholed as culture producers. By forming their own union, they tried to recast their concerns and demands within the realm of small-scale industrial production. The following ethnographic narrative traces the effects of state intervention and the effort to accumulate cultural means of production in the hands of the cultural bureaucracy for those families and individuals involved in the performance of *El Güegüence* in Masaya-Carazo. Given the play's central role in the construction of Nicaraguan cultural identity for elites and Sandinistas alike, such intervention was both inevitable and unavoidable, illustrating this critique of the state as a patron of cultural production.

In 1995, Flavio and I traveled around Masaya-Carazo and the northern highlands trying to find as many different textualizations of *El Güegüence* as we could, but also in search of people who acted in, organized, or provided key materials for the play's performance. In the towns of Masaya-Carazo, we found individuals who were doing all of these things. "We will have to spend some time in Monimbó, in Niquinohomo, in Diriomo, and in Diriamba," Flavio told me, naming towns of the ancient Mangue-speaking heartland surrounding San Juan de Oriente, where I had worked for so long.

My long-standing work with artisans led me to ask Flavio about the wood carvers who made the masks used in the performance of *El Güegüence,* and to try to follow the trail from artisans to texts rather than the other way around. After driving around Diriamba's potholed streets, Flavio guided us to the house of the man he called the finest mask carver in Diriamba, José Flores Romero. José Flores told us that his family had been making masks "for a very long time," that unspecified period familiar to me from conversations with San Juaneros that usually means at least three generations. His family's masks appeared in performances of *El Güegüence, Torovenado,*[2] *Los Gigantes,* and other street theater performed in the towns he identified as Masaya-Carazo's cultural centers: Diriamba, Monimbó, Niquinohomo, Diriomo, and Nindirí. The day we visited, José Flores and his nephews were carving several Macho Ratón masks of various sizes, all made of wood from the increasingly scarce *palo de agua* tree, which mostly grows around La Boquita, a village on the Pacific Ocean. As far as he knew, *El Güegüence* was performed regularly only in Diriamba, and infrequently, usually only partially, in Monimbó, where I had seen one scene enacted in 1984. I asked José Flores about the texts used in the play's performance in Diriamba. By way of reply he showed us not scripts or texts but rather photographs he had taken of the last performance given in town that showed the masks he had carved in use. Whatever I asked about the play, his response was to show masks, photographs, carving tools, or other material evidence of his involvement with the performance.

In retrospect, the gap between my questions about texts and his recourse to materials other than textual ones may have had less to do with different cognitive maps in our respective heads than with another issue to which he referred only obliquely. In several asides, José Flores made clear that the past few years had seen fewer and far less elaborate performances of the play, and that demand for his masks was dwindling. At one point he remarked that during the Sandinista years, at least the foreigners, especially Europeans, had trekked to Diriamba to buy his masks. Now the foreigners did not come and no one had money to put on performances anymore. Just as we were leaving José Flores's house, it occurred to me that he had been frantic to show us just how important his role in the play really was, not only so that I would buy a mask, but so that he might appear in the book Flavio told him I was writing as a man without whom the play could not be performed in Diriamba, its last redoubt. He also referred to the unhappy relationship between the Church and the Frente as a factor that had contributed to the decline of the play. But before I could inquire further, José Flores was suggesting the names of people in town we should talk to about *El Güegüence* and Flavio was scribbling down directions to their houses.

First, we tried to find Jaime Serrano, a man José Flores had told us performed in *El Güegüence*. I later realized we were looking for the son of Leopoldo Serrano Gutierrez, the local historian and cultural authority quoted by the folklorist Enrique Peña Hernandez in chapter 1. We were not able to talk to Jaime Serrano; another actor José Flores mentioned, Marcia Avendaño, had moved to Managua. Instead, we ended up in the home of Juan Carlos Muñoz, a local historian (he showed us a pamphlet he had published about Diriamba's history) and a cultural figure, an elderly man from an old, prominent family and a force for some fifty years behind the tenacious hold *El Güegüence* has exercised in Diriamba. Juan Carlos Muñoz came to Diriamba from Masatepe in 1945 and became, according to his own testimony, one of most active individuals in the community in matters of culture and education. From his wheelchair, he was more than willing to discuss the mixed effects of the Sandinista Revolution upon the performance of *El Güegüence*.

Many of Muñoz's resentful feelings stemmed from the expropriation of a private secondary school he had founded during the 1950s, in which he acted as both a teacher and the principal. The school had been nationalized by the Frente Sandinista soon after their triumph. Muñoz wondered why that had been necessary, given that he had personally extended scholarships to children of poor families. During the Sandinista years the school had deteriorated, and now was vacant. Bitter about this outcome, Muñoz nevertheless told us in no uncertain terms: "I was not a Somocista, I never supported the Contra, and I was for the insurrections that led to the triumph [of the Frente]." He expressed what Flavio called a "realistic" assessment of Sandinista cultural policy and its effects on the performance of *El Güegüence*.

"I had been involved with the *cofradía* [religious brotherhood] of San Sebastián [patron saint of Diriamba], which organizes the performance [of *El Güegüence*] for many years: I was the stage manager," Muñoz told us. "During the insurrections, the triumph [of the Frente], then the war, participation in the *cofradía* was dropping off. People anyway had less and less [money] to give, or even to buy costumes or to get the materials to make costumes if they could find such things in the market." He did not blame the Frente for the crises affecting the performance of the play, recognizing the lengths to which the Sandinista Ministry of Culture had gone to record the performance of *El Güegüence* in Diriamba for posterity. One of Muñoz's children scoured his office and found a six-record set of music from the play recorded by the Ministry's ethnographic staff during performances in Diriamba. The records were elegantly boxed with lyrics, musical score, and detailed accompanying text. Yet at the same time that the Ministry was collecting, preserving, and salvaging the music of *El Güegüence*, the battles between the hierarchy of the Catholic Church and the Frente made the operation of *cofradías* increasingly difficult. Participating in a *cofradía*, he said, became "a political statement of opposition to the government."

Muñoz moved on in his discussion: "I was against the politicization of folkloric dances such as *El Güegüence*, which the people from the Ministry of Culture were doing. The way they would reinterpret the dance so that it had Sandinista politics, was just about Sandinismo; and so if you participated it had to be through something that the Ministry sponsored, not the *cofradía*. I think this destroyed the purity, the originality of the work." I asked Muñoz to talk about the history of the play, amazed that he would use the term "purity" to describe the composition of *El Güegüence*. His responses to my questions were surprising to me, coming from a conservative (in the Granadino sense) mestizo gentleman.

"This work comes from the seventeenth century," he said, "an era of transition, and this work is nothing more than a protest against domination and oppression from a long time before Sandinismo. Also a remembrance of what was lost because of the Conquest: *el tiempo del hilo azul.*" He laughed. "So we are not even supposed to remember about that time anymore, except through the words of Carlos Fonseca?"[3]

The influence of Dávila Bolaños's interpretations seemed clear in Muñoz's words, and Flavio asked him about the manuscripts from the past century and their role in the performance of the play in Diriamba.[4] Flipping through a tall stack of papers brought to his side by his children, he pulled out the actual script with handwritten stage directions used by the actors in Diriamba performing *El Güegüence*. It was a computer-printout copy of Walter Lehmann's original Nahuatl-Spanish manuscript as recovered by Arellano. It had come into his possession through Leopoldo Serrano Gutierrez and Arellano himself.

Muñoz's words represented an amalgamation of the many influences bearing upon the translation and performance of *El Güegüence*, and therefore his position was one in which political boundaries were difficult to draw. But during the years of Sandinismo, politically complex positionings could become an increasing liability, especially for those individuals involved in the field of culture production. In light of this conversation, the Frente's battle with the Church, the rivalry between two different institutions and their power to deploy and mandate the interpretation of symbols, can be seen as part of the Frente's general efforts to accumulate the means of cultural production, and a specifically restrictive control over the multiple meanings of *El Güegüence*. Muñoz's discourse suggested that the Ministry's apparently admirable salvage of the play's music could also be understood as draining some of the vitality out of the play's ambiguities.

For the next week, Flavio and I tried unsuccessfully to track down individual actors in Diriamba, and our quest finally led us to the outlying *comarcas* (rural districts) of Niquinohomo. Guided by Manuel Garay Vivas, the leader of the indigenous identity movement in Niquinohomo, we drove out to the house of Carlos Sotelo Potosme. Don Carlos, now seventy-five years old, belongs to a family that has been the lifeblood of local theater for at least four generations, as we were to discover. He no longer performs or directs his own troupe, and although some of his memories have faded, many were jogged when Flavio recalled the connections between their two families. Amid much laughter and head shaking, it turned out that his father, Carlos Sotelo Garcia, had helped Flavio's mother, Salvadora, put on a performance of *El Güegüence* in Monimbó in the year 1915 during the fiestas of mid-August.

Carlos Sotelo Potosme told us he had helped to reintroduce the play into the national limelight during Somocismo, when his troupe performed the play in the Teatro Nacional Rubén Darío in Managua, one of the few examples of significant public architecture constructed during the Somoza dynasty. His involvement in theater proved an asset, not a liability, in the Sandinista era. Ernesto Cardenal's Ministry of Culture recruited Sotelo's troupe for the Teatro Nacional de Nicaragua. In the early 1980s, Don Carlos performed *El Güegüence* in the Teatro and in Matagalpa, and then the Ministry flew the actors to Caracas as part of a cultural exchange with Venezuela. In his recollections, Sotelo expressed considerable bitterness about representing Nicaraguan culture for the revolutionary state in Venezuela.[5] They had been required to perform on a grueling schedule, but the Ministry officials appeared to have believed that the flight to Caracas constituted the actors' payment. "Can you imagine," he said wryly, "there we were in Caracas with one cordoba in our pockets: prisoners to poverty and the Ministry of Culture!" He smiled ruefully. "I suppose we were a good example of Nicaraguans, working hard, full of comedy, paid nothing at all."

What did you enjoy most about putting on *El Güegüence?* I asked.[6] His eyes lit up and he said, "For my part, the way that what the characters say has two and three meanings fascinated me, and has always caused me to laugh." I asked for an example. "At the end of the play, Güegüence is sad, and he asks Don Forsico: Are we going forward or backward? So then Don Forsico replies, We are going forward, papa. But at the same time, Don Forsico and the constable and the others are dragging Güegüence backwards, trying to get him on the macho to bring him to [Don Forsico's] wedding. It is completely absurd." Then for a while Don Carlos spoke about the total lack of funds for theater in the current time. "Before, we worked for the Ministry, but at least we had work," he declared in a eulogy to the cultural bureaucracy likely heard throughout formerly socialist states. That eulogy was necessarily tempered by the restrictions working with the Ministry had imposed.

The next day Flavio and I decided to spend some time in Diriomo, trying to find people who knew about the performance of *El Güegüence* in that old Mangue town. As usual, Flavio ended up in extended conversations with an assortment of old-timers who had been involved in the production of the play for many years. His meanderings eventually brought us to the house of Eusebio Chevo Mena, a ninety-five-year-old man who, like Juan Muñoz, had worked with the Cofradía de San Sebastian and had helped to bring performances of *El Güegüence* to Diriomo from Diriamba, Monimbó, and Nandaime. Don Chevo's conversation featured mixed praise for Sandinista cultural policies, a life-long adherence to the small-town conservatism of the Granadinos, and an attachment to the symbolism of *El Güegüence,* that recurred among older generations of individuals involved in things cultural in Masaya-Carazo. Don Chevo also told us that he did not mind that the Sandinistas had involved themselves in the matter of *El Güegüence,* but then asked with evident frustration, "Must we only have things one way?" It was difficult to pursue this line of questioning, as he tired easily, had very few teeth left, and perhaps I read too much into his words. Before we left, I asked Chevo Mena to name his favorite part of the play. "The end," he said. "Can you imagine? Something for nothing, he [Güegüence] says. They got something for nothing from the old governor. It could never happen, right? But this is how we are, we Nicaraguans. It doesn't matter what kind of a government we have." Flavio added: "And the joke is probably on us."

Flavio discussed these interviews with me at some length. I said that it was difficult to blame the Sandinistas for the fact that performances of the play had been dwindling since the late 1980s. No one had any money, and less so under post-Sandinista governments than under the Frente. The war, the blockade, the intense hostility the United States had directed against Nicaragua had far more to do with the play's decline, I contended. Flavio agreed, but observed: "Look, before, the state had nothing to do with *El Güegüence.* It was a protest against the state. Then the Sandinistas reinterpret the play, and they say it is about the revolutionary history of the Nicaraguan people. This is not wrong; Dávila Bolaños also thought this, and his interpretation is the best. Sure, the crisis is mostly to blame. But I think the involvement of the state in this, in what was [originally] against the state, also had an effect."

The Sandinista state's urge to accumulate cultural symbols and the means to perform them, a strategy of socialist states in general, emerged as a coefficient of *El Güegüence*'s decline in these conversations. Perhaps too, the anti-authoritarian sentiments readily apprehended in the play made it a cultural artifact particularly important to control and delimit. In that light, the Ministry of Culture's efforts to record, preserve, and otherwise categorize the play as a national "tradition" might also be seen as a corollary feature of the revolutionary state's instinct to own cultural production.

The critique of socialist cultural policy and its application to the Sandinista period is illustrative of the profound problems state patronage of cultural production incurs, both locally and nationally. The fact that these problems occurred under the democratizing guidance of Cardenal as well as the more obviously elitist influence of Murillo could lead one to seriously doubt whether state patronage of cultural production is a goal worth struggling for, at least in the nation-building contexts of Central America. Notwithstanding the application of socialist models of accumulation during the Sandinista period, the post-Sandinista state is not taking shape in the same ways postsocialist states appear to be doing in Eastern Europe (Verdery 1996: 225–27). Whether due to a longer history of coherent and cohesive state-led nation-building in these areas of Europe, or the large amounts (at least relative to Central America) of capital being dumped in a few of the former Warsaw Pact countries, or both, the post-Sandinista state does not resemble either the reconstituted "spoiler state" or the incipient corporatist state Verdery describes for Romania and Poland, respectively. Instead, the post-Sandinista state is a weak, vastly underfunded rerun of an old-style, agro-export-driven state, obsessed with the machinations of elite factions and fashions, in which the poor majority are almost entirely left to fend for themselves: something like a late-twentieth-century version of the Zelaya state, minus any manifestation of nationalist pride in reference to the United States.[7] But if a general attack is to be made upon the state as a current or future sponsor for producing culture in Nicaragua and elsewhere in Latin America, this does not mean that the state can simply be ignored with respect to the production of and the relationships between local and national cultural forms and identities.

Critique of the State as a Site for Changing the Nation: The Framework of the New Social Movements

Since the end of the cold war, the left in Central America and in other parts of the increasingly obsolescent Third World have questioned the value of taking state power, and indeed of the state itself, as a vehicle for social transformation in their impoverished societies. In one trenchant critique published in *Envío,* a Nicaraguan news and analysis magazine, authors Grigsby and Alvarado write: "In reality, Central America's [governments] have very little space in which to define a national or regional strategy. The path toward reconstruction has already been drawn by the International Monetary Fund or the World Bank . . . All the region's countries are applying stabilization and structural adjustment programs designed by these multi-lateral institutions . . . Is [the struggle for power] thus reduced to a simple dispute over who can best administer this model designed from the outside? Is the left's only alternative to enter the election race under the banner of progressive administration of this same model?" (1993, quoted in Sinclair 1995: 13). The evident irrelevance of the state in Central America means that states, of whatever ideological coloring, do not possess the financial means or geopolitical importance to substantively address either the causes or the effects of social inequalities. The failure of the Nicaraguan case, where an initially idealistic and energetic revolutionary state's nation-building project applied concepts of identity and culture derived from nationalism, socialism, and *indigenismo,* highlights the crisis of state-led nation-building projects in Latin America since the 1970s. North American analysts have not necessarily taken stock of the degree to which the current models of state and nation have been exhausted, and the need to imagine beyond these models if only in solidarity with the subaltern. Martin (1994: 76–77), for example, argues that "the legacy of the Sandinista revolution was to make the articulation of national identity, and of a cultural terrain that might forge it, finally viable." Yet his own research on new theater and dramatic performance describes cultural movements that have sidestepped both elite and revolutionary constructions of nation and national cultural identity. In the conclusion to Whisnant's (1995) encyclopedic overview of Nicaraguan culture, he favors an even stronger association between Nicaraguan culture and Nicaraguan national identity:

Since Nicaragua has never had an extended period of cultural tranquillity or unity, many of the perennial internal conflicts have occurred not between long-established and well-defined cultural sectors or groups, but between those that were themselves in flux, struggling to define themselves, to bring themselves into being, to establish themselves in relation to others. In some respects, then, with regard to Nicaragua one might usefully think in terms of a protocultural system or a system in process of formation rather than a cultural system in the usual sense . . . The poignancy of this emergent rather than fully resolved situation in Nicaragua is underscored by the fact that—in view of its small size, economic and political marginality, and continual susceptibility to economic and political interventions—Nicaragua has been especially needful of having a reasonably integrated national culture, however pluralistic in its local details. (443–44)

Whisnant's observations suggest that a "real" national culture would help Nicaragua advance. This assumption, so akin to the arguments of Latin American elites since the previous century, is precisely what recent authors analyzing the new social movements of Latin America have argued against.

The social movements literature addresses the post-1980 proliferation of diverse social actors in Latin America—women; indigenous peoples; students; environmentalists; gay people; urban artists; people struggling for regional autonomy, against development, for democracy and human rights, against military abuses—who live within national territories, but whose movements struggle against the state and many aspects of the national projects of states. In much of this literature, authors attempt to disengage the state from the nation, especially with regard to the economic development projects modern Latin American states have imposed on diverse national societies. They view social movements as the result of tension between rigid states and the growing, changing societies within them, as Calderón, Piscitelli, and Reyna (1992) have described. Authors in Escobar and Alvarez's edited volume (1992) agree that a number of factors that converged in the late 1970s conspired to shape the explosion of social movements all over Latin America: the theology of liberation; new ideas in the mainstream left; the complex networks between urban and rural areas sparked by massive immigration to the cities; expansion of the state's role in provision of social services and in development; and the expanded role of international development organizations among indigenous peoples and women. All these phenomena and the explosion of social movements describe Nicaragua from the period just prior to the Sandinista triumph to the present. These authors agree that although the appearance of these social movements has fragmented political goals, social movements have underscored the need for "collective imaginaries capable of orienting social and political action" (Escobar 1992: 68), such that "social actors [can] reconstruct a system that enables them to relate to each other, project themselves into the political arena, and participate actively in discussions about development alternatives" (Calderón, Piscitelli, and Reyna 1992: 29).

Escobar's focus on the cultural aspect of these social movements is intriguing in the Nicaraguan context. Using a broad understanding of Touraine's (1988) and Certeau's (1984) work, Escobar finds that for divergent dominated groups in Latin American nation-states, cultural practices are sites where strategies of resistance to power, particularly state power, can emerge. Social movements organized around cultural practices that in effect resist the power of the state generate tactics for resistance that are deeply rooted within the daily lives of dominated groups. Escobar's analysis makes it necessary to elaborate the parameters of the concept of "daily practices," their relationship to identity and resistance, and what sorts of phenomena constitute a social movement. His framework usefully appends Appadurai's (1996: 15) discussion of "culturalist movements," which are defined as "identity politics mobilized at the level of the nation-state." Both authors stress the importance of resistance to the state and the nation in defining such movements and in describing their relationship to local and global levels of discourse that are not limited by national boundaries. Their analyses illustrate the utilization of cultural forms to create collective political subjects.

The framework of the new social movements literature further elucidates differences between the goings-on I have described in San Juan de Oriente and in the northern highlands regions. The indigenous movement of the highlands clearly composes a new social movement that is also culturalist in its efforts to "re-Indianize" the highlands[8] through the reestablishment of land and farming practices that the movement marks as Indian traits. I want to argue that the San Juaneros have also been involved in a social movement of a substantially different kind, left mostly unaccounted for in the frameworks elaborated by both Escobar and Appadurai. This social movement, as chapter 2 related, first took shape three or four years prior to the Sandinista triumph and coalesced shortly thereafter. During the late 1970s, a group of San Juaneros, both men and women from several families, began to develop a neo-Chorotega style of pottery design and decoration. Their work in design and technique formed the basis for the work of the early Co-op and its instructional courses, which has since revolutionized ceramics production in the village. Clearly, the activities of these San Juaneros constituted resistance to the overall decline of *artesanía* that was the direct result of the economic policies of the Somocista state; just as clearly, the transformation of the production of ceramics was also a transformation of the practices of daily life, and was made possible by the deep roots ceramics production has maintained in San Juan, roots that most observers, Nicaraguan and foreign, have deemed "indigenous." If we consider the transformation of ceramics production, and consequently of daily life in San Juan, a social and culturalist movement, then it is clearly a movement that does *not* essentialize cultural forms as identity traits. The San Juaneros' movement is about an identity that does not depend on marked traits or cultural forms. This is underscored in the changes I have witnessed: from the 1980s, when San Juaneros threw pots on the wheel and painted them with inspiration from pre-Columbian art found in their backyards or in books of Maya, Mixtec, or Aztec artifacts, to the 1990s, when they have changed their designs to birds, frogs, orchids, zodiacal symbols, and concocted abstractions. The new forms and symbols used do not constitute explicit statements about cultural or ethnic identity but instead derive from relationships between artisans and the conditions of work, the work process and the marketing of their products, which speak to the realities of artisan identity.

This kind of social movement and the nonessentialized cultural production to which it is related are characteristic, I would argue, of several other successful artisan communities in Latin America. The weavers of Otavalo (see Meisch 1987) and the Zapotec weavers of highland Oaxaca (see Stephen 1993a) have developed markets for their goods outside of their home regions and countries by advancing production techniques and technologies and experimenting widely with their products in response to market demand. For these artisans, the goods they produce, which consumers associate with cultural identity, are actually less important than the process of production itself as a source of cultural identity. Insofar as artisans encounter state opposition to their efforts, artisanal social movements are also all about resistance to states and their national projects that have excluded, categorized, and persecuted such communities on both the individual and collective levels.

In rejecting the various unhelpful state interventions in their affairs, as well as their exclusion from the nation, Nicaraguan artisans in the 1990s have increasingly tied themselves into the global handicrafts market. This has introduced the fundamental incongruencies in the relationship between First World patrons and Third World clients, with the inherent distortions and inequalities associated with global marketing, especially through tourism and in the tourist market. Unlike Ecuador or Mexico, Nicaragua's integration into the world of tourism has been marginal, and in its rather minuscule heyday during Sandinismo the country attracted an odd sort of traveler, the *internacionalista,* who did not spend money or consume local culture in conventional tourist ways. Yet, even with a marginal tourist influx, Nicaraguan artisans have had to make the requisite adaptations artisans must make to produce what is considered marketable in the industrialized countries. In the Nicaraguan case, these adaptations have been impelled by the well-intentioned interventions of First World patrons trying to "develop" *artesanía* to help the artisans. This was brought home to me during my last visits to the *cerámica negra* women in Matagalpa, who in 1992 had finally fulfilled their dream of organizing a production cooperative, with funding from the Canadian version of AID (Agency for International Development). These funds had purchased a building in Matagalpa that also included a large retail store selling *cerámica negra.*

The Canadians had insisted on locating the cooperative-store on a beautiful and very old street in the city, which received little traffic. The women had offered other suggestions to the Canadians, informed by their knowledge that Matagalpa was not a city associated with *artesanía* by either Nicaraguans or foreigners: the production cooperative could stay in Matagalpa, perhaps closer to their house, but they insisted that a store selling *cerámica negra* should be located in Managua, maybe in or near the huge Huembes Market. Alternatively, they proposed, the store could be built near the bus station in Matagalpa, a heavily trafficked area. The Canadians demurred, and bought the large house on the beautiful street for the women and their cooperative-store, sending money every month to pay electricity, water, and other utilities. In 1995, the store was ready to close. "At the time," María Esthela told me, "I thought, should we refuse this money? But we decided to try because maybe we would never get another chance." When sales persistently stayed negligible, the women attempted to export their ceramics directly by setting up contracts with the Oxfam catalogue. But Oxfam would only purchase small and easily shipped items such as earrings, and the cooperative could not sell enough of those to make ends meet. The *cerámica negra* women had sidestepped the vagaries of state patronage and the marginalization of artisans in the nation, but fallen victim to the exigencies of reliance on international development agencies.

The difficulties encountered by social movements whose means to resist the state and reject exclusion from the nation derive from forging relations with international sponsors are likely to recur. This is clear even when the sponsorship is less clearly guided by profit and the market or by mainstream concepts of development. In El Salvador, refugees who fled their villages in the guerrilla-occupied zones created new communities in exile and are now returning to their old territories as a result of the war's end. Their attempts to reconstitute their villages on the basis of new concepts of leadership, cooperation, collectivity, and democracy, concepts realized in exile and through their relationship to the revolutionary left, have been in large part marginalized by the state and funded instead by external sources, primarily leftist solidarity groups in the United States and Europe. According to Salvadoran and non-Salvadoran observers (see Thompson 1995; Lungo Uclés 1995), this has put these communities into a relationship of dependency on these external sources, leading to their isolation from the majority of exploited and marginalized sectors of the population who do not live in the repopulated villages. Lungo Uclés (1995: 178) points out that this circumstance forces a realization that El Salvador needs a new national project "which involves both the wealthy and the poor in a process of consensus-building . . . not a revolutionary or popular project."

Such observations from Central American analysts force the question of how to go about changing the nation, the project the indigenous movement in western Nicaragua has not undertaken and for which I criticized it, without getting trapped in a revolutionary project of conquering an ineffectual state. Insofar as metropolitan academics are concerned, addressing this question may bring out a tendency on their part to unconsciously seek a new revolutionary subject in new social and culturalist movements in order to replace the working class or the peasantry, who, with the demise of conventional twentieth-century socialism, are no longer available to fit the bill. Insofar as subaltern groups are concerned, it is likely impossible for any kind of social movement to completely avoid confrontation with the state, however much their tactics in redefining the nation attempt to create new spaces for autonomy by sidestepping both. Two indigenous movements mentioned in the previous chapter have demanded a reconfiguration of the nation without necessarily aiming to conquer state power. The Otavaleño artisans are important participants in the national indigenous movement in Ecuador, whose goals are precisely those of reimagining the nation as *plurinacional* (see CONAIE 1989). This demand implies a drastic restructuring of the state to accommodate the power sharing a new Ecuadorean nation would require, but CONAIE does not conceive of itself as commanding this transformation. Likewise, the Zapatista movement, based in one of the major artisanal and indigenous areas of Mexico, has explicitly demanded a reconstruction of the Mexican nation by ending the monopoly of the ruling party, the PRI, over the state, without proposing itself as the new leading force.

In Nicaragua, the legacy of Sandinismo bequeathed thriving social movements of various kinds to the post-Sandinista period, but the party of the revolution (the Frente Sandinista) so far still confines its purview to the attainment of state power and limits its imagination with respect to the nation. The legacy of elite demarcation of national culture and identity remains strong for both the left and the right, and without a new approach to the questions of nation and national identity a new Sandinista state may be bound to repeat previous errors. Yet, I think it is mistaken to see only a sickening recycling of the same cultural themes and identities in Nicaraguan history, for which Whisnant (1995: 448–49) has argued. Nicaraguan social movements, particularly the women's movement, the indigenous movement, the campesinos' movement, and labor unions (see Randall 1994; Rizo Zeledón 1992; O'Kane 1995; Criquillon 1995; Baumeister 1995; and Quandt 1995), are demanding a radical revision of their relationship to the Frente Sandinista. Nicaraguan social movements are pressuring the Frente in ways that would require a new sensibility about the Nicaraguan nation and its diverse citizenry, a new structure for the party, and consequently a different sort of state, if the Sandinistas hope to win a national election in the future (see Quandt 1995). Neither the Frente nor the Nicaraguan people need be reminded about the severe constrictions on such projects because of Nicaragua's abject subalternity in the global economy.

Let us for a moment imagine cultural policy in a neo-Sandinista state in which the Frente (or several allied political forces) had significantly transformed the conceptualization of the nation. If we take the neoliberal economic and political policies that have become the guiding forces throughout Latin America in the post–cold war era and push them to their logical extremes, it may be possible to imagine a state that disengages from numerous functions that culturally favor either the elite or the poor majority. A state that does not represent itself as a cultural arbiter or intellectual wellspring of national culture and identity would not spend funds, create favorable tax structures, or publicly endorse either local popular cultures or the "Miami culture" of the rich. Who would get excited enough to work or struggle for such a neutralized state? How long would it take for such a state to shed its neutrality and make decisions that favor the rich minority over the poor majority? But then, there may be few other choices, given the U.S. track record in militarily suppressing revolutionary states in Latin America and the financial strangulation a new revolutionary state would be sure to suffer in the global economy. If we are to allow the possibility of a strategy of neutralizing the state, the work of reimagining the nation must still be addressed at other levels, both local and global.

No to the Nation-State: Toward a New Terrain

A hypothetical neutralized state—if such an entity could really function—would neither impede nor patronize the emergent local identities out of which postnational regions might develop. To "think ourselves beyond the nation," as Appadurai (1996: 158) calls for, I would argue that such local identities must be loosely bounded, non-essentialized, shaped by the experience of daily work, and connected to place without the mediation of either national or minority ethnicity—that is, more like the San Juanero artisans than the western Nicaraguan indigenous movement. But I do not consider San Juan a model, for a postnational future could "not be a system of homogeneous units (as with the current system of nation-states) but a system based on relations between heterogeneous units (some social movements, some nongovernmental organizations, some armed constabularies, some judicial bodies)" (23).[9] Myriad ideas will be necessary to think up a postnational political structure in Central America or anywhere else in the world, and local conditions will dictate the possibilities therein for both metropolitan and local intellectuals. Thus, although Kearney (1997) writes of a postnational Ireland in which the problems of two irreconcilable competing nationalisms in the north are subsumed by greater integration into supranational, capital-rich Europe, capital-starved Central American nations probably do not have this option.

In Central America, the new social, political, and economic imaginings probably have to start locally. By contrast, Appadurai has stressed features of the global sociopolitical and economic landscape that he contends form the foundations for the emerging postnational world. Two of his neologisms are useful to illuminate how little the global context offers for the Nicaraguan case at hand. "Ideoscapes," as he defines them, are political concepts either promoted by nation-states or social movements in opposition to states, but which have global, transnational currency. Appadurai (1996: 36) lists concepts such as "freedom, welfare rights, sovereignty, representation, and the master term, democracy," the transcendent power of which stems from their place in the Enlightenment master-narratives of the great imperialist powers that have dominated the world for some time now. The fact that he omits "socialism," "social justice," or "revolution," terms that have had and still retain considerable transnational significance in Latin America and Africa, may speak to Appadurai's focus on South Asia, the Middle East, and Europe. Alternatively, the omission may reflect the actual process by which the global ideoscape is slimming down to just a few limited and limiting concepts in the post–cold war-era afterglow of the ultimate "victory" of capitalism and the free market. The slimming process is no doubt facilitated by what Appadurai calls the global "mediascape," which refers to the technological apparatus by which information and images are conveyed. Neither the conveying technology nor the way information is organized and narrated is neutral. Both are saturated with values and norms directly derivative from the ideoscape, although, as Appadurai points out, in less obviously ideological ways, that is, in a Gramscian hegemonic sense.

Obviously, the global ideoscape served up by the global mediascape did not provide either the rulers or the ruled with a way to reimagine Nicaragua in the past three decades. This may be so because the Sandinista Revolution occurred at the very end of the cold war, just as socialism was about to fall apart; or perhaps the conceptual frameworks of the old elite state, such as the myth of Nicaragua mestiza, were just too entrenched to be undermined during the all too brief revolutionary period. During the almost eleven years of Sandinismo, I would argue, the Nicaraguan state and many of the Nicaraguan people were discovering the limits in the already existing ideoscape, in the concepts of nation, state-led socialism, and revolutionary change. Nicaragua under Sandinismo was flung into an extremely diverse mediascape, much more diverse than what currently exists, due to the efforts of multiple competing powers to exert influence over the revolutionary ideoscape. For example, Nicaraguan bookstores stocked a motley collection of ideological texts. The Soviet Union dumped as many tons of the Spanish versions of the works of Marx, Engels, and Lenin as Nicaragua would accept. The eleven-volume set of Kim Il-Sung's philosophical exegesis of *zuche* (self-reliance) were for sale for a brief time in two Masaya bookstores after the North Korean embassy held a small trade fair in the town. Spanish translations of Muammar Qaddafi's *Green Book* made their way to Masaya from the cafés of Managua, where in one, copies were left on every table for patrons to peruse. None of these items from the global ideoscape interested the San Juaneros, Masayas, or other Nicaraguan people we knew.

In addition, the Sandinista period in general engendered little of what I would call speculative literature, or literature intent upon changing the ideoscape, even though many people we knew were searching for new ideas, ways to think themselves, their localities, and their country out of poverty, war, and increasingly shrill political rhetoric. Agustín, Gia, and I found one Masaya bookstore that stocked a few science fiction novels from Cuba, which Agustín stopped reading after a while. Catalina scoured the library in nearby Niquinohomo and found the book about Quetzalcoatl published in Mexico. Her readings fueled both the new pottery designs she produced at home, mentioned in chapter 3, as well as several extended conversations about the pre-Columbian past and the aspects of that time she felt should be part of the future Nicaraguan society—reverence for women and closeness to natural forces. Catalina's imagination, she told us, rebelled against both the repetitiveness of political sloganeering by the Frente as well as the elite Miami culture served up by the opposition newspaper *La Prensa*. Both poles of the ideoscape made many of the people with whom we worked feel intellectually hopeless and disempowered.[10] By contrast, the Western European and North American *internacionalistas* had come to Nicaragua to find in Sandinismo a unique and beautiful form of socialism. They brought along their own social analysis, poetry, fiction, film, and other inspirational media, which they tried to map onto what they saw in Nicaragua.[11]

With the Sandinista defeat, and the postsocialist shrinking of the global ideoscape, the global mediascape transmits unadulterated Miami culture to Nicaraguans and their slavish local media. But in this environment, a few Nicaraguans have begun writing speculative and mytho-novelistic works expressing their capacity to imagine beyond the increasingly insurmountable limitations constricting their nation. I think of these texts as "schools" in the sense that Gramsci used the metaphor of schools and schooling to express the long-term strategies necessary to bring about the profound social, political, and economic transformations he envisioned. Along these lines, during the first two years of Sandinismo, one slogan found on walls was "Nicaragua es una escuela" (Nicaragua is a school). Flavio has consistently explained his work to me as one of pedagogy and instruction, and in San Juan the transformation of production, of creativity, and of daily life started with the Co-op's school. Current and former *socios* still recount the past decades of history by marking time according to the courses of instruction at the Co-op's school. Certain texts can also bring groups of people who read them through a process of learning that results in transformative political activity, and I argue that it is this process that is more likely to bring about a reconceptualization of nation or postnation than any arrival from the global ideoscape.

Montenegro, Belli, and the radical feminist intellectuals have schooled one another and a larger group of women through their novels, poems, and manifestos, which has resulted in the establishment of journals, bulletins, research institutions, and publishing houses (Montenegro in Randall 1994: 307–8). These intellectuals have undertaken ever bolder works of imagination to inspire the reconstruction of state and nation and the inscription of women within both. For example, Belli's novel, *Sofía de los presagios* (Sofía of the omens) (1990), clearly mined the local history and lore of Masaya-Carazo to create an almost self-contained geographic and psychological region of magic and intrigue in which the state becomes irrelevant to local understandings and lives. *El Libro de la nación Qu* (The book of the Qu nation) (1990) by Alan Bolt provides the most trenchant critique of the nation-state and extraordinary vision of postnational identity. Bolt, a playwright and theater organizer whose Nixtayolero performance group was at first financially and politically sponsored by the Frente and later became independent of Sandinista oversight, became attentive to the problematics of state patronage of culture in the construction of Nicaraguan national identity. Using sacred narrative, political allegory, poetic chant, parable, and manifesto, Bolt's book struggles to move Nicaraguan history forward toward new thematics, which in their emphasis on local identities, the power of women, and the bankruptcy of the state, act as a school par excellence for thinking "beyond the nation."

The political allegory in the book is its most straightforward facet. The complex civilizations of the Qu nation are conquered and victimized by the Spaniards through treachery and betrayal. A dictator named Misésboy and his progeny, clearly the Somozas, plunder the country in the style of the Spaniards, until the Liga del Quetzal (League of the Quetzal), that is, the Frente Sandinista, triumph and begin the Transformation (Revolution). But from the very start, the leaders of the League are infected by the arrogance and greed of the Spaniards. For example, these leaders decide, against the advice of their oldest and wisest supporters, that the people with the best ability to lead the country are those who can speak the most rhetorically, because "he who can best twist words together, like in a holiday wreath, is the best" (101). In its battle with the diabolical opponents of the Transformation, the contra Mictlantexotes (Death Warriors), the League ends up concentrating all power in the ugly, torpid City Between Waters (Managua), which had been the city of Misésboy and now becomes the city of the League. The book closes as the League and the Transformation are stymied by the contra Mictlantexotes.

Beyond transparent allegory, the book also reconfigures tropes from *El Güegüence* in a way Nicaraguans, perhaps, can best appreciate. The Qu nation, like the Nicaragua of Güegüence, is populated by diverse peoples speaking many languages, among whom the mestizos remain a minority concentrated in the City Between Waters. The book starts with a weary Sandinista, a political activist and writer, fleeing Managua for the healing effects of the northern highlands and its wild rivers. There, he encounters an ancient herbalist named Juan, who is in fact awaiting him. Juan is an old man who is actually wise, knowledgeable, and able to perform magic: a true **Huehuentzin,** or honored elder, unlike the ironic derivative of that title and persona, Güegüence. Juan tells the unnamed Sandinista that by eating sacred mushrooms he was able to pass through "the Blue Door." The blue thread is thus metamorphosed into a portal of time and knowledge, still a connecting thread but imbued with tremendous power. Beyond the Blue Door, Juan has encountered Ma-Chinda, a woman condemned to "death by silence" for having told the truth about the fate of the Qu nation, for having collected the stories of its downfall and put them together in a book. Ma-Chinda tells Juan the stories, including the political allegory of Misésboy, the League, and the Mictlantexotes, and Juan tells the Sandinista the stories. Ma-Chinda, unlike Suche-Malinche, is thus unsuccessfully silenced. However, Ma-Chinda dies as a result of her sentence, and the silence of women thematizes this book as much as it does the old play. For although the women of the League had been instrumental in defeating Misésboy, the men of the League and of Qu resent them, and eventually figure out ways to ignore, abuse, and blame the women. The women continue to serve men as they had been trained to do formerly, and among themselves are unable to break the silence about the misdoings of the League and of men. In this narrative, the book acts as a call to consciousness-raising for Nicaraguan women.

A third level at which the book acts as a school is through the parables Ma-Chinda tells, especially the erotic tales from a place called Temachalco. In one, Don Forsico's sexual ambiguity finally becomes permissible. Two male friends get drunk at the performance of the ancient play *Torovenado,* and one man decides to have sex with the other. He proudly penetrates his friend and reaches his climax, even as women run in and scorn him—not because of the act itself, but because he has apparently anticipated the correct moment to pursue carnal pleasure according to the protocol of the performance. Unsure of himself, the next day he tells another man what has transpired; this man laughs and tells him he must marry his lover now. In another parable, an old woman falls in love with a beautiful youth and sexually educates him. The youth's mother defends the older woman, proclaiming that it is only the idiocy of the Spanish culture that censures such experiences.

Finally, the book acts a series of open-ended programmatics for changing Nicaragua through its alter ego, the Qu nation. Bolt admits this in no uncertain terms, writing in a synopsis at the end of the book: "To establish parallelisms with the Nicaragua of today is not only inevitable but absolutely desirable" (209). Bolt extends the critique of Nicaragua's post-Conquest theology initiated by Dávila Bolaños. In a brilliant syncretism of Mesoamerican and Hispanic theology, Quetzal, the Supreme Being, marries the Virgin of Guadelupe, who is also Couatl, or Death. They beget Cipalmatal the Great Mother and Tamagastad the First Man, who beget Adaneva (Adameve) and the Virgin of Mercy. They in turn beget twins: Jesús, the "friend of the Spaniards who helps those who kill, and protects them in their wars, thefts and abuses," and Demonio, "lord of knowledge, humble artisan without pride, father of science and of the marvel of the mind, who is allied with the Indians and all the persecuted and humiliated, to help them leave behind their troubles" (21). The teachings of Quetzal are meant to drive home Bolt's critique of colonialism, the elite state, and the revolutionary process under the Sandinistas:

> There truly is no single truth.
> To speak of unity as the greatest knowledge
> is to not know of the light behind all things.
> The diversity of the rhythms of the light
> makes life diverse.
> And the rhythm of the light in things,
> and deeds and people
> changes constantly.
> Change is their essential characteristic. (29)

At the book's end, an apprentice of the art of learning offers a neoanarchist vision of the state: "The best government is that which impels the Marvel of the Mind, such that there will be no necessity of government" (200). In the meantime, the state must be guided by diversity, doubt, and a profoundly critical mind. The weary Sandinista decides to identify with "the magic that has to do with the energy and harmony of everything, with the knowledge of plants, roots, leaves, flowers, and stones, the meridians of energy in the world and in the body, the labyrinths through which the Universes communicate" (206). New identities for the peoples of Qu would thus be totemic (rather than ethnic), based on the kinlike alliance among human groups and places and natural forces, and the symmetric structure of these groups with respect to one another.

These are bizarre and fantastical visions and ideas that no one should really take seriously. But by reading and performing them, in conjunction with the ideas of many other local Nicaraguan intellectuals such as Flavio, individuals from San Juan, and elsewhere, a school for transforming personhood, the state, culture, and the nation could be initiated. If *El Güegüence* has been performed for centuries as a parable to inspire the ironic grimace of forbearance with the intolerable, then the tales of the Qu nation might be performed to drive away that grimace, replacing it with unforeseen inspirations for daily living. It is astonishing indeed that at this century's close, anyone could suggest that the artisans might still be a wellspring out of which not one but many Nicaraguan identities could emerge; or that the historic symbols of Masaya-Carazo enshrined in an ancient vulgar play could narrate the production of a twenty-first-century Nicaraguan postnation; or that the many kinds of Nicaraguan women might finally be breaking their silence in multiple ways. Then again, maybe none of this will occur. Macho Ratón could still grimace, and Güegüence's progeny could steal away wealth, hope, honor, and fertility from themselves for nothing in return. In Nicaragua, the choice has never been clearer or more impossible to make.

Notes

All English translations of Spanish materials in this book are mine.

Prologue

1 This summary relies on three historical sources: Millett (1977); Radell (1969); and Teplitz (1973).
2 Expansionist in the sense that Zelaya successfully removed the British presence from the eastern third of what is now Nicaraguan territory. This vast coastal plain became the Department of Zelaya, more frequently known as the Costa Atlantica (Atlantic Coast).
3 Somocismo refers to the social system and historical period dominated by the Somoza family.
4 For the purposes of this synthetic synopsis, I rely heavily on Brinton (1883). I also use aspects of the interpretations put forward by Arellano (1985), although probably not in ways he would phrase them, based on his reading of Lehmann's 1908 manuscript. Differences in interpretation among these and other intellectuals will be elaborated in chapter 1.

Introduction: Regarding Macho Ratón

1 For example, for all the hypothesizing about the authorship of *El Güegüence,* which I review extensively in chapter 1, it is very unlikely that the identity of the author will ever be known. In another vein, I find that reconstructions of pre-Columbian political history, intellectual discourse, and cultural identities in what is now Nicaragua are not merely speculative, but far more reflective of preoccupations and the specific analytical inclinations of the writers in question. The way individuals and social groups perceived their social and cultural realities before the arrival of the Spaniards and other Europeans is, at least in Nicaragua, for the most part unreachable. Pre-Columbian texts that survived the Conquest in Mexico, even though they are necessarily reinterpreted in the fundamentally alien contexts of the post-Conquest, provide the few tenuous threads to those other realities in that place. In the case of Nicaragua, the Spaniards incinerated *all* the books of the Nicarao and

Chorotega peoples, so such threads are not part of the fabric of interpretation.

2 I will refer to the play *El Güegüence* using italicized letters, but when discussing the play's main character, Güegüence, delete the italics and the "el." Similarly, I will refer to other characters from the play without italicizing their names. Names, words, and phrases from Nahuatl, Mangue, and other indigenous languages appear in bold lettering.

3 In Nicaragua, "mestizo" signifies persons of mixed heritage, both Spanish and Indian, who speak Spanish and are culturally Hispanic or Latin. The term is culturally rather than racially descriptive, because an Indian can become a mestizo by leaving behind her or his indigenous language, presentation of self, and religious customs. Guatemalans use "ladino" to describe the same cultural identity. Chapter 4 focuses in detail on conceptualizing and reconceptualizing mestizo identity and *mestizaje,* the process of becoming mestizo, so the reader must be content with this very preliminary description.

4 As I show, the business of indigenous identity in Matagalpa is not finished, although its problematics differ considerably from those extant in Masaya-Carazo and elsewhere in western Nicaragua. I am indebted to the work of Jeffrey Gould (1993) for my insights into the historical richness of the Matagalpa region, as will become clear in chapter 4.

5 This book certainly makes ample use of texts to discuss the demarcation of Nicaraguan culture by elite intellectuals, but in no way am I a partisan of the view that culture *is* a text. My view of the world/culture/existence-as-text theories coincides with those of Ahmad (1992), who worries that such an expanded claim for textuality

> suppress[es] the very conditions of intelligibility within which the fundamental facts of our time can be theorized; and in privileging the figure of the reader, the critic, the theorist as guardian of the texts of the world, where everything becomes a text, it recoups the main cultural tropes of bourgeois humanism—especially in its Romantic variants, since the dismissal of class and nation as so many "essentialisms" logically leads towards an ethic of non-attachment as the necessary condition of true understanding, and because breaking away from collective socialities of that kind leaves only the "individual"—in the most abstract sense epistemologically, but in the shape of the critic/theorist concretely—as the locus of experience and meaning, while the well-known poststructuralist skepticism about the possibility of rational knowledge impels that same "individual" to maintain only an ironic relationship with the world and its intelligibility. (36)

6 My intention here is, of course, not to lay a load of belated criticism on Adams's doorstep for work he did long ago. His later work little re-

sembles *Cultural Surveys*, and he has been an active and critically astute advocate for indigenous rights (see Adams 1970, 1990). Still, notwithstanding the character of his later work, I contend that his old book has played an important role in characterizing Nicaragua and western Nicaraguan identity, especially to the anthropological community, and thus in shaping anthropologists' historical attention to various regions of the country. Anthropologists certainly have not neglected the Atlantic (i.e., Caribbean) Coast of eastern Nicaragua, where there are readily identifiable, unassimilated Indians. From Nietschmann (1973, 1979) to Helms (1971) to the post-1979 work of Bourgois (1981), Dennis and Olien (1984), Diskin (1991), Hale (1994), and others, the Atlantic Coast has been a persistent anthropological site, underscoring, by contrast, anthropologists' avoidance of the rest of the country. Although this volume and the work of Lancaster (1988, 1992) and Higgins (1992) represent the reentry of anthropologists into western Nicaragua, ethnographic work is still minimal compared to the interventions of literary critics and essayists.

7 Another culture critic, Greg Dawes (1993), argues that a direct link exists between class background and the style and content of a poet's work. He concludes that the rise and fall of the Ministry related to the reemergence of bourgeois culture, itself a by-product of what he identified as long-standing and profound bourgeois penetration of the Frente. His analysis successfully linked changes in economic policies by the revolutionary state with changes in cultural policy during the late 1980s, which I also discuss in chapter 2. Yet his conclusions are so broad and far-reaching, they beg for some sort of ethnographic evidence, at least more than the denunciations of metaphoric erotica in the poetry of Gioconda Belli, a prominent Nicaraguan writer discussed in Dawes's book. Class, I will show, has been a key factor shaping social, economic, and political relations in Nicaragua as well as local identities. Disregarding the arena of the nation and national identity, an arena that also concerns much of my analysis, keeps Dawes ideologically pure, but collapses his analysis of cultural transformation and struggle in Sandinista Nicaragua into a flat portrayal.

8 David Craven is another author who has used rich ethnographic detail to describe the Frente's cultural policies. In *The New Concept of Art and Popular Culture in Nicaragua since the Revolution in 1979* (1989), he shows that the Ministry of Culture's nurturance of the intellectual and aesthetic creativity of the Nicaraguan masses was part of the Sandinistas' project aimed at reconfiguring the nation-state and national identity. The data substantiating his conclusions came from three main sources: the Popular Poetry Workshops and the rural cultural centers set up by the Ministry of Culture, the professional painters of Managua,

and the mural and graffiti artists working all over the country. Craven's defense of Sandinista cultural policy and its benefits to the Nicaraguan masses is impassioned as well as theoretically argued. Through a mobilization of Gramscian theory and the Latin American Marxisms of Ché Guevara and José Carlos Mariategui, Craven maintains that the Sandinistas were able to foster the cultural empowerment of the masses without dictating an "official culture." In his brief consideration of artisans, Craven collapses the differences between historically enduring artisan communities on the one hand, and the popular art movements sponsored by the Ministry and the urban professional artists on the other. This is noteworthy because the Ministry itself tended to perform exactly the same operation in its policies, as the artisans with whom I worked came to understand early in the 1980s. Moreover, Craven sometimes shortchanges the indeterminacies and contradictions suffusing Nicaraguan cultural production, as in his description of *El Güegüence*. Although he is undoubtedly aware of the deep controversies among Nicaraguan intellectuals over the significance of the play, he details only the insurrectionary interpretation that the Sandinistas favored.

9 Whisnant's (1995) cultural history of revolutionary Nicaragua is also worthy of note. Whisnant seeks to trace the historical construction of the cultural paradigm the Sandinistas utilized as a part of their overall revolutionary project. Like many other North American scholars', however, Whisnant's history is based entirely on information and testimony from high officials in the Ministry of Culture, who I will contend functioned on the basis of notions quite derivative of established elite cultural concepts. Moreover, I am particularly interested in the perspectives and testimonies of people outside the corridors of state power, such as artisans and local intellectuals. These people were acted upon by elite and revolutionary notions of Nicaraguan culture, and I focus on what they did with and against those notions.

10 This term was often used by Sandinista officials to describe revolutionary politics that were supposed to favor a number of disparate classes and social groups, which together composed the majority of Nicaraguans. This national politics, as chapter 2 shows, conflicted with the class politics that also played its role in the revolutionary transformation.

1. A Class Project: *El Güegüence*, Masaya-Carazo, and Nicaraguan National Identity

1 Ahmad's discussion traces the changes in literary theory from the cultural nationalist tendency many Marxists in the 1950s and '60s pro-

fessed in defense of the bourgeois national revolutions of that era, to the post-1980s poststructuralist theory that has favored a deconstructionist reading of texts and has denounced all nationalisms as the products of bankrupt Enlightenment rationalism.

2 Western Nicaragua presents a distinctive and somewhat baffling profile in this regard. Before A.D. 1000, jade was the material that marked status and prestige both to the north and to the south of what is now Nicaragua, that is, in the Mayan zone and in the Nicoya peninsula of modern Costa Rica, respectively. Yet jade ornaments simply are absent from the archaeological record in Nicaragua (Bishop and Lange 1993). Some of the jade worked in Nicoya originated in the Motagua valley of contemporary Guatemala. It must have been traded through what is now western Nicaragua, yet there are no traces even of trade much less of possession of jade in Carazo-Masaya and elsewhere in the region (Lange and Bishop 1988). Similarly, although after A.D. 1000 gold ornaments occur prominently in much of Costa Rica (although less so in Nicoya) and in the Mesoamerican civilizations to the north as a marker of wealth and status, very few such ornaments have been discovered in Nicaragua (Day 1988). In the case of gold, the elaborate ceramics buried with high-status individuals often display representations of high-status persons adorned with gold earrings, nose-rings, and so on, but the actual gold ornaments do not occur in such graves. Jane Day (personal communication) theorizes that western Nicaragua acted as a transshipment area for gold ornaments on their way from Costa Rica and Panama to western Mexico, but that little gold stayed in Nicaragua. She confirms my own suspicion that high-quality pottery was indeed the primary symbol of status and elite power among the Mangue and Nicarao civilizations, even though these peoples knew about and traded jade and gold.

3 Another, much smaller pre-Hispanic civilization of Mesoamerican derivation was extant on the Pacific seaboard of modern Nicaragua. The speakers of Maribio, related to the Tlapaneca languages of western Mexico and also suspected of affiliations to the Hokan language family, populated chiefdoms in northwestern Nicaragua. Their descendants are the Sutiavas, who live in a sector of the city of León also called Sutiava. Sutiava and Monimbó constitute the largest communities of self-identified indigenous people in contemporary western Nicaragua. In the following chapters, the role of the Sutiavas in overthrowing Somoza and in the indigenous movement of the 1990s will be mentioned briefly.

4 According to Brinton, *logas* are "scenic recitations with music, by a single actor . . . peculiar to the Mangues. A small theatre is extemporized, music is provided, and the actor comes forward, arrayed in old garb, and recites a sort of poem, with gestures and dancing" (1883:

xxiv–xxv). The *Loga del Niño Dios* was republished in Pablo Antonio Cuadra's literary journal *El Pez y la Serpiente,* no. 9 (1968): 145–51.

5 Harrison (1989) has shown that Quechua became the lingua franca for Spanish colonial and religious authorities in the Andean zone after the 1580s in a manner identical to Nahuatl's role in Mexico and Central America. Thus, both Quechua and Nahuatl became *more* widely spoken in the aftermath of the Conquest than before the Spanish arrived.

6 For example, Angel María Garibay, a Mexican literary historian, praised *El Güegüence*'s merits as a linguistic and literary tour de force reflective of the achievements of Nahuatl literature.

7 Lejarza's text reads:

Gobernador Tastuanes: Pues, Güegüence, ¿quién te ha dado licencia para entrar a presencia del representante del rey en la provincia?

Güegüence: Válgame Dios, señor gobernador Tastuanes, pues qué, ¿es menester licencia?

Gobernador: Es menester licencia, Güegüence.

Güegüence: ¡Oh, válgame Dios, señor gobernador Tastuanes! Cuando yo anduve por esas tierras adentro, por los caminos de México, por Veracruz, Verapaz, Tecuantepec, arriando mi recua, guiando a mis muchachos, ora don Forsico llega donde un mesonero y le pide nos traiga una docena de huevos; vamos comiendo y descargando y vuelto a cargar y me voy de paso; y no es menester licencia para ello, señor gobernador Tastuanes.

Gobernador: Pues aquí sí es menester licencia para ello, Güegüence.

Güegüence: Válgame Dios, señor gobernador Tastuanes, viniendo yo por una calle derecha me columbró una niña que estaba sentada en una ventana de oro, y me dice: Qué galán el Güegüence, qué bizarro el Güegüence. Aquí tienes bodega, Güegüence; entra Güegüence; siéntate, Güegüence, aquí hay dulce, Güegüence; aquí hay limón. Y como soy un hombre de tan gracejo, salté a la calle en un "cabriollé", que con sus adornos no se distinguía de lo que era, lleno de plata y oro hasta el suelo; y así una niña me dio licencia, señor gobernador Tastuanes.

Gobernador: Pues una niña no puede dar licencia, Güegüence.

8 Lejarza's text reads: "¡Ah! mi tiempo, cuando era muchacho, en el tiempo del hilo azul," cuando me veía en aquellos campos de los Diriomos, alzando fardos de guayabas, ¿no es verdad, muchachos?"

9 Lejarza's text reads: "Oh, válgame Dios, señor gobernador Tastuanes, no seremos amigos y negociaremos mis fardos de mercaderías de ropas. En primer lugar tengo cajonería de oro, cajonería de plata, ropa de Castilla, ropa de contrabando, güipil de pecho, güipil de pluma, medias de seda, zapatos de oro, sombrero de castor, estribos con lazos de oro y plata, que puedan satisfacer al hábil gobernador Tastuanes."

10 Foucault wrote with admiration of a strangely heterogeneous list from

one of Borges's stories, recalling " 'a certain Chinese encyclopedia' in which it is written that 'animals are divided into: a) belonging to the Emperor, b) embalmed, c) tame, d) sucking pigs, e) sirens, f) fabulous, g) stray dogs, h) included in the present classification, i) frenzied, j) innumerable, k) drawn with a very fine camelhair brush, l) *et cetera,* m) having just broken the water pitcher, n) that from a long way off look like flies' " (1970: xv).

11 In May 1995, Flavio Gamboa and I spent a week traveling all over western Nicaragua in search of Dávila Bolaños's books, especially his edition of *El Güegüence.* In Managua, Masaya, Niquinohomo, San Juan de Oriente, Diriamba, and Matagalpa we spoke to many people—local historians, actors, artisans—who had read his "Introducción Dialectica," although none of these individuals possessed a copy of Dávila Bolaños's volume. Finally, we found a worn-out old copy in the public library in Estelí; inside the back cover of the book, the publisher had recorded that a mere two hundred copies had been printed. More about my travels with Don Flavio are detailed in chapter 4. Thanks to Flavio, who returned to Estelí at my request in 1997 and spoke to Dávila Bolaños's son, I also received the bibliographic information about this unique intellectual which I have related here.

12 The works of both Carlos Mántica and Alejandro Dávila Bolaños inspired another philologist, Jaime Incer Barquero, who investigated the Nahuatl roots of Nicaraguan place-names and colloquialisms in his publications (see Incer Barquero 1964, 1985, 1990).

13 In colonial Spanish America, outside of the Caribbean, creole (*criollo* in Spanish) referred to persons of Spanish descent born in this hemisphere. By contrast, the *peninsulares* were Spaniards born and raised in Spain.

14 The idea of a clandestine anticolonial conspiracy composed of indigenous peoples in possession of pre-Conquest knowledge and wisdom has obvious appeals for many, including myself. But I know of no corroborating evidence to support Dávila Bolaños's claims. An allusive dialogue in Carlos Castaneda's *Tales of Power* (1974) seems to resonate with Dávila Bolaños's evocation of Los Naguales, even if Castaneda's work is seen by many anthropologists as fictionalized or simply fiction:

"For the sorcerer the Conquest was the challenge of a lifetime. They were the only ones who were not destroyed by it but adapted to it and used it to their advantage."

"How was that possible Don Juan? I was under the impression that the Spaniards left no stone unturned."

"Let's say that they turned over all the stones that were within the limits of their own **tonal.** In the Indian life, however, there were things that were incomprehensible to the white man; those things he did not even notice. Perhaps it was the sheer luck of the sorcerers, or perhaps it was their knowledge that saved them. After the **tonal** of the time and the personal **tonals** of every Indian was obliterated, the sorcerers found themselves holding onto the only thing left uncontested, the **nagual**. In other words their **tonal** took refuge in their **nagual**. This couldn't have happened had it not been for the excruciating conditions of a vanquished people. The men of knowledge of today are the product of those conditions and are the ultimate connoisseurs of the **nagual** since they were left there thoroughly alone. There, the white man has never ventured. In fact, he doesn't even have the idea that it exists." (140)

15 "Azul" is Darío's most famous poem.

16 In both Spanish and English, Selser's (1978, 1983) classics should be consulted, and Hodges (1986, 1992) probably provides the most comprehensive overview of Sandino's political and cultural legacies. In the vast literature about Sandino in Nicaragua itself, I have found Sergio Ramírez's work (1984, 1988a, 1988b) to be the most informative, notwithstanding my disagreements with him regarding *El Güegüence*.

17 The use of the dye-bearing mollusk, also known scientifically as *Purpura pansa,* to color cloth continues in Oaxaca. The technology used combines both the indigenous traditions with colonial-era and more contemporary modifications and has been beautifully documented by the Mexican institute La Dirección General de Culturas Populares in a volume entitled *El caracol púrpura: Una tradición milenaria en Oaxaca* (1988), written by Marta Turok.

2. Nobody has to give me permission for this, Lord Governor Tastuanes, or Why the Artisans Did Not Become a Revolutionary Class, 1979–1990

1 Diriangén was an indigenous *cacique,* or chieftain, who fought against and died at the hands of the Spaniards. That the artisans' union, which claimed a revolutionary class identity for the artisans, should invoke an indigenous warrior in its name highlights the complex interweaving of ethnicity and class for the union, the Ministry of Culture, and the Sandinistas.

2 If Western Nicaragua composes the Pacific littoral, the northern mountain region, and a large inland grassy plateau, the Department of Zelaya, also known as the Atlantic Coast, or Costa Atlantica, comprises the rest. The two regions, Pacific and Atlantic, feature sharply divergent colonial histories, ethnic compositions, and relationships to the Sandinista Revolution. Indigenous identity, and artisanal production as linked to indigenous ethnic groups, on the Atlantic Coast are entirely

different matters, both analytically and in the history of the Nicaraguan Revolution. Overt ethnic tensions involving black Creoles, indigenous Miskitu, Sumu, and Rama, and mestizos from western Nicaragua were ignited into armed conflict in this region both by the policies the Sandinistas pursued during the early 1980s and the manipulative proxy politics of the United States and its various mercenary armies. For this reason, the study of ethnicity in Nicaragua has focused on the Atlantic Coast (see Ethnic Groups and the State: The Case of the Atlantic Coast in Nicaragua, by the C I D C A Development Study Group 1987, and Hale 1994 for the most insightful and intimate looks at the conflicts on the Atlantic Coast in the 1980s).

3 I use the Spanish term *artesanía*, which means the form of production in which artisans are engaged as well as the products they manufacture. I also use *artesanas*, the female form of the Spanish *artesano*, to refer to the women who make *cerámica negra*.

4 Sandino's followers, as I wrote in the prologue, called themselves Sandinistas in the 1920s and '30s. Three radicalized young men—Tomás Borge, Carlos Fonseca, and Silvio Mayorga—conspired to overthrow Somocismo, and in 1961 revived the word Sandinista for their new group, the Frente Sandinista de Liberación Nacional (F S L N).

3. Breaking the Silence: Suche-Malinche, Artisan Women, and Nicaraguan Feminism

1 As in chapter 1, my rendering of dialogue here from *El Güegüence* departs markedly from Brinton's often wooden translation of the rhymes, alliterations, and wordplay in the original. Instead, I have gone to the recent reprint (1993) of Lejarza's text and attempted to preserve the playfulness of the original in an English vernacular. Below, Lejarza's Spanish version of this dialogue:

Güegüence: Pues, señor gobernador Tastuanes, ¿haremos un trato y un contrato entre este "tuno sin tunal" y doña Suche-Malinche?
Gobernador Tastuanes: ¿No lo sabe usted, ya, Güegüence?
Güegüence: No lo sé, señor gobernador Tastuanes.
Gobernador: Hijo mío, capitán alguacil mayor, suspéndase el trabajo en la residencia del escribano real y que obedezca nuestra orden; que entre a mi presencia con doña Suche-Malinche.
(El Alguacil se dirige a hablar con el Escribano Real)
Alguacil: Ruego a Dios que proteja a usted, señor escribano real.
Escribano Real: Ruego a Dios por su prosperidad, capitán alguacil mayor, ¿está usted bien?
Alguacil: Estoy como es debido, señor escribano real. Usted entrará en la

presencia real del señor gobernador Tastuanes para obedecer sus órdenes, lo mismo que doña Suche-Malinche.

Escribano Real: Bueno, entonces hijo mío, capitán alguacil mayor, suspenda en las residencias de los señores principales la música "Los Rujeros" y cosas parecidos para que yo pueda obedecer, lo mismo que doña Suche-Malinche.

Alguacil: A sus órdenes, señor escribano real.

(Tocan "El Rujero", bailando los dos)

Escribano Real: Ruego a Dios que proteja a usted, señor gobernador Tastuanes.

Gobernador: Ruego a Dios por su prosperidad, señor escribano real; ¿está usted bien?

Escribano Real: Estoy como es debido y vengo a obedecer sus órdenes, lo mismo que doña Suche-Malinche.

Gobernador: Pues, señor escribano real, hay un trato entre este inútil del Güegüence, que es hombre rico, y doña Suche-Malinche.

Escribano Real: Señor gobernador Tastuanes, que el trato sea el de vestirla con saya de la china, güipil de pecho, güipil de pluma, medias de seda, zapatos dorados, un sombrero de piel de castor, para todo un yerno del señor gobernador Tastuanes.

Gobernador: ¡Ah! ¡Güegüence! me indigna que escojas tan presuntuosamente.

Güegüence: ¿Desmonte?

Gobernador: Presuntuosamente, Güegüence.

Güegüence: Yo no he hecho ningún trato ni contrato con el señor gobernador Tastuanes; solo que sea mi muchacho.

Gobernador: Eso no lo sé, Güegüence.

Güegüence: ¡Ah! ¡muchachos!, ¿qué trato o contrato tienen ustedes con el señor gobernador Tastuanes?

Don Forsico: En cuanto a mí, el de casarme, tatita. (39–41)

2 Lejarza's version of the text is:

Don Forsico: No vaya, tatita. Ya he conseguido yo las dos botijas de vino.

Güegüence: ¿Dónde las obtuviste, muchacho?

Don Forsico: En casa de un "amigo."

Güegüence: ¿Quién te enseñó a hacerte de un amigo?

Don Forsico: Usted, tatita.

Güegüence: Cállate, muchacho. ¿Que dirá la gente si sabe que yo te enseñaré a hacerte de un amigo? (45)

It was Brinton who translated the Spanish phrase *hacer amigo,* or "to make a friend" in a sexual sense: "This is the phrase which is used by courtezans [sic] with reference to securing a male patron to pay their expenses, and for that reason Güegüence affects to be shocked by the employment of it by Don Forsico" (Brinton 1883: 81).

3 Matagalpa's water supply has been historically sporadic: water was available only during the wet months, and even then it was often brackish and of questionable hygienic quality. Carrying water, storing water, and purifying water have been the concerns of Matagalpinos for decades, concerns that the *cerámica negra* women also shared. At the end of the 1980s, the Dutch government funded a municipal water system that has changed life in this city dramatically.

4 Maxine Molyneux (1986) cites statistics showing that by the 1960s, the effects of the Somocista "development" of the Nicaraguan economy left two-thirds of women below the official poverty line, and that by 1977, women constituted 40 percent of the "economically active workforce," that is, women who were paid wages for their work as opposed to women not paid for working in the home. Putting the statistical information together, it is clear that by 1979, almost half of Nicaraguan women were wage earners and heads of household, having been abandoned by men who followed the labor migrations of the agro-export harvests or sometimes simply left their wives and children. This situation was unparalleled in all of Latin America.

5 Juanita Bracamonte and Catalina Bracamonte allowed us to arrange formal, recorded life-history interviews with them in 1985. Ena Bracamonte and Ester Bracamonte spoke with us informally over a series of months, but less intimately. Patricia Gallegos declined to have conversations recorded, but spoke with us at great length on many occasions, basically giving a full life history.

6 The deterioration of the market for ceramics and other *artesanías* post-1990 has meant that San Juaneros and other artisans in the Masaya-Carazo region are chronically short of cash. This has led San Juaneros, who in the majority own at least small pieces of land where tree crops such as bananas and plantains, oranges and other citrus, avocados, and a variety of native fruits as well as a few rows of the staple yuca are grown, to rely much more on what they can produce than in the past. San Juaneros commonly maintain a clutch of chickens, perhaps a pig, goats, and several cows on their plots, whose importance as sources of food has also grown. Commensurately, there has been an upsurge in rural criminality, which, I was told with alacrity, had never occurred before. Current and former *socios* informed me that chickens had disappeared from their households, that cows had been stolen, branches laden with ripe plantains and even yuca plants lifted from their plots. This means that in the 1990s San Juanero families never leave their houses and plots unguarded—at least one older child must stay behind to discourage theft.

7 Paola Pérez Alemán and Mercedes Olivera draw upon a number of U.S. socialist-feminist sources, such as Jaggar (1983), Rubin (1975), Hartman (1981), and especially Eisenstein (1978).

4. The Time of the Blue Thread: Knowledge and Truth about Ethnicity in Western Nicaragua

1 The proposed creation of an antifeminist, antigay, "traditional family values" Ministry of the Family by the new ultraconservative Alemán administration, publicized by an e-mail campaign from the feminist collective called the Grupo Venancia (1997), is symptomatic of the revitalization of the elitist gender-nation matrix. Such a move forms the crucible for a revitalization of the myth of Nicaragua mestiza.

2 The Lejarza text reads: "Déjame recordar mis tiempos pasados, que con eso me consuelo. Ah, muchachos, ¿para dónde vamos, para atrás o para adelante?" (Lejarza 1993: 49).

3 García Bresó, *Monimbó: Una comunidad Índia de Nicaragua* (1992: 51). Flavio included eight references in his manuscript; three of his sources, by García Bresó, Romero Vargas, and Dávila Bolaños, can also be found in my bibliography, but the others are not available to me.

4 *Revista de Historia* #1 of the *Instituto de Historia de Nicaragua,* n.d. (p. 23).

5 *Revista; Por el desarrollo de una conciencia crítica,* n.d. (p. 5).

6 *Enciclopedia Temática, Volumen 12: Los Anahuac.*

7 Ibid.

8 Romero Vargas, *Las estructuras sociales de Nicaragua en el siglo XVIII,* (1988: 163).

9 Dávila Bolaños, *El Güegüence* (1974a: 31).

10 Adolfo Bonilla y Sn. Martín, *Los mitos de la América Precolombina* (n.d.: 41).

11 Flavio has worked extensively with both the Spanish anthropologist Javier García Bresó and with the historian Jeffrey Gould.

12 Whereas during colonial times Jalteva seems to have been an indigenous community that resembled Sutiava and Monimbó, indigenous identity appears to have dwindled during the nineteenth century. Perhaps the utter destruction wrought upon Granada by the adventurer William Walker played a role in the decline of the Jalteva community, which represents one of the major instances in which an indigenous community that regrouped in the wake of the Conquest did not emerge into the twentieth century.

13 The strangest form Somocista *indigenismo* assumed occurred when, confronted with Sutiava assaults on the properties of local large land-

owners, Luis Somoza suggested that the government fund the teaching of the Maribio language to the people of Sutiava, even though the last speaker of that language had probably died two decades earlier (Gould 1990b).

14 "We" means the intervening metropolitan author and her or his audience. Flavio, as usual, cedes no ground to social constructionist views, but sees what I call "fluidity" as the ultimate evidence for the strength of tradition.

15 The National Federation of Indigenous Communities (FENACIN) and the Indigenous-Black-Peoples' Movement, of which Flavio became the secretary-general, became rivals on the national level, and, particularly in the Matagalpa region, local rival organizations surfaced, among which Flavio maintained his particular loyalties. In response to indigenous organizing on both coasts, the UNO government seated a representative delegation from several of these indigenous organizations in the newly created Comisión de Asuntos Etnicos y de las Comunidades Indígenas (Commission for Ethnic Affairs and Indigenous Communities), part of the National Assembly; although the Commission seemed designed to represent the interests of indigenous communities, by 1995 it had done little to address the basic demands of the indigenous movement. In any event, my perspectives about the indigenous movement in western Nicaragua have clearly been molded by my association with Flavio and his particular analyses and experiences.

5. Whither the Grimace? Reimagining Nation, State, and Culture

1 See Grant (1995) for a resonant case study among a small indigenous Siberian people in the former USSR.

2 Flavio has written about the *Torovenado* dance-drama (see Gamboa 1989).

3 I remind readers that Fonseca was cofounder of the Sandinista Front and during the 1979–90 period became a revolutionary icon second in importance only to Sandino himself.

4 His response affirmed all that Flavio had told me. As far as he knew, de la Rocha had copied the play from originals in 1833, originals in which anonymous scribes had translated the play from Mankeme, the Mangue language, to Nahuatl. De la Rocha's text, in turn, marked the translation of the play from Nahuatl to the Nahuatl-Spanish dialect still current in the early 1800s in western Nicaragua.

5 Martin (1994: 54–55) represented the cultural mission to Venezuela and Sotelo's role in it in rather glowing terms, which I found ironic after talking to Sotelo himself.

6 Recalling our visit with Juan Carlos Muñoz, I wanted to know more about the script of *El Güegüence* used by Sotelo's actors. He told us that they used Lejarza's Spanish translation of Brinton's text, which underscored the great likelihood that Diriamba was the only place where actors performed the play in Nahuatl-Spanish.

7 Gioconda Lucia Robinson (personal communication) relates that the main difference between the current state and the pre-Somoza elite state is that instead of the old elite rivalry between Leonese and Granadino aristocrats, the current internecine struggle among the elites is between a national group and a group that fled to Miami during Sandinismo. The former group is composed of elites from all over the country, and the latter has access to and is highly influenced by capital from the United States.

8 Charles Hale is responsible for naming the thrust of indigenous organizing in the highlands a "re-Indianization" of this region. He was also instrumental in helping me to see much more clearly how the San Juaneros fit and did not fit into the new social movements framework.

9 This musing brings to mind one exchange between a criminal and an authority in a recent science fiction novel:

Then the constable turned to Bud and said, very fast: "Are you a member of any signatory tribe, phyle, registered diaspora, franchise-organized quasi-national entity, sovereign polity, or any other form of dynamic collective security claiming status under the C[ommon]E[conomic]P[rotocol]?"

"Are you shitting me?" Bud said. (Stephenson 1995: 28)

10 People we knew did purchase the local works published by a press financially supported by the Frente (Editorial Nueva Nicaragua) and by other small presses (Editorial Vanguardia and Vientos del Sur). Editorial Nueva Nicaragua's books mostly focused on the political philosophy of Sandino and his war against the U.S. Marines, the formation of the Frente Sandinista and the insurrections against Somoza that led to the Frente's victory, and the analysis of Nicaragua's contemporary political and economic predicaments. The press also printed works of fiction and poetry: new editions of Darío and also prose and poetry written by Sergio Ramírez, Daisy Zamora, Gioconda Belli, and others.

11 In my personal journal, I scrawled pages of bleak predictions for the short-term future of the Revolution, predictions betrayed a few years later by the economic collapse of the Revolution, the electoral demise of the Frente, and the end of the socialist bloc. I also allowed myself to imagine a distant Nicaraguan future shaped by the eclectic influences of Georg Lukacs, Shulamit Firestone, Marge Piercy, Ursula LeGuin, William Morris, and Antonio Negri. These authors filled the small

bookshelf in our house in Masaya, and were read and discussed by the many visitors who passed through. Most of the authors are familiar enough, with the exception of Antonio Negri, the premier theorist of the Italian Autonomia Movement, an urban workers' movement of the late 1970s and early 1980s (see "Italy: Autonomia" 1980).

Bibliography

Abel-Vidor, Suzanne. 1988. "Gonzalo Fernandez Oviedo y Valdes: His Work and His Nicaragua." In *Costa Rican Art and Archaeology,* ed. Frederick W. Lange. Denver: University of Colorado Regents.

Abu-Lughod, Lila. 1992. "Writing against Culture." In *Recapturing Anthropology: Working in the Present,* ed. Richard G. Fox. Santa Fe, NM: School of American Research Press.

Adams, Richard. 1957. *Cultural Surveys of Panama-Nicaragua-Guatemala-El Salvador-Honduras.* Washington, DC: Pan American Sanitary Bureau, Regional Office of the World Health Organization.

———. 1970. *Crucifixion by Power: Essays on Guatemalan National Social Structure, 1944-1966.* Austin: University of Texas Press.

———. 1990. "Ethnic Images and Strategies in 1944." In *Guatemalan Indians and the State, 1540-1988,* ed. Carol A. Smith. Austin: University of Texas Press.

Adamson, Walter. 1980. *Hegemony and Revolution: A Study of Antonio Gramsci's Political and Cultural Theory.* Berkeley: University of California Press.

Ahmad, Aijaz. 1992. *In Theory: Classes, Nations, Literatures.* London: Verso.

Alarcón, Norma. 1990. "The Theoretical Subject(s) of 'This Bridge Called My Back' and Anglo-American Feminism." In *Making Face, Making Soul/Haciendo Caras,* ed. Gloria Anzaldúa. San Francisco: Aunt Lute Foundation.

Alonso, Ana María. 1994. "The Politics of Space, Time and Substance: State Formation, Nationalism, and Ethnicity." *Annual Review of Anthropology* 23: 379–405.

Anderson, Benedict. 1983. *Imagined Communities: Reflections on the Origin and Spread of Nationalism.* London: Verso.

Angel, Adriana, and Fiona Macintosh. 1987. *The Tiger's Milk: Women of Nicaragua.* New York: Henry Holt.

"The Anti-imperialist Darío." 1986. *Barricada International,* February 20.

Anzaldúa, Gloria. 1987. *Borderlands/La Frontera.* San Francisco: Spinsters/Aunt Lute.

Appadurai, Arjun. 1996. *Modernity at Large: Cultural Dimensions of Globalization.* Minneapolis: University of Minnesota Press.

Arellano, Jorge Eduardo. 1969. *El movimiento de vanguardia de Nicaragua:*

Gémenes, desarollo, significado, 1927–1932. Managua: Imprenta Novedades.

———. 1984–85. *El Güegüence o Macho Ratón: Bailete dialogado de la época colonial.* Managua: Ediciones Americanas. 2 vols.

———. 1985. "El Güegüence o la esencia mestiza de Nicaragua." *Cuadernos Hispanoamericanos,* no. 416: 19–51.

———. 1991. "La primera expresión literaria del genio popular de Nicaragua." In *El Güegüence: Bailete dialogado en español-náhuat de Nicaragua,* ed. Jorge Eduardo Arellano. México DF: Editorial Limusa.

"Los artesanos son parte fundamental de sociedad nicaragüense." 1984. *Barricada,* December 12.

Avilés, Jeannette. 1992. "La Concesión Taiwanesa y los sumos." In *Persistencia indígena en Nicaragua,* ed. German Romero Vargas et. al. Managua: CIDCA-UCA.

Babb, Florence E. 1997. "Women, Informal Economies, and the State in Peru and Nicaragua." In *Women and Economic Change: Andean Perspectives,* vol. 14, ed. Ann Miles and Hans Buechler. N.p.: Society for Latin American Anthropology Publication Series.

Bakhtin, Mikhail. 1953. "Discourse in the Novel." In *The Dialogic Imagination,* ed. Michael Holquist. Austin: University of Texas Press, 1981.

Baumeister, Eduardo. 1995. "Farmers' Organizations and Agrarian Transformation in Nicaragua." In *The New Politics of Survival: Grassroots Movements in Central America,* ed. Minor Sinclair. New York: Monthly Review Press.

Baumeister, Eduardo, and Oscar Neira Cuadra. 1986. "The Making of a Mixed Economy: Class Struggle and State Policy in the Nicaraguan Transition." In *Transition and Development: Problems of Third World Socialism,* ed. Richard R. Fagen et al. New York: Monthly Review Press.

Behar, Ruth. 1993. *Translated Woman: Crossing the Border with Esperanza's Story.* Boston: Beacon Press.

Behar, Ruth, and Deborah A. Gordon, eds. 1995. *Women Writing Culture.* Berkeley: University of California Press.

Belli, Gioconda. 1987. *De la costilla de Eva.* Managua: Editorial Nueva Nicaragua.

———. 1988. *La mujer habitada.* Managua: Editorial Vanguardia.

———. 1990. *Sofia de los presagios.* Managua: Editorial Vanguardia.

Belt, Thomas. 1911. *The Naturalist in Nicaragua.* New York: Dutton.

Berendt, Karl Hermann. 1874. *"Nota" in Apuntamientos de la lengua mangue. Don Juan eligio de la rocha.* Copy of original unpublished ms. Van Pelt-Dietrich Library, University of Pennsylvania.

Beverley, John, and Marc Zimmerman. 1990. *Literature and Politics in the Central American Revolutions.* Austin: University of Texas Press.

Biondi-Morra, Brizio N. 1993. *Hungry Dreams: The Failure of Food Policy in Revolutionary Nicaragua.* Ithaca, NY: Cornell University Press.

Bishop, Ronald L., and Frederick W. Lange. 1993. "Sources of Maya and Central American Jodeites: Data Bases and Interpretations." In *Precolumbian Jade: New Geological and Cultural Interpretations,* ed. Frederick W. Lange. Salt Lake City: University of Utah Press.

Black, George. 1981. *Triumph of the People.* London: Zed Press.

Bolt, Alan. 1990. *El libro de la Nación Qu.* Mangua: Vientos del Sur.

Bonfil Batalla, Guillermo. 1992a. *Identidad y pluralismo cultural en America Latina.* San Juan, Puerto Rico: Editorial de la Universidad de Puerto Rico.

———. 1992b. *Decadenica y auge de las identidades.* Tijuana: El Colegio de la Frontera Norte.

Booth, John A. 1982. *The End and the Beginning.* Boulder, CO: Westview Press.

Bourgois, Philippe. 1981. "Class, Ethnicity, and the State among the Miskitu Amerindians of Northeastern Nicaragua." *Latin American Perspectives* 8 (2): 22–39.

Bransford, J. F. 1881. *Archaeological Researches in Nicaragua.* Washington, DC: Smithsonian Institute.

Braverman, Harry. 1974. *Labor and Monopoly Capital: The Degradation of Work in the Twentieth Century.* New York: Monthly Review Press.

Brettell, Caroline, ed. 1996. *When They Read What We Write: The Politics of Ethnography.* Westport, CT: Bergin and Garvey.

Brinton, Daniel G. 1885. "Notes on the Mangue: An Extinct Dialect Formerly Spoken in Nicaragua." Proceedings of the American Philosophical Society, November 20.

Brinton, Daniel G., ed. 1883. The Güegüence: A Comedy Ballet in the Nahuatl-Spanish Dialect of Nicaragua. Reprint, New York: AMS Press, 1969.

Brundenius, Claes. 1987. "Industrial Development Strategies in Revolutionary Nicaragua." In *The Political Economy of the Nicaraguan Revolution,* ed. Rose Spalding. Boston: Allen and Unwin.

Burns, E. Bradford. 1991. *Patriarch and Folk: The Emergence of Nicaragua, 1798-1858.* Cambridge, MA: Harvard University Press.

Cabezas, Omar. 1985. *Fire from the Mountain.* New York: Crown Publishers.

Calderón, Fernando, Alejandro Piscitelli, and José Luis Reyna. 1992. "Social Movements: Actors, Theories, Expectations." In *The Making of Social Movements in Latin America: Identity, Strategy and Democracy,* ed. Arturo Escobar and Sonia E. Alvarez. Boulder, CO: Westview Press.

Canclini, Néstor García. 1982. *Las culturas populares en el capitalismo.* La Habana: Ediciones Casa de las Americas.

Cardenal, Ernesto. 1973. *Homage to the American Indian.* Baltimore: Johns Hopkins University Press.

———. 1974. *In Cuba.* New York: New Directions.

―――. 1986. "The Democratization of Nicaraguan Culture." In *Nicaragua: Unfinished Revolution,* ed. P. Rosset and J. Vandermeer. New York: Grove Press.

Castaneda, Carlos. 1974. *Tales of Power.* New York: Simon and Schuster.

Castegnaro de Foletti, Alessandra. 1992. "La alfarería tradicional de La Paz Centro." In *Persistencia indígena en Nicaragua,* ed. German Romero Vargas et al. Managua: CIDCA-UCA.

Castells, Manuel. 1986. "High Technology, World Development, and Structural Transformation: The Trends and the Debate." *Alternatives* 11(3): 297–344.

Certeau, Michel de. 1984. *The Practice of Everyday Life.* Berkeley: University of California Press.

CIDCA Development Study Group. 1987. *Ethnic Groups and the State: The Case of the Atlantic Coast in Nicaragua.* Stockholm: University of Stockholm.

CIERA. 1989. *La vida cotidiana de la mujer campesina.* Managua: Author.

CIERA-MIDINRA. 1984a. *La mujer en las cooperativas agropecuarias en Nicaragua.* Managua: n.p.

―――. 1984b. *Nicaragua y por eso defendemos la frontera: Historia agraria de las segovias occidentales.* Managua: Author.

Chatterjee, Partha. 1986. *Nationalist Thought and the Colonial World: A Derivative Discourse.* Minneapolis: University of Minnesota Press.

Clifford, James. 1986. "On Ethnographic Allegory." In *Writing Culture,* ed. James Clifford and George Marcus. Berkeley: University of California Press.

―――. 1988. *The Predicament of Culture.* Cambridge, MA: Harvard University Press.

Comaroff, John, and Jean Comaroff. 1992. *Ethnography and the Historical Imagination.* Boulder, CO: Westview Press.

CONAIE. 1989. *Las nacionalidades indigenas en el Ecuador.* Quito: Ediciones Tincui-Abya Yala.

"Contra Viento y Marea." 1987. *Barricada,* September 24.

Coraggio, José Luis. 1986. "Economics and Politics in the Transition." In *Transition and Development: Problems of Third World Socialism,* ed. Richard R. Fagen et al. New York: Monthly Review Press.

Craven, David. 1989. *The New Concept of Art and Popular Culture in Nicaragua since the Revolution in 1979: An Analytical Essay and Compendium of Illustrations.* Lewiston, NY: Edwin Mellen Press.

Criquillon, Ana. 1995. "The Nicaraguan Women's Movement: Feminist Reflections from Within." In *The New Politics of Survival: Grassroots Movements in Central America,* ed. Minor Sinclair. New York: Monthly Review Press.

Cuadra, Pablo Antonio. 1963. "Introducción a la literatura nicaragüense." *El Pez y la Serpiente,* no. 4.

———. 1981. *El Nicaragüense*. 10th ed. Managua: Ediciones El Pez y la Serpiente.

Cuadra, Pablo Antonio, and Emilio Alvarez Lejarza. 1942. "El Güegüence o Macho Ratón: Comedia bailete de la época colonial." *Cuaderno del Taller de San Lucas* 1(18): 7–22.

Cypess, Sandra Messenger. 1991. *La Malinche in Mexican Literature: From History to Myth*. Austin: University of Texas Press.

"Darío: The Poet and His Times." 1983. *Barricada International,* January 24.

Dávila Bolaños, Alejandro. 1974a. *El Güegüence o Macho Ratón: Drama épico indígena: Traducción directa del original en náhuat-castellano*. Estelí: Tipografía Géminis.

———. 1974b. *Medecina indígena pre-colombina de Nicaragua*. Estelí: Editorial de la Imprenta.

———. 1977. *Indice de la mitología Nicaragüense*. Estelí: Editorial de la Imprenta.

Dawes, Greg. 1993. *Aesthetics and Revolution: Nicaraguan Poetry, 1979–1990*. Minneapolis: University of Minnesota Press.

Day, Jane. 1988. "Golden Images in Greater Nicoya." In *Costa Rican Art and Archaeology,* ed. Frederick W. Lange. Denver: University of Colorado Press.

de la Cadena, Marisol. 1995. "Women Are More Indian: Ethnicity and Gender in a Community of Cuzco." In *Ethnicity, Markets and Migration in the Andes: At the Crossroads of History and Anthropology,* ed. Olivia Harris and Enrique Tandeter. Durham, NC: Duke University Press.

———. 1996. "The Political Tensions of Representations and Misrepresentations: Intellectuals and Mestizas in Cuzco (1919–1990)." *Journal of Latin American Anthropology* 2(1): 112–48.

de la Selva, Salomón. 1931. "El Macho-Ratón." *Repertorio Americano* 21(21): 188–89.

———. 1984. *Sandino: Free Country or Death*. Compiled by Jorge Eduardo Arellano. Managua: Biblioteca Nacional de Nicaragua.

Dennis, Philip A., and Michael D. Olien. 1984. "Kingship among the Miskito." *American Ethnologist* 11(4): 719–37.

di Leonardo, Micaela. 1991. "Introduction: Gender, Culture, and Political Economy: Feminist Anthropology in Historical Perspective." In *Gender at the Crossroads of Knowledge: Feminist Anthropology in the Postmodern Era,* ed. Micaela di Leonardo. Berkeley: University of California Press.

Dirección de Artesanía. 1985. *El Artesano*. Bulletin no. 1.

Diskin, Martin. 1991. "Ethnic Discourse and the Challenge to Anthropology: The Nicaraguan Case." In *Nation-States and Indians in Latin America,* ed. Greg Urban and Joel Sherzen. Austin: University of Texas Press.

Dominguez, Virginia. 1989. *People as Subject, People as Object: Selfhood and Peoplehood in Contemporary Israel.* Madison: University of Wisconsin Press.

Dunkerly, James. 1988. *Power in the Isthmus: A Political History of Modern Central America.* London: Verso.

Eisenstein, Zillah. 1978. *Capitalist Patriarchy and the Case for Socialist Feminism.* New York: Monthly Review Press.

Eisler, Riane. 1987. *The Chalice and the Blade: Our History, Our Future.* Cambridge, MA: Harper & Row.

Elliott, Marshall. 1884. "The Nahuatl-Spanish Dialect of Nicaragua." *American Journal of Philology* 5: 54–67.

Escobar, Arturo. 1992. "Culture, Economics, and Politics in Latin American Social Movements Theory and Research." In *The Making of Social Movements in Latin America: Identity, Strategy, and Democracy,* ed. Arturo Escobar and Sonia Alvarez. Boulder, CO: Westview Press.

Escobar, Arturo, and Sonia E. Alvarez, eds. 1992. *The Making of Social Movements in Latin America: Identity, Strategy and Democracy.* Boulder, CO: Westview Press.

Esteva-Fabrigat, Claudio. 1995. *Mestizaje in Ibero-America.* Tucson: University of Arizona Press.

Field, Les. 1987. "'I Am Content With My Art:' Two Groups of Artisans in Revolutionary Nicaragua." Ph.D. diss. Anthropology Department, Duke University.

———. 1994a. "Who Are the Indians? Reconceptualizing Indigenous Identity, Resistance, and the Role of Social Science in Latin America." *Latin American Research Review* 29(3): 237–48.

———. 1994b. "Harvesting the Bitter Juice: Contradictions of Páez Resistance in the Changing Colombian Nation-State." *Identities:* 1(1): 89–108.

———. 1995. "Constructing Local Identities in a Revolutionary Nation: The Cultural Politics of the Artisan Class in Nicaragua, 1979–90." *American Ethnologist* 22(4): 786–806.

———. 1996. "Mired Positionings: Beyond Metropolitan Authority and Indigenous Authenticity." Introduction to *Ma'cayuuya'za'nu: We see each other: The Politics of Zapotec and Anthropological Understandings.* Special issue of *Identities* 3(1, 2): 137–54.

———. 1998. "Knowledge and Truth about Post-Sandinista Ethnic Identities in Western Nicaragua." *American Anthropologist* 100(2): 47–69.

Fitzgerald, E. V. K. 1985. "Agrarian Reform as a Model of Accumulation: The Case of Nicaragua since 1979." *Journal of Development Studies* 22(1): 208–26.

Foucault, Michel. 1970. *The Order of Things.* New York: Random House.

———. 1980. *Power/Knowledge: Selected Interviews and Other Writings, 1972–1977.* New York: Pantheon Books.

Fox, Richard G. 1992. "Introduction: Working in the Present." In *Recapturing Anthropology: Working in the Present,* ed. Richard Fox. Santa Fe, NM: School of American Research Press.

Fox-Genovese, Elizabeth. 1993. "From Separate Spheres to Dangerous Streets: Postmodernist Feminism and the Problem of Order." *Social Research* 60: 235–54.

Frente Sandinista de Liberacion Nacional. 1986. "The Historic Program of the FSLN." In *Nicaragua: Unfinished Revolution,* ed. P. Rosset and J. Vandermeer. New York: Grove Press.

Friedlander, Judith. 1975. *Being Indian in Hueyapan: A Study of Forced Identity in Contemporary Mexico.* New York: St. Martin's Press.

Friedman, Jonathan. 1994. *Cultural Identity and Global Process.* London: Sage Publications.

Gamboa, Flavio. 1989. "Tescatlipoca o torovenado." *Ventana (Barricada Literary Supplement)* October 28: 5.

García Bresó, Javier. 1992. *Monimbó: Una comunidad India de Nicaragua.* Managua: Editorial Multiformas.

García Canclini, Néstor. 1981. *Las culturas populares en el capitalismo.* Havana: Ediciones Casa de las Américas.

Garibay, Angel María. 1971. *Historia de la literatura náhuatl, segunda parte: El trauma de la conquista.* 2d ed. México DF: Editorial Porrúa.

Gentile, Frank W. 1989. *Interview with Sergio Ramírez in Nicaragua.* New York: Norton.

Gilbert, Dennis, and David Block, eds. 1990. *Sandinistas: Key Documents/ Documentos Claves.* Latin American Studies Program, Cornell University.

Gossen, Gary H. 1996. "Who Is the Comandante of Sub-comandante Marcos?" In *Indigenous Revolts in Chiapas and the Andean Highlands,* ed. Kevin Gosner and Arij Ouwenweel. Amsterdam: CEDLA.

Gould, Jeffrey. 1990a. *To Lead As Equals: Rural Protest and Political Consciousness in Chinandega, Nicaragua 1912–1979.* Chapel Hill: University of North Carolina Press.

———. 1990b. "La raza rebelde: Las luchas de la comunidad indígena de Sutiava, 1900–1960." *La Revista de Historia* (Costa Rica) 21–22: 69–117.

———. 1993. " 'Vana Ilusión!': The Highland Indians and the Myth of Nicaragua Mestiza 1880–1925." *Hispanic American Historical Review* 73(3): 393–431.

———. 1995. "Y el buitre respondió: La cuestión indígena en Nicaragua occidental, 1920–1960." *Mesoamérica* 30: 327–54.

Grant, Bruce. 1995. *In the Soviet House of Culture: A Century of Perestroikas.* Princeton, NJ: Princeton University Press.

Grupo Venancia. 1997. "An Urgent Call for Action from the Women's Movement in Nicaragua," E-mail transmission.

Guerrero, Julián C., and Lola Soriano de Guerrero. 1965. *Monografía de Masaya.* Managua: Colección Nicaragua.

———. 1982. *La rebelión indígena de Matagalpa en 1881 y la expulsión de los Jesuitas.* Managua: n.p.

Guzmán-Bockler, Carlos. 1975. *Colonialismo y revolución.* Mexico City: Siglo XXI.

Hale, Charles. 1994. *Resistance and Contradiction: Miskitu Indians and the Nicaraguan State, 1894-1987.* Palo Alto, CA: Stanford University Press.

Haraway, Donna. 1991. *Simians, Cyborgs and Women.* New York: Routledge.

Harrison, Regina. 1989. *Signs, Songs, and Memory in the Andes.* Austin: University of Texas Press.

Hartman, Heidi. 1981. "The Unhappy Marriage between Marxism and Feminism: Towards a More Progressive Union." In *Women and Revolution: A Discussion of the Unhappy Marriage between Marxism and Feminism,* ed. Lydia Sargent. Boston: South End Press.

Harvey, David. 1989. *The Condition of Postmodernity: An Enquiry into the Origins of Cultural Change.* Oxford: Basil Blackwell.

Helms, Mary W. 1971. *Asang: Adaptations to Culture Contact in a Miskito Community.* Gainesville: University of Florida Press.

Henriksen, Marta. N.d. "The Self as a Metaphorical Journey: A Performance." Unpublished ms., Albuquerque, NM.

Higgins, Michael. 1992. *Oigame! Oigame! Struggle and Social Change in a Nicaraguan Urban Community.* Boulder, CO: Westview Press.

Hill, Jane H. and Kenneth C. Hill. 1986. *Speaking Mexicano: Dynamics of Syncretic Language in Central Mexico.* Tucson: University of Arizona Press.

Hobsbawm, Eric J. 1990. *Nations and Nationalism since 1780.* Cambridge, UK: Cambridge University Press.

Hodges, Donald. 1986. *The Intellectual Foundations of the Nicaraguan Revolution.* Austin: University of Texas Press.

———. 1992. *Sandino's Communism: Spiritual Politics for the Twenty-First Century.* Austin: University of Texas Press.

Incer Barquero, Jaime. 1964. *Geografía de Nicaragua.* Managua: Banco Central de Nicaragua.

———. 1985. *Toponomías indígenas de Nicaragua.* San José, Costa Rica: Libro Libre.

———. 1990. *Viajes, rutas, y encuentros.* San José, Costa Rica: Libro Libre.

Industrial Division, Department of Technical Services of the Banco Central Nicaragüense. 1976. *La situación de la artesanía Nicaragüense.* Managua.

Institute for the Study of Sandinismo. 1981. *La insurección popular sandinista en Masaya.* Managua: Editorial Nueva Nicaragua.

Irvin, George. 1983. "Nicaragua: Establishing the State as the Centre of Accumulation." *Cambridge Journal of Economics* no. 7: 125-39.

"Italy: Autonomia: Post Political Politics." 1980. *Semiotext(e)* 3 (3).

Jaffe, Alexandra. 1993. "Involvement, Detachment, and Representation in Corsica." In *When They Read What We Write: The Politics of Ethnography*, ed. Caroline B. Brettell. Westport, CT: Bergin and Garvey.

Jaggar, Alison. 1983. *Feminist Politics and Human Nature*. Totowa, NJ: Rowman and Allanhela.

Kafka, Franz. 1976. "On Parables." In *Kafka: The Complete Stories*, ed. Nahum N. Glatzer. New York: Schocken Books.

Kaimowitz, David. 1986. "Nicaraguan Debates on Agrarian Structure and Their Implications for Agricultural Policy and the Rural Poor." *Journal of Peasant Studies* 14(1): 100–117.

Kaminsky, Amy. 1994. "Gender, Race, Raza." *Feminist Studies* 20: 7–31.

Kcarney, Richard. 1997. *Post-Nationalist Ireland: Politics, Literature, Philosophy*. New York: Routledge.

Klor de Alva, Jorge. 1995. "The Postcolonization of the (Latin) American Experience: A Reconsideration of 'Colonialism,' 'Postcolonialism,' and 'Mestizaje.'" In *After Colonialism: Imperial Histories and Postcolonial Displacements*, ed. Gyan Prakash. Princeton, NJ: Princeton University Press.

Kondo, Dorinne. 1990. *Crafting Selves: Power, Gender, and Discourses of Identity in a Japanese Workplace*. Chicago: University of Chicago Press.

Lancaster, Roger N. 1988. *Thanks to God and the Revolution: Popular Religion and Class Consciousness in the New Nicaragua*. New York: Columbia University Press.

———. 1992. *Life Is Hard: Machismo, Danger, and the Intimacy of Power in Nicaragua*. Berkeley: University of California Press.

Lange, Frederick W., and Ronald L. Bishop. 1988. "Abstraction and Jade Exchange in Precolumbian Southern Mesoamerica and Lower Central America." In *Costa Rica Art and Archaeology*, ed. Frederick W. Lange. Denver: University of Colorado Regents.

LaRamée, Pierre, and Erica Polakoff. 1990. "Transformation of the CDSs and the Breakdown of Democracy in Revolutionary Nicaragua." *New Political Science*, fall/winter: 103–23.

Lehmann, Walter. 1920. *Zentral Amerika*. Berlin: D. Reimer. 2 vols.

Lejarza, Emilio A. 1993. *El Güegüence: Comedia-bailete de la epoca colonial*. 1940. Reprint, with introduction, commentary and bibliography by Jorge Eduardo Arellano. Managua: Ediciones Distribuidora Cultural.

Llopesa, Ricardo. 1988. "Algunos aspectos de la poesia de Eduardo Zepedíquez." *Cuadernos Americanos (Nueva Epoca)* 5(11): 205–14.

Lomnitz-Adler, Claudio. 1992. *Exits from the Labyrinth*. Berkeley: University of California Press.

López, Hector. N.d. *Proyecto vajilla arahuac*. Internal document written for the Ministry of Culture, Nicaragua.

Lothrop, Samuel K. 1926. *Pottery of Nicaragua and Costa Rica.* New York: Museum of the American Indian.

Lungo Uclés, Mario. 1995. "Building an Alternative: The Formation of a Popular Project." In *The New Politics of Survival: Grassroots Movements in Central America,* ed. Minor Sinclair. New York: Monthly Review Press.

Mallon, Florencia. 1995. *Peasant and Nation: The Making of Postcolonial Mexico and Peru.* Berkeley: University of California Press.

"Managua's Economic Crisis: How Do the Poor Survive?" 1986. *Envío,* report no. 66.

Mántica Abaunza, Carlos. 1968–69. "El Güegüence o Macho Ratón." *El Pez y el Serpiente* no. 10, winter. Original by Daniel Brinton, translated with notes by Carlos Mántica.

Martin, Emily. 1996. "Meeting Polemics with Irenics in the Science Wars." *Social Text* 46–47: 43–61.

Martin, Randy. 1994. *Socialist Ensembles: Theater and State in Cuba and Nicaragua.* Minneapolis: University of Minnesota Press.

Martinez Cuenca, Alejandro. 1992. *Sandinista Economics in Practice.* Boston: South End Press.

Marx, Karl. 1847. *The Poverty of Philosophy.* 1963 ed. New York: International Publishers.

———. 1852. *The Eighteenth Brumaire of Louis Bonaparte.* 1972 ed. Moscow: Progress Publishers.

———. 1895. *Class Struggle in France 1848-1850.* 1976 ed. New York: International Publishers.

Mason, J. Alden. 1973. "The Native Languages of Middle America." In *The Maya and Their Neighbors,* ed. Clarence L. Hay et al. New York: Cooper Square Publishers.

Meisch, Lynn. 1987. *Otavalo: Weaving, Costume, and the Market.* Quito: Ediciones Libri Mundi.

Melucci, Alberto. 1988. "Getting Involved: Identity and Mobilization in Social Movements." In *International Social Movements Research.* Vol. 1: *From Structure to Action: Comparing Social Movements Research across Cultures,* ed. Hansperter Kriesi, Sidney Tarrow, and Bert Klandemans. London: JAI Press.

Membraño Idiaquez, Marcos. 1992. "Persistencia etnica en Sutiava y Monimbó." In *Persistencia Indígena en Nicaragua,* ed. German Romero Vargas et al. Managua: CIDCA-UCA.

———. 1994. *La estructura de las comunidades étnicas: Itinerario de una investigación teórica desde Nicaragua.* Managua: Editorial Envio.

Menchaca, Martha. 1993. "Chicano Indianism: A Historical Account of Racial Repression in the United States." *American Ethnologist* 20(3): 583–604.

Millett, Richard. 1977. *Guardians of the Dynasty*. Maryknoll, NY: Orbis Books.

Ministry of Culture, Nicaragua. 1985a. *Cerámica Negra*. Managua: Dirección de Artesanía.

———. 1985b. *Qué es la cerámica*. Managua: Dirección de Artesanía.

Molyneux, Maxine. 1986. "¿Movilización sin emancipación? Intereses de la mujer, el estado, y la revolución." In *La transición difícil: La autodeterminación de los pequeños países periféricos*, ed. José Luis Coraggio, Carmen Diana Deere, and Orlando Nuñez Soto. Mexico DF: Siglo XXI.

Montenegro, Sofía. 1992. "Nuestra madre. La Malinche." *Gente* 3(138): 11.

———. N.d. "Identidad y colonialismo: El retorno de la Malinche." Unpublished manuscript.

Moraga, Cherríe, and Gloria Anzaldúa, eds. 1981. *This Bridge Called My Back: Writings by Radical Women of Color*. Watertown, NY: Persephone.

Nandy, Ashis. 1987. "Cultural Frames for Social Transformation." *Alternatives* 12(1): 113–24.

Nash, June. 1993. "Maya Household Production in the World Market: The Potters of Amatenango del valle, Chiapas, Mexico." In *Crafts in the World Market: The Impact of Global Exchange on Middle American Artisans*, ed. June Nash. Albany, NY: State University of New York Press.

Newson, Linda A. 1987. *Indian Survival in Colonial Nicaragua*. Norman: University of Oklahoma Press.

Nietschmann, Bernard. 1973. *Between Land and Water: The Subsistence Ecology of the Miskito Indians of Eastern Nicaragua*. New York: Seminar Press.

———. 1979. *Caribbean Edge: The Coming of Modern Times to Isolated People and Wildlife*. Indianapolis: Bobbs-Merrill Co.

Novelo, Victoria. 1976. *Artesanías y capitalismo en México*. México City: SEP-INAH.

Nuñez Soto, Orlando. 1987. *Transición y lucha de clases en Nicaragua, 1979–1986*. México City: Siglo Veintiuno.

O'Kane, Trish. 1995. "New Autonomy, New Struggles: Labor Unions in Nicaragua." In *The New Politics of Survival: Grassroots Movements in Central America*, ed. Minor Sinclair. New York: Monthly Review Press.

Olivera, Mercedes, and Ana María Fernández. 1991. *Subordinación de genero en las organizaciones populares nicaragüenses: Un estudio sobre la participación política de las mujeres*. Managua: Cenzontle.

Olivera, Mercedes, et al. 1992. *Nicaragua: El poder de las mujeres*. Managua: Cezontle.

Oquist, Paul. 1992. "Sociopolitical Dynamics of the 1990 Nicaraguan Elections." In *The 1990 Elections in Nicaragua and Their Aftermath*, ed. Vanessa Castro and Gary Prevost. Lanham, MD: Rowman and Littlefield.

Ouwenweel, Arij. 1996. "Away from the Prying Eyes: The Zapatista Revolt of 1994." In *Indigenous Revolts in Chiapas and the Andean Highlands,* ed. Kevin Gosner and Arij Ouwenweel. Amsterdam: CEDLA.

Oviedo y Valdés, Gonzalo Fernández. 1976. *Nicaragua en los cronistas de indias: Oviedo.* Serie Cronistas no. 3. Managua: Banco de América, Fondo de Promoción Cultural.

Palma, Milagros. 1984. *Por los senderos míticos de Nicaragua.* Managua: Editorial Nueva Nicaragua.

Patai, Daphne. 1991. "U.S. Academics and Third World Women: Is Ethical Research Possible?" In *Women's Words: The Feminist Practice of Oral History,* ed. Sherna Berger Glick and Daphne Patai. New York: Routledge.

Paz, Octavio. 1959. *El laberinto de la soledad.* Mexico City: Fondo de Cultura Económica.

Peña Hernandez, Enrique. 1986. *Folklore de Nicaragua.* 1968. 2d ed. Managua: Republica de Nicaragua.

Pérez Alemán, Paola. 1990. *Organización, identidad, y cambio: Las campesinas de Nicaragua.* Managua: CIAM.

Pérez Alemán, Paola, Diana Martínez, and Crista Widmaier. 1989. *Industria, genero, y mujer en Nicaragua.* Managua: Instituto Nicaragüense de la Mujer.

Pérez Estrada, Francisco. 1954. "Historia y geografía del Güegüence." In *Cuatro estudios sobre folklore.* Managua: Editorial Novedades.

————. 1968. "El hilo azul: La frase del Güegüence." *La Prensa Literaria,* December 1.

————. 1992. *Ensayos Nicaragüenses.* Managua: Editorial Vanguardia.

Pfeffer, Richard. 1979. *Working for Capitalism.* New York: Columbia University Press.

Probyn, Elspeth. 1993. *Sexing the Self: Gendered Positions in Cultural Studies.* New York: Routledge.

Quandt, Midge. 1995. "Unbinding the Ties That Bind: The FSLN and the Popular Organizations." In *The New Politics of Survival: Grassroots Movements in Central America,* ed. Minor Sinclair. New York: Monthly Review Press.

Quijano, Aníbal. 1980. *Dominación y cultura: Lo cholo y el conflicto cultural en el Peru.* Lima: Mosca Azul Editores.

Radell, David Richard. 1969. "An Historical Geography of Western Nicaragua: The Spheres of Influence of Léon, Granada, and Managua, 1519–1965." Ph.D. diss. University of California, Berkeley.

Ramírez, Sergio. 1984. *El pensamiento vivo de Sandino.* Managua: Editorial Nueva Nicaragua.

————. 1988a. *El muchacho de Niquinohomo.* Managua: Editorial Vanguardia.

————. 1988b. *Pensamiento político*. Caracas, Venezuela: Biblioteca Ayacucho.

Randall, Margaret. 1978. *Doris Tijerino: Inside the Nicaraguan Revolution*. Vancouver: New Star Books.

————. 1981. *Sandino's Daughters: Testimonies of Nicaraguan Women in Struggle*. Vancouver: New Star Books.

————. 1984. *Risking a Somersault in the Air: Conversations with Nicaraguan Writers*. San Francisco: Solidarity Publications.

————. 1985. *Christians in the Nicaraguan Revolution*. Vancouver: New Star Books.

————. 1994. *Sandino's Daughters Revisited: Feminism in Nicaragua*. New Brunswick, NJ: Rutgers University Press.

Rapp, Reyna. 1992. "Anthropology: Feminist Methodologies for the Science of Man?" In *Revolutions in Knowledge: Feminism in the Social Sciences*, ed. Faye Ginsburg and Anna Tsing. Boston: Beacon.

Rappaport, Joanne. 1990. *The Politics of Memory: Native Historical Interpretation in the Columbian Andes*. Cambridge, UK: Cambridge University Press.

————. 1994. *Cumbe Reborn: An Andean Ethnography of History*. Chicago: University of Chicago Press.

Rappaport, Joanne, and Robert V. H. Dover. 1996. "The Construction of Difference by Native Legislators: Assessing the Impact of the Colombian Constitution of 1991." *Journal of Latin American Anthropology* 1(2): 22–45.

Rasnake, Roger. 1988. *Domination and Cultural Resistance: Authority and Power among an Andean People*. Durham, NC: Duke University Press.

"Rescate de Arte Indígena." 1987. *Barricada*, July 22.

Rizo Zeledón, Mario. 1992. "Etnicidad, legalidad y demandas de las comunidades indígenas del norte, centro, y del pacífico de Nicaragua." In *Persistencia Indígena en Nicaragua*, ed. German Romero Vargas et al. Managua: CIDCA-UCA.

Romero Vargas, German. 1988. *Las estructuras sociales de Nicaragua en el Siglo XVIII*. Managua: Editorial Vanguardia.

Romero Vargas, German, et al. 1992. *Persistencia indígena en Nicaragua*. Managua: CIDCA-UCA.

Rosset, Peter, and John Vandermeer. 1986. *Nicaragua: Unfinished Revolution. The New Nicaragua Reader*. New York: Grove Press.

Rubin, Gayle. 1975. "The Traffic in Women: Notes on the 'Political Economy' of Sex." In *Toward an Anthropology of Women*, ed. Rayna R. Reiter. New York: Monthly Review Press.

Said, Edward W. 1983. *The World, the Text, and the Critic*. Cambridge, MA: Harvard University Press.

Sandoval, Chela. 1991. "U.S. Third World Feminism: The Theory and

Method of Oppositional Consciousness in the Postmodern World." *Genders* 10: 1-24.

Sarris, Greg. 1993. *Keeping Slug Woman Alive: A Holistic Approach to American Indian Texts*. Berkeley: University of California Press.

Scheper-Hughes, Nancy. 1992. *Death without Weeping: The Violence of Everyday Life in Brazil*. Berkeley: University of California Press.

Selser, Gregorio. 1978. *Sandino, general de hombre libres*. México City: Editorial Diogenes.

———. 1983. *El pequeño ejército loco: Sandino y la operación México-Nicaragua*. 5th ed. Managua: Editorial Nueva Nicaragua.

Sheehan, Elizabeth A. 1993. "The Student of Culture and the Ethnography of Irish Intellectuals." In *When They Read What We Write*, ed. Caroline B. Brettell. Westport, CT: Bergin and Garvey.

Sider, Gerald. 1994. "Identity as History: Ethnohistory, Ethnogenesis, and Ethnocide in the Southeastern United States." *Identities* 1(1): 109-22.

Sinclair, Minor. 1995. Introduction to *The New Politics of Survival: Grassroots Movements in Central America*, ed. Minor Sinclair. New York: Monthly Review Press.

Smith, Carol. 1990. *Guatemalan Indians and the State: 1540-1988*. Austin: University of Texas Press.

———. 1996. "Race-Class-Gender in Guatemala: Modern and Anti-Modern Forms." In *Women Out of Place: The Gender of Agency and the Race of Nationality*, ed. Brackette F. Williams. New York: Routledge.

Sociedad Colectiva de Cerámica Negra. 1990. Untitled pamphlet. Matagalpa, Nicaragua.

Solórzano, Porfirio R., compiler. 1993. *The NIREX Collection: Nicaraguan Revolutionary Extracts, 1979-1990*. Vols. 3, 5, 6, 8. Austin: LITEXT Inc.

Sommer, Doris. 1991. *Foundational Fictions: The National Romances of Latin America*. Berkeley: University of California Press.

Spalding, Rose J. 1994. *Capitalists and Revolution in Nicaragua: Opposition and Accommodation, 1979-1993*. Chapel Hill: University of North Carolina Press.

Spivak, Gayatri. 1988. "Can the Subaltern Speak?" In *Marxism and the Interpretation of Culture*, ed. C. Nelson and L. Grossberg. Urbana: University of Illinois Press.

Squier, Ephraim. 1860. *Nicaragua: Its People, Scenery, Monuments, Resources, Condition and Proposed Canal*. New York: Harper.

———. 1990. *Observations on the Archaeology and Ethnology of Nicaragua*. 1853. Culver City, CA: Labyrinthos. Reprint, *Transactions of the American Ethnological Society* 3: 83-158.

Stanislawski, Dan. 1983. *The Transformation of Nicaragua, 1519-1548*. Berkeley: University of California.

Stephen, Lynn. 1991. *Zapotec Women*. Austin: University of Texas Press.

———. 1993a. "Weaving in the Fast Lane: Class, Ethnicity, and Gender in Zapotec Craft Commercialization." In *Crafts in the World Market: The Impact of Global Exchange on Middle American Artisans,* ed. June Nash. Albany, NY: State University of New York Press.

———. 1993b. "Anthropological Research on Latin American Women: Past Trends and New Directions for the 1990s." In *Researching Women in Latin America and the Caribbean,* ed. Edna Acota-Belén and Christine E. Bose. Boulder, CO: Westview Press.

Stephens, Beth. 1988. "Women and Nicaragua." *Monthly Review* 40 (September): 1–18.

Stephenson, Neal. 1995. *The Diamond Age, or, A Young Lady's Primer.* London: Viking.

Stonc, Samuel Z. 1990. *The Heritage of the Conquistadors: Ruling Classes in Central America from the Conquest to the Sandinistas.* Lincoln: University of Nebraska Press.

Stutzman, Ronald. 1981. "El mestizaje: An All-Inclusive Ideology of Exclusion." In *Cultural Transformations and Ethnicity in Modern Ecuador,* ed. Norman E. Whitten. Urbana: University of Illinois Press.

Tedlock, Barbara. 1995. "Works and Wives: On the Sexual Division of Textual Labor." In *Women Writing Culture,* ed. Ruth Behar and Deborah A. Gordon. Berkeley: University of California Press.

Teplitz, Benjamin. 1973. "The Political and Economic Foundations of Modernization in Nicaragua: The Administration of José Santos Zelaya, 1893–1909." Ph.D. diss. Howard University.

Thompson, Martha. 1995. "Repopulated Communities in El Salvador." In *The New Politics of Survival: Grassroots Movements in Central America,* ed. Minor Sinclair. New York: Monthly Review Press.

Tixier y Vigil, Yvonne, and Nan Elsasser. 1976. "The Effects of the Ethnicity of the Interviewer on Conversation: A Study of Chicana Women." In *The Sociology of the Language of American Women,* ed. Betty L. DuBois and Isabel Crouch. San Antonio, TX: Trinity University Press.

Touraine, Alain. 1988. *The Return of the Actor.* Minneapolis: University of Minnesota Press.

Trouillot, Rolph. 1991. "Anthropology and the Savage Slot: The Poetics and Politics of Otherness." In *Recapturing Anthropology: Working in the Present,* ed. Richard G. Fox. Santa Fe, NM: School of American Research Press.

True, Jacqui. 1996. " 'Fit Citizens for the British Empire?' Class-ifying Racial and Gendered Subjects in 'Godzone' (New Zealand)." In *Women Out of Place: The Gender of Agency and the Race of Nationality,* ed. Brackette F. Williams. New York: Routledge.

Turok, Marta. 1988. *El caracól púrpura: Una tradición milenaria en Oaxaca.* Mexico DF: Secretaría de Educación, Dirección de Culturas Populares, Programa de Artesanías y Culturas Populares.

UNADI. 1985. Governing Memoranda of Our Commercial Activity. Managua: Authór.

Urban, Greg. 1991. "The Semiotics of State-Indian Linguistic Relationships: Peru, Paraguay, and Brazil." In *Nation-States and Indians in Latin America,* ed. Greg Urban and Joel Sherzer. Austin: University of Texas Press.

Urtecho, José Coronel. 1962. *Reflecciones sobre la historia de Nicaragua.* 2 vols. León, Nicaragua: Editorial Hospicio.

Verdery, Katherine. 1991. *National Ideology under Socialism: Identity and Culture in Ceausescu's Romania.* Berkeley: University of California Press.

———. 1996. *What Was Socialism, and What Comes Next?* Princeton, NJ: Princeton University Press.

Vilas, Carlos M. 1986. *The Sandinista Revolution.* New York: Monthly Review Press.

———. 1991. "Nicaragua: A Revolution That Fell from the Grace of the People." In *Socialist Register 1991,* ed. Ralph Miliband and Leo Paritch. London: Merlin Press.

———. 1992. "Family Affairs: Class, Lineage and Politics in Contemporary Nicaragua." *Journal of Latin American Studies* 24(2): 309–42.

Visweswaran, Kamala. 1994. *Fictions of Feminist Ethnography.* Minneapolis: University of Minnesota Press.

Walker, Thomas W. 1991. *Nicaragua: The Land of Sandino.* Boulder, CO: Westview Press.

Walter, Knut. 1993. *The Regime of Anastasio Somoza, 1936–1956.* Chapel Hill: University of North Carolina Press.

Warren, Kay. 1992. "Transforming Memories and Histories: The Meanings of Ethnic Resurgence for Mayan Indians." In *Americas: New Interpretive Essays,* ed. Alfred Stepan. New York: Oxford University Press.

———. 1996. "Reading History as Resistance: Mayan Public Intellectuals in Guatemala." In *Mayan Cultural Activism in Guatemala,* ed. Edward Fischer and McKenna Brown. Austin: University of Texas Press.

Wheelock Roman, Jaime. 1981. *Las raices indígenas de la lucha anti-colonialista en Nicaragua.* 1974. 2d ed. Managua: Editorial Nueva Nicaragua.

Whisnant, David. 1995. *Rascally Signs in Sacred Places: The Politics of Culture in Nicaragua.* Chapel Hill: University of North Carolina Press.

White, Steven. 1986. *Culture and Politics in Nicaragua: Testimonies of Poets and Writers.* New York: Lumen Books.

Williams, Brackette. 1989. "A Class Act: Anthropology and the Race to Nation across Ethnic Terrain." *Annual Review of Anthropology* 18: 401–44.

———. 1991. *Stains on My Name, War in My Veins: Guyana and the Politics of Cultural Struggle.* Durham, NC: Duke University Press.

———. 1995. "Skinfolk, Not Kinfolk: Comparative Reflections on the

Identity of the Participant-Observer in Two Field Situations." In *Feminist Dilemmas in Fieldwork,* ed. Diane L. Wolf. Boulder, CO: Westview Press.

———. 1996. "Introduction: Mannish Women and Gender after the Act." In *Women Out of Place: The Gender of Agency and the Race of Nationality,* ed. Brackette F. Williams. New York: Routledge.

Williams, Philip J. 1989. *The Catholic Church in Nicaragua and Costa Rica.* Pittsburgh: University of Pittsburgh Press.

Williams, Raymond. 1977. *Marxism and Literature.* Oxford: Oxford University Press.

Williams, Robert G. 1986. *Export Agriculture and the Crisis in Central America.* Chapel Hill: University of North Carolina Press.

Wolf, Diane L. 1995. "Situating Feminist Dilemmas in Fieldwork." In *Feminist Dilemmas in Fieldwork,* ed. Diane L. Wolf. Boulder, CO: Westview Press.

Wolf, Margery. 1992. *A Thrice-Told Tale: Feminism, Postmodernism, and Ethnographic Responsibility.* Stanford, CA: Stanford University Press.

———. 1995. "Afterward: Musings from an Old Gray Wolf." In *Feminist Dilemmas in Fieldwork,* ed. Diane L. Wolf. Boulder, CO: Westview Press.

Woodward, Ralph. 1985. *Central America: A Nation Divided.* 2d ed. New York: Oxford University Press.

Wright, Erik Olin. 1985. *Classes.* New York: Schocken Books.

Zamora, Daisy. 1981. *La violenta espuma/The Violent Foam.* Managua: Ministry of Culture.

———. 1988. *En limpio se escribe la vida/Clean Slate.* Managua: Editorial Nueva Nicaragua.

———. 1992. *La mujer nicaragüense en la poesía/ Nicaraguan Women's Poetry.* Managua: Editorial Nueva Nicaragua.

Zamora, Marta. 1985. "La artesanía hoy: Una busqueda de definiciones." *Barricada Literary Supplement,* July 20.

Zepeda-Henríquez, Eduardo. 1987. *Mitología Nicaragüense.* 1976. 2d ed. Managua: Editorial Monolo Morales.

Zwerling, Philip, and Connie Martin. 1985. *Nicaragua: A New Kind of Revolution.* Westport, CT: L. Hill.

Index

Index

2666

Les W. Field is Assistant Professor in the Department of Anthropology at the University of New Mexico.

Library of Congress Cataloging-in-Publication Data

Field, Les W.

The grimace of Macho Ratón : artisans, identity, and nation in late-twentieth-century western Nicaragua / Les W. Field.

p.   cm.

Includes bibliographical references and index.

ISBN 0-8223-2255-2 (cloth : alk. paper). —

ISBN 0-8223-2288-9 (paper : alk. paper)

1. Güegüense.   2. Nicaragua—National characteristics.
3. Nationalism—Nicaragua.   4. Nicaragua—Politics and government.   I. Title.

PM4070.Z77.F54   1999

897'.4—dc21   98-21619